1999

361.37
PIDGEON

The Universal Benefits of Volunteering

The NSFRE/Wiley Fund Development Series

The Universal Benefits of Volunteering

A PRACTICAL WORKBOOK FOR NONPROFIT ORGANIZATIONS, VOLUNTEERS, AND CORPORATIONS

Walter P. Pidgeon, Jr.

John Wiley & Sons, Inc.

NEW YORK • CHICHESTER • WEINHEIM • BRISBANE • SINGAPORE • TORONTO

This publication is designed to provide accurate and authoritative information in regard to the subject matter covered. It is sold with the understanding that the publisher is not engaged in rendering legal, accounting, or other professional services. If legal advice or other expert assistance is required, the services of a competent professional person should be sought.

Library of Congress Cataloging-in-Publication Data:

ISBN 0-471-18505-1

Printed in the United States of America.

10 9 8 7 6 5 4 3 2 1

Volunteering is learned. The first time I recall an act of volunteering was in the early 1950s when my mother, Lucille Robinson Pidgeon, volunteered to collect, door-to-door, for the March of Dimes. In time, my mother became the chief collector of funds for a number of health charities in our neighborhood.

When my sister, Patricia, was old enough to join the Girl Scouts, my mother helped organize the troop and became one of its first leaders. My mother was also active in politics as an elected committee woman. Through that process, she became the person who could solve local problems.

She was a wonderful mother. She was always there when I needed her. Yet, she also found the time to give something back to the community through a lifetime of service.

My father, Walter Paul Pidgeon, Sr., also showed, by example, the important role of volunteering. His key volunteer positions in the Boy Scout troop at our church made it possible for me to have my first leadership and volunteer experiences. These experiences introduced me to a professional career of serving humanity through various leadership positions within the not-for-profit sector.

For these reasons, I dedicate this book to the memory of my loving mother and father who provided me with all of my core values and who taught me about the important role that volunteering can play in our lives.

The NSFRE/Wiley Fund Development Series

The NSFRE/Wiley Fund Development Series is intended to provide fund development professionals and volunteers (including board members and others interested in the not-for-profit sector) with top-quality publications that help advance philanthropy as voluntary action for the public good. Our goal is to provide practical, timely guidance and information on fund raising, charitable giving, and related subjects. NSFRE and Wiley each bring to this innovative collaboration unique and important resources that result in a whole greater than the sum of its parts.

The National Society of Fund-Raising Executives

The NSFRE is a professional association of fund-raising executives which advances philanthropy through its more than 18,000 members in 149 chapters throughout the United States, Canada, and Mexico. Through its advocacy, research, education, and certification programs, the Society fosters development and growth of fund-raising professionals, works to advance philanthropy and volunteerism, and promotes high ethical standards in the fund-raising profession.

1997 NSFRE Publishing Advisory Council

About the Author

Walter (Bud) Pidgeon, Jr. is a recognized authority on volunteering. He has years of experience in volunteering and has conducted extensive research on the benefits that individuals and society receive from volunteering. He is a published author and consultant in the areas of volunteering, fund raising, strategic planning, membership enhancement, and health-related issues.

Dr. Pidgeon has had a distinguished career as a not-for-profit manager. He held positions that required expertise in finance, membership development, program enhancement, fund raising, meeting planning, and education. He served as the chief executive officer of four not-for-profit organizations (one regional, three national). Dr. Pidgeon is currently President of Trans-American Associates, a national management services organization, that assists businesses, academic institutions, and not-for-profit organizations with strategic planning, fund development, and other management issues.

Dr. Pidgeon earned his bachelor's degree in Human Relations and Non-Profit Administration at Salem-Teikyo University in Salem, West Virginia. His major was an American Humanics, Inc., sponsored program. Dr. Pidgeon earned his doctoral degree in Philanthropy, Leadership, and Voluntary Behavioral Studies at the Union Institute in Cincinnati, Ohio.

Dr. Pidgeon is currently certified by the National Society of Fund Raising Executives as a Certified Fund Raising Executive (CFRE). He has also been certified by the American Society of Association Executives as a Certified Association Executive (CAE).

Dr. Pidgeon is an active volunteer in a number of professional, business, and social service organizations.

▼ Foreword

It is clear that Americans are increasingly disconnected from one another and from the institutions in their communities that could help them lead productive, fulfilling lives. In fact, a recent Points of Light Foundation survey found that 80 percent of us agree that disconnection is an underlying characteristic of many of our social problems. Through volunteering, we can make a difference in others' lives. From the simplest act of community crime watch, Americans are working together, moving past their differences and building shared understanding that can lead to resolution of conflicts and the reuniting of "community."

The Points of Light Foundation applauds the work set forth in *The Universal Benefits of Volunteering*. This publication acknowledges, "The most valuable asset of a not-for-profit is its ability to provide an instant 'community' for those who participate (as volunteers)." We feel that volunteering and the involvement of the organizations in the community—whether nonprofit, government, business, or civic—are the essential building blocks to reconnecting Americans. That's why we've launched Connect America, a national effort that involves more than 40 national nonprofits and their local affiliates to remind all Americans of what we can accomplish when we work together. This movement builds on the concept that volunteering benefits all those involved—the givers, the receivers, and society at large.

As set forth in the goals developed at the Presidents' Summit for America's Future in April, 1997, every American has a role to play in the well-being of this society and its future—our youth. *The Universal Benefits of Volunteering* is a valuable tool to help us reach these goals and to help people connect through volunteer service.

Robert K. Goodwin
President and CEO
The Points of Light Foundation

▼ Preface

Volunteering benefits all of our lives. We began to receive these benefits quite early in life: Volunteering may have made it possible for the hospital where you were born to perform an easier delivery because of a successful volunteer-driven capital fund drive that provided the resources to install a state-of-the-art delivery room; volunteer tutors may have been available at your elementary school to improve your reading skills; volunteers may have helped you learn teamwork and leadership skills through youth organizations.

Volunteering's benefits are achieved through a variety of local, national, and international organizations that provide an infinite array of services from collecting blood to representing important political issues. This vast network of not-for-profit organizations and the services that they offer would not be possible if no one volunteered their time. Volunteering has enriched our personal and professional lives.

Volunteering has been one of the most productive and positive energies created in our society. In 1995, a Gallup survey conducted for the Independent Sector reported that 48.8 percent of households engaged in some kind of volunteer activity. The survey also revealed that the average volunteer contributed 4.2 hours a week.[1] If everyone in the United States stopped volunteering, the cost of getting the same amount of work done would be at least $201.5 billion per year.[2]

Another benefit of volunteering is often overlooked, however. It is the benefit or value that volunteering provides to the individual volunteer. What does a person derive from a volunteering experience? Can the experience be measured and, if so, who could benefit from the data?

HISTORY OF VOLUNTEERING

The most important group of individuals within a nonprofit are volunteers. Volunteers are people who, for a number of reasons, wish to donate their time and often their financial resources to a particular organization or cause. Volunteering is a part of most of our lives. We are products of individuals who have volunteered to make us happier and more productive. We have volunteered to help others as well. Volunteering is so ingrained in our culture that it would be impossible to think of our communities without thousands of individuals doing good works for others.

You might be surprised to know that volunteering isn't new. The act of volunteering has been around for a long time. It can be traced back to ancient cultures. Philanthropy and charitable work are often substituted for the word volunteering and in that context the philanthropic tradition is older than democracy, older than Christianity, older than even formal education.[3] The Egyptian civilization provides the first documented evidence of charity. In the *Book of the Dead*, which dates back to around 4000 B.C., you can find passages praising those who gave bread to the hungry and water to the thirsty.[4]

Throughout the ages, volunteering has played a part in most civilizations. The American tradition can be traced back to origins in Europe before the colonization of America began.[5] As individuals immigrated to America, they brought these traditions with them. In America, however, the act of good works began to expand or mature to a higher level. This was due to a number of factors including less government and an increased need to help each other survive in the new world.

The early settlers of the new world were the pioneers of what American philanthropy or volunteering is today. In fact, it was acts of volunteering by hundreds of individuals that formed the United States of America. "Volunteerism is crucial to a functioning democracy because it mobilizes enormous energy. Volunteering is so pervasive in the United States that it can be observed daily in almost every aspect of life."[6] This is a case where the individual counts.

VOLUNTEERING TODAY

The decision to volunteer is not often made in a systematic fashion. Individuals volunteer when interest is generated to get involved with an organization or the individual is asked to serve. Not-for-profits attract volunteers by promoting their cause and by alerting the community to the services that they need. For-profit businesses promote employee volunteering as a way of creating favorable links with the community. While these methods may have worked in the past, there are signs that the traditional methods of attracting and retaining volunteers may not be as effective today.

A 1996 study by the Independent Sector reported that volunteer activities were up by one percent (to 48.8 percent) in 1995 as compared to 1993. However, a closer review of the Independent Sector's statistics reveals that volunteering was down by 3.4 percent in 1993 from the numbers in the 1991 report. Therefore, the one percent gain in 1995 did not overcome the drop in 1993. A decline in volunteering first appeared in the Independent Sector's 1991 report where a drop of 3.3 percent was recorded based on the findings of the 1989 report.[7] Overall, the current level of volunteering is about equal to the level that was recorded in 1987, 45.3 percent.[8] Speculation on the cause of this phenomenon ranges from the reduction of time that individuals have to volunteer to job security issues. Whatever the cause, it is clear that the traditional methods of attracting and retaining volunteers are not working as well. A new focus is needed that identifies the causes of the reduction in volunteering and suggests action which will increase volunteering levels. In addition, the motivations for volunteering have begun to change. Individuals, not-for-profits, and for-profits need to recognize and take advantage of these changes.

THE GOAL OF THIS BOOK

The Universal Benefits of Volunteering: A Practical Workbook for Nonprofit Organizations, Volunteers, and Corporations provides individuals, not-for-profit leaders, for-profit business executives, and community managers with a practical and systematic approach to volunteering, to make a difference and to fulfill individual and collective goals. This workbook is designed to be used by each of these segments as an individual entity, as well as to benefit all segments through a unified and collective plan involving the entire community.

The workbook is organized in four parts:

Part I: The Individual's Relationship to the Volunteer Process

This section provides an in-depth analysis of how an individual can use volunteering to help others and to improve individual skills.

Part II: How Not-For-Profits Can Increase the Quality and the Quantity of Volunteering

This section provides not-for-profits with a method of attracting and retaining volunteers through the promotion of return value volunteering.

Part III: The Important Role That Volunteering Can Play in a For-Profit Business

This section encourages for-profit businesses to institute or adapt employee volunteer programs to fulfill community relation goals and to increase the skills of their employees.

Part IV: The Community: An Opportunity to Form Volunteer Partnerships for the Common Good

This section outlines a method of using parts I, II, and III to create a comprehensive community plan that attracts and retains volunteers.

Individuals who volunteer can benefit a great deal more from the experience if they employ a plan that uses return value to determine how they wish to volunteer. Such a plan can be used by a first-time volunteer or a seasoned volunteer. Return value refers to the benefits that a volunteer can receive from the volunteer experience.

Individuals can use this workbook to receive the maximum benefit from each volunteer experience. This book will assist individuals to determine the kinds of volunteer experiences that are best for them as well as showing how to select the appropriate institutions to approach, the proper method of approach, what to ask for, and how to evaluate each experience.

Not-for-profit organizations need to implement new methods of attracting and retaining quality volunteers at all levels. This workbook will show not-for-profit leaders a method of increasing volunteering by emphasizing return value. The method will also significantly increase the visibility of the institution to the business community, will increase volunteer levels, and create new fund-raising opportunities.

For-profit businesses have gone through dramatic changes in the past decade and they are eager to educate employees with the necessary skills to take advantage of these changes. Often, these skills cannot be fully developed in the workplace. Employers who want to educate their employees through creating skills and enhancing their employee volunteer program can do so by utilizing the plan outlined in the workbook. For businesses, return value refers to the benefits that the business receives from the enhanced skills of employees and the good publicity that such a plan can generate. A good volunteer program will also help a business determine the most appropriate not-for-profits to associate or partner with.

The community can gain great benefits through a unified and centralized volunteer effort on behalf of individuals, not-for-profits, and for-profits. While the process can and does work through numerous individual and unrelated plans, the process can be much more successful if it is a single, community-wide effort. This is one of those circumstances where the whole is more than the sum of the parts. Chapter 10 will highlight a method for creating a community volunteer plan.

One of the unique features of this book is the computer disk found in the inside back cover. This disk contains:

- Blank versions of the worksheets;
- Listings of local and national groups that can provide advice and support on the process of volunteering;
- Forms and data provided by forward-thinking corporations who have pioneered successful employee volunteer programs that focus on return value;
- A brief review of *The National College Graduate Study on Volunteering.*

The *National College Graduate Study on Volunteering* was a study conducted in 1991 as part of my doctoral dissertation. The study verified a number of past assumptions on volunteering but it revealed a significant new finding, namely that "individuals who actively volunteer gained leadership traits regardless of the type of volunteer experience or profession that they pursued."[9] This was the beginning of my journey in documenting the enormous return value that individuals receive when they volunteer.

Although the plans contained in the workbook and disk are under copyright, each individual who purchases the workbook may use the materials for his or her personal use. Not-for-profits and for-profit businesses who want to implement the plan are respectfully asked to purchase additional copies of the workbook and disk for each principal user.

The world we live in has changed dramatically in the last decade. In order to keep up, we must change our approach in helping individuals, not-for-profits, and for-profit businesses cope with the changes taking place. We must find new ways of attracting and retaining volunteers. Including return value in a volunteer plan will enhance individual skills, preserve the philanthropic tradition, and increase the competitive edge of the entities involved.

Walter P. Pidgeon, Jr., PhD, CAE, CFRE

Washington, DC

ENDNOTES

[1]*Giving and Volunteering in the United States,* Independent Sector, Washington, D.C., 1996.

[2]Payton, Robert H., *Philanthropy: Voluntary Action for the Public Good,* Collier MacMillan Publishers, New York, NY, 1988, p. 44.

[3]Fisher, James L. and Gary H. Quehl, *The President and Fund Raising,* MacMillan Publishing Company, New York, NY, 1989, p. 19.

[4]Brenner, Robert H., 1988, *American Philanthropy,* University of Chicago Press, Chicago, IL, p. 3.

[5]Ellis, Susan J. and Katherine H. Noyes, *By the People,* Jossey-Bass Publishers, San Francisco, CA, 1990, XII.

[6]*Giving and Volunteering in the United States,* Independent Sector, Washington, D.C., 1996.

[7]"America's Independent Sector in Brief," *The Nonprofit Almanac,* Independent Sector, Washington, D.C., Winter 1996.

[8]Ibid.

[9]Pidgeon, Walter P., *Volunteering: The Leader's Competitive Edge,* The Union Institute, Cincinnati, OH, 1991.

▼ Acknowledgments

Volunteering has been a part of humankind since the beginning. The name for the process has varied but it is part of our nature for people to help people. So, it is appropriate to thank everyone who has come before me who has ever helped another person. These are the people who have developed the art of volunteering and who have made a difference in the lives of those they have encountered.

This publication would not have been possible if it were not for a number of individuals who have been instrumental in my professional life. These people include: Weaver Marr and Forest Witcraft, Salem College, Salem, West Virginia; Margaret A. Halstead, American Humanics, Kansas City, Missouri; Al Smith and Frank R. Fultz, Boy Scouts of America, Reading and Valley Forge Councils in Pennsylvania; and Robert C. Whitney, Combined Health Appeal, Baltimore, Maryland.

A special thanks to James L. Fisher, Robert T. Conley, Virginia Hodgkinson, Stephen W. Carey, John R. Miltner, and Charles G. Rodriguez who served on my doctoral committee and inspired me to devote my future research to the return value of volunteering.

This workbook is based on a study that I conducted in 1990 and 1991 to complete my doctoral degree titled *The National Graduate Study on Volunteering*. This study would not have been possible without a grant from the American Society of Association Executives Foundation and the special help of Jon P. Grove, CAE, ASAE's Executive Vice President.

A special thanks must go to the National Society of Fund Raising Executives' volunteer leadership for helping to publish this work. To Patricia F. Lewis, ACFRE, President & CEO, and Maurice Levite, CFRE, Senior Vice President, for encouraging the publication, to James Greenfield, ACFRE, for his advice and assistance. Thanks to the NSFRE Publishing Advisory Council including Suzanne Hittman, CFRE, Committee Chair, and the members of the committee, Nina Berkheiser, CFRE; Linda Chew, CFRE; Samuel N.

ACKNOWLEDGMENTS

Gough, CFRE, Ann Hyatt, ACFRE; James A Reid, Ph.D., CFRE, G. Patrick Williams, ACFRE, and Marie A. Reed, Ed.D, CNAA for making this publication part of the NSFRE/Wiley Fund Development Series.

Thanks must go to the Points of Light Foundation's leadership including Robert Goodwin, President & CEO, Mimi Galligan, Vice President Business Outreach; Barbara Louman and Jeffrey Hough who provided valuable information and assisted me in finding and accessing key corporations who understand the value of volunteering.

Thanks to the businesses leaders who provided me with example after example of how volunteering enriched the lives of their employees. These leaders include Reatha Clark King, General Mills Foundation; Jonie Johnson, Aid Association for Lutherans; Barbara Alfrey, Pillsbury Company; Jeff Hoffman, The Walt Disney Company; Roger G. Hancock, Bank of America; John T. Batty, General Electric; Judy Shober, Calvert Group; Carol Reiser, Federated Department Stores; Julie Hennessy, Dayton Hudson (Target Stores); Julie Bergman, Eli Lilly and Company; Rebecca Felsen, Chase Manhattan Bank; Laurie Heiser, Adams and Reese; Diane Spradlin, Electronic Data Systems (EDS), and Libby Alkire, Freddie Mac.

Thanks to the Wiley team who smoothly assisted in the production of this workbook. To Marla Bobowick, my initial acquisition editor, who believed in the book and was instrumental in obtaining approval for publication and to Martha Cooley who became the final acquisition editor and assisted me in expanding the market potential of the publication.

I have saved the final thank you for my family who, above all, had to endure the nights and weekends I spent working on this publication. To Susan Wallace Pidgeon, my wife of 28 years, who was at my side as my chief partner, critic, and editor on the project. To my son Walter (BJ) Pidgeon, III, who provided sound suggestions and editing support and to my son Spencer W. Pidgeon who provided computer support to the project. It was a team effort and the workbook would not have been completed without their help.

▼ Contents

8 Volunteering's Return Value to the Business World / 143

9 A Strategic Approach for Maximizing Volunteering's Value for the For-Profit Organization / 224

PART IV THE COMMUNITY: AN OPPORTUNITY TO FORM VOLUNTEER PARTNERSHIPS FOR THE COMMON GOOD

10 A Community Approach That Can Increase the Rate and the Worth of Volunteering / 273

▼ Definition of Terms

Acts of Good Work Another way to describe volunteering.

Calculated Risk A strategic move that is planned and well-thought-out. While it has an element of risk, it also has a genuine link to the mission of the organization and a chance to make a significant difference.

Family Volunteering A method of volunteering where the entire family unit volunteers to perform a project or activity together. This is one of the fastest growing developments in the current volunteer movement.

Farm Club A pool of volunteers who are being trained and developed for greater service opportunities.

Formal Volunteering Assisting others through acts organized and operated by a not-for-profit organization.

For-Profit Businesses Organizations designed to operate for personal or corporate monetary gain. They can issue stock.

Gifts-In-Kind The donation of a commodity instead of cash.

Group Volunteering Circumstances where a volunteer commitment is made as a group and not as an individual. This method is often used by for-profits who have employee volunteer programs.

Guide A term used to describe a volunteer who supervises another volunteer.

Informal Volunteering Assisting others through acts or good works on your own.

Market Segmentation The ability to find a niche in the market and to capitalize on this niche to improve the entity's competitive position by subdividing donor lists or prospect lists into smaller groupings with similar characteristics.

Not-For-Profit Organizations Organizations classified under the Internal Revenue Code as 501(c) organizations. These groups are formed to serve a designated purpose. These groups provide services of benefit to the public without financial incentive and are qualified by the Internal Revenue Service as tax-exempt. They cannot issue stock.

Partnership The association of two or more individuals or entities formed for the purpose of working together for mutual benefit.

Philanthropy The act of giving to make lasting change. This includes financial gifts to and/or personal involvement with causes such as charities, service clubs, youth groups, arts, education, environmental, or religious groups.

Public Sector The area of a nation's economy that is under governmental, rather than private, control. This includes all governmental agencies and functions within the community.

Return Value The direct benefits that an individual can receive from an act of volunteering.

Risk Taker A person who understands that certain calculated risks need to be taken in order to orchestrate change.

Self-spirituality The inner peace and perspective of an individual. How an individual perceives their position in life and their surroundings.

Strategic Thinker An individual who has the ability to see beyond the day-to-day activities of an organization to envision the future. A person who can guide an organization through calculated and planned steps to turn this vision into a reality.

Team A self-contained, multi-disciplinary group of individuals working together to produce an end result.

Volunteering Giving personal time freely for the purpose of assisting others. An act of good will for the betterment of the community.

The Universal Benefits of Volunteering

The Individual's Relationship to the Volunteer Process

The benefit that volunteering provides has traditionally been thought of as the good works given by the individual to the nonprofit organization and the community. While this is and should remain the main reason for volunteering, there is another reward that is created when an individual volunteers, namely, the return value that the individual who volunteers receives from the process. Return value has not been discussed a great deal but most individuals who volunteer understand that they receive value in return for their volunteering, including the "great feeling" that is received from helping others.

However, although this great feeling is often reward enough, a number of other benefits are often derived. An individual can enhance personal skills and make important professional contacts through volunteer experiences to maximize the return value of volunteering. Individuals can develop a step-by-step process or plan to seek the maximum personal benefit from each volunteer experience. Part I will explore the ways an individual can gain return value from volunteer experiences.

If you are new to the world of volunteering, Part I will help you develop lifetime skills that will enrich your personal life and professional career. If you are a more seasoned volunteer, scan the materials and take the time to critique your own volunteer experiences. Perhaps there is a technique or two that can help you increase the return value of future volunteer opportunities.

The act of volunteering is one of the most beneficial acts that any human can perform. Volunteering provides help to countless others. It can also benefit individuals who unselfishly give of their time as well. I encourage you to volunteer and to help others to explore the ways to maximize the return value of the volunteer process.

▼1 Planning the Volunteer Experience

1.1　INTRODUCTION

Volunteering can be conducted as either an informal or formal process. Informal volunteering can be provided in a number of ways, from helping an elderly neighbor to picking up trash on a vacant lot. Formal volunteering is conducted through a not-for-profit organization. For the most part, the procedures suggested in this chapter will be directed toward formal volunteering.

This chapter will illustrate how to engineer a more effective formal volunteer experience that increases the contribution to the community while maximizing the personal benefits that a volunteer receives from the experience. When seeking a volunteering position, an individual must first understand the overall process. Keep in mind that the average not-for-profit is continually looking for quality volunteers, which is an immense advantage if a volunteer is willing to make a genuine commitment. It is not difficult to find a volunteer position. The hard part is finding the volunteer position that provides the excitement and the return value desired by the volunteer.

In order to find the best position, a prospective volunteer will need to create a systematic approach for selecting a volunteer position. Here are the recommended steps:

1. Develop a listing of volunteer benefits that you wish to receive.
2. List the types of volunteer experiences that you would like to seek.
3. Determine the possible not-for-profit organization prospects that you wish to investigate.

4. List the knowledge, skills, and abilities that can assist you in volunteering.
5. Develop a plan to approach and to gain access to the top not-for-profit prospects.
6. Create an agenda and a list of objectives that you want to discuss when you initially meet with the not-for-profit representative.
7. Develop a one-page brief on the volunteer position desired.
8. Create an agenda and a list of objectives that you want to discuss for the second meeting with the not-for-profit representative.
9. Institute the volunteer agreement.
10. Create an agenda and a list of objectives that you want to discuss for the final meeting with the not-for-profit representative.

Throughout this chapter, a fictitious person named James Jones will be going through the volunteer process. Your volunteer aspirations may not be an exact match to his, but the systematic approach outlined in this chapter can work for most positions you will want to seek.

James Jones is new in town. He is thirty-seven years old, married, and has a son who is thirteen years old and a daughter who is eight years old. He has just started his third professional position since graduating from SME University. Jim is used to moving; he had to move the last time a new career opportunity became available. His first two positions dealt primarily in the public relations field and the companies he worked for specialized in health-related activities. He discovered that sales was where the action, fun, and promotions seem to generate, so Jim sought a position as a sales manager at XYZ, Inc., a major company that provides goods to health care institutions in the region. He was quickly hired. Jim very much wants to volunteer, and he wants to choose a position and organization that will meet his personal and professional needs. At each step along the way, Jim Jones will serve as an example of how to approach the volunteering process. He will show you how he filled out the worksheets, which are provided in the Appendix to this chapter and are also included on the disk.

1.2 DEVELOP A LISTING OF VOLUNTEERING BENEFITS THAT THE VOLUNTEER DESIRES

The first step prospective volunteers should take is to develop a list of the benefits that they wish to receive in their next volunteer position. For those who have volunteered in the past, this may sound rather basic, but it can provide some surprising results. Spend a few minutes thinking of the positive benefits, and also the areas that should be avoided.

On occasion, individuals are recruited to volunteer by being given misleading information. "It is an easy job. You only have to attend one meeting a month and assist in activities for one or two hours between meetings." Then the volunteer finds out that "one meeting a month" means that the eight gatherings held each month constituted one meeting and that "one or two hours between meetings" means eight times two. Since they were unable to recruit the fifteen other volunteers for the committee, the lone volunteer is now the chair for the committee and will need to "double-up a bit" to ensure that the goals of the committee are achieved.

This may sound like an exaggeration, however it is not an unfamiliar experience for those who are seasoned volunteers. Does this mean that most not-for-profits are poorly run? Not at all. Most not-for-profits are well managed and they will welcome any inquiry from an individual who wishes to use a systematic approach to choosing a volunteering opportunity.

Let us look at how James Jones has approached this process in Exhibit 1.1. Note that the form is divided into three areas: general requirements, personal requirements, and career requirements.

(a)   General Requirements

This is the area in which the type of volunteer experience should be detailed, the geographical location should be determined, and the type of not-for-profit that fits the volunteer's needs, unique requirements, and general interests should be outlined.

Jim has listed what he felt were his basic overall needs. Note that Jim wishes to focus on health-related organizations with a mission focused on the disadvantaged. He wants the group to be financially sound and to have liability insurance protection for its volunteers. Jim wishes to volunteer for a not-for-profit that minimizes his risk. Jim is new in town and is in a new professional position and does not want to become involved in a negative situation. Jim's time is at a premium, therefore, he wants the volunteer experience to be near his office and home.

(b)   Personal Requirements

This is an area that should also be explored. What kind of skills would you like to gain? Do you wish to have a socialization aspect with the experience? Do you want to receive visual recognition for your efforts? You can also list any other particular requirements that are unique to you.

Jim has indicated that he is interested in having an experience that increases his team work skills. Now that he has become a supervisor, he feels

EXHIBIT 1.1 The Volunteer Benefits Requirements Form

Name:	James Jones
Type of Volunteer Experience Sought:	To work with a health not-for-profit
Date:	12/4/97

The following listing contains the benefits or "return value" that I wish to receive from my next volunteer experience. They represent both my personal desires/needs and the career enhancements I seek.

General Requirements

1. To be a member of a highly visible committee and to seek a volunteer chair's position within one year;
2. The position needs to be within ten miles of my office;
3. The organization has to be well known, respected, and financially sound;
4. The organization must carry liability protection for its volunteers; and
5. The organization must be health-related and provide services to the disadvantaged of the city.

Personal Requirements

1. I want to gain additional team working skills;
2. Since I am new in town, I want to associate with an organization that has major social events that will assist me to assimilate into the social structure of the community
3. I want a position that will primarily provide volunteering experiences during business hours; and
4. It would be a plus if the volunteer experience provided a recognition program that will increase my visibility in the community.

Career Requirements.

1. I wish to meet and associate with the leadership in the health field in our community;
2. I wish to gain a better understanding of the health care needs of those who are not insured;
3. I want to help explore the possible partnership between my company and the health organization that I select; and
4. I want to make sure that the volunteer position that I select will open doors to greater volunteer opportunities.

that this will assist him in managing his sales staff. He is particularly interested in the social aspects of the volunteer position. This will be an advantage for both him and his wife. He also wants to have most of his volunteer experiences during the work day. This reflects his need to spend time with his children. While the recognition factor is often overlooked, this is an important factor for Jim, because it will assist him in gaining visibility quickly within the community.

(c)   Career Requirements

This can be the most interesting listing of all. Can the volunteer position that you seek provide a meaningful return to your career? The answer is a resounding yes if you fully understand what you wish to gain from a volunteer experience and seek an appropriate volunteer position to gain the requirements sought.

Jim wants to gain access to the health care leadership in his community. He wants to seek a volunteer position in a not-for-profit organization that attracts a number of volunteers who are health care leaders. He wants to know more about health care for the uninsured. Not-for-profit organizations who offer health care to the poor will be his leading candidates.

Jim has a lot to offer the prospective not-for-profit institution for which he will volunteer. Indeed, it might provide a possible partnership opportunity with his company. This can be a great "calling card" when he begins his visitations to prospective not-for-profits.

Partnerships between not-for-profit and for-profit organizations are a growing trend. Not all not-for-profits will welcome the thought, however. Organizations that have vision and understand the need for closer ties within the entire community will welcome such an opportunity.

Jim made an important statement when he set a requirement that the volunteer position he would select needed to "open doors" to greater volunteer opportunities. He is stating that he is willing to volunteer for a particular position for a period of time with the expectation that he will be asked to assume a new and more challenging volunteer position in the future. This progression is important to him and to his career pursuits. James Jones has listed his desires well.

When you begin the process yourself, do not hesitate to list all the requirements that you seek. You may not obtain all that you wish from your next volunteer position but you will have a better understanding of what you seek from the volunteering experience. This will help you to begin your journey towards finding the volunteer positions that will provide increased return value for you.

1.3 LIST THE TYPES OF VOLUNTEER EXPERIENCES THAT YOU WOULD LIKE TO SEEK

The next step is to list the types of volunteer experience you would like to seek. James Jones' choices are illustrated in Exhibit 1.2. This step in the process provides an opportunity to translate your requirements onto a form that can be used for public consumption. Note that the sample provides five areas or focus points. These will be areas that can be explained or reviewed quite easily when the appropriate time arrives.

(a)   Area Sought

This provides an opportunity to clearly state the particular volunteer position sought. Jim wants to volunteer for a health-related position in a well respected health organization. This statement eliminates the need to review any non-health-related not-for-profit in his community.

(b)   Level of Responsibility Required

This provides an opportunity to focus on the type of position sought. In Jim's case, he wishes to be involved in the upper level of an organization. He wants to be a committee member and to chair a committee within one year. This is a smart move on Jim's part. It is unlikely that an organization will have a chair's position open when he is seeking a volunteer position. It will be easier and more prudent to seek a committee position while also making it clear that he would really like a chair position.

(c)   Description of the Type of Position Requested

This section provides an opportunity for the prospective volunteer to create a base or a concept of the volunteer position desired. Often a volunteer position's title may not reflect the real nature of the position. By highlighting the value you seek in the volunteer position desired, an organization leader can locate or even develop a new position that fits your needs. Jim clearly states that he wants a position that increases his knowledge concerning local health care needs while also linking him with key opinion makers in the community. This provides Jim with a clearly defined need that is easily explained.

EXHIBIT 1.2 Types of Volunteer Experiences Sought

Name:	James Jones
Date:	12/4/97

Volunteer experiences can vary. One not-for-profit can provide a wonderful experience at the committee level while another organization may offer an experience at the board level that is filled with problems and disappointments. That is why it is important to clearly articulate the type of experience that you seek.

Area Sought

I wish to volunteer for a health-related position in a well respected health organization.

Level of Responsibility Required

I want to be involved in the upper level of the organization. At minimum, a committee member level with an opportunity to chair a key committee in one year.

Description of the Type of Position Requested

I want to have a position that not only increases my knowledge about the state of health care in the community but also links me to the key opinion makers in the community.

Time and Location Sought

I wish to perform most of my volunteer duties during business hours and within ten miles of my business location.

Other Areas *(List particular areas or concerns that you may have.)*

I would like to have an orientation session conducted prior to my first meeting to make sure that I am up to speed and that I fully understand my role in the function that I select.

(d)   Time and Location Sought

This provides a simple and direct way of stating when and where you wish to perform your volunteer duties. Jim wants to volunteer during business hours so he can spend the evening hours with his children. He also wants his volunteer position to be near his office due to the time restraints placed on him at work.

(e)   Other Areas

This section is designed to list additional areas of concern or need. Note that Jim would like to have an orientation session before he starts his volunteer experience. This is a good idea for Jim since he is new in town and he wants to make a good impression at the first meeting or gathering that he attends as a volunteer.

Upon reviewing and focusing on the types of volunteer experiences sought, the prospective volunteer now has a general idea of the type of volunteer experience to seek, the kind of not-for-profit to investigate, and the overall needs required.

1.4   DETERMINE THE POSSIBLE NOT-FOR-PROFIT ORGANIZATION PROSPECT THAT YOU WISH TO INVESTIGATE

The next step in the process is to locate the organizations that best fit your needs. Exhibit 1.3 provides a way to list, in a consistent fashion, the prospects that fit your requirements. Not-for-profits vary a great deal in size, culture, and use of volunteers, so it is important to obtain the core information on each prospective organization in order to make an educated decision based on up-to-date data. Note that the listing includes a contact or referral person. If you can obtain a name or talk to someone who has influence with the not-for-profit, it will help you a great deal in obtaining the position desired. It helps to know the mission statement which will tell a great deal about the organization and will act as a guide to your decision. Also try to discover the areas that may fulfill your volunteer goals. This information will be useful when you meet with the prospect organization.

There are a number of ways to identify which not-for-profits you want to investigate. The methods will vary depending on the type, the size, and the geographical reach of the organization. Jim focused on the local area near his office and found two possibilities, which is a low number to start with. It is best to begin with three to five prospects.

James Jones had a bit of good luck. A client of his, John Smith, Vice President of DFL, Inc., is currently on the board of the Southeastern Chapter of the American Health Association. Smith provided him with all the information that he needs on the organization. This will help Jim to determine if American Health Association should be an organization prospect.

Henry Johnson, Area Health Coordinator, Health Plus, Inc., is Jim's neighbor. He volunteered for the Northwest Area Health Center's last

EXHIBIT 1.3 The Not-For-Profit Organization Prospects

Name:	James Jones
Date:	12/4/97

Name/location: American Health Association - Southeastern Chapter, 125 Main Street

Contact/referral: John Smith, Vice President, DFL Inc.

Budget and financial condition: $13,500,000 The organization has had a surplus for three years and has a $2,000,000 reserve.

Number of staff: 48

Number of volunteers: 3150

Mission: To provide disaster relief and a quality blood supply to the community.

Programs: 47 programs (Note additional information attached.)

Areas that fulfill my volunteer goals: Several committees relate to community health issues. The organization also has high visibility and has among its list of volunteers key opinion makers in the community.

Other: It is an organization that I would be proud and honored to be a volunteer for.

Name/location: Northwest Area Health Center, 1350 Elm Street

Contact/referral: Henry Johnson, Area Health Coordinator, Health Plus, Inc.

Budget and financial condition: $2,100,000 Organization ended in the red last year and is running a $500,000 deficit.

Number of staff: 17

Number of volunteers: 321

Mission: To provide the residents of the northwest with basic primary health care.

Programs: 14 programs (Note additional information attached.)

Areas that fulfill my volunteer goals: The organization needs quality volunteers and they have programs that fulfill my goal of discovering the health needs of residents throughout my community.

Other: There may be a risk to volunteering for this organization. It is not fiscally sound. Yet, I would enjoy the challenge.

Name/location:

Contact/referral:

Budget and financial condition:

Number of staff:

Number of volunteers:

Mission:

Programs:

Areas that fulfill my volunteer goals:

Other:

capital campaign. Mr. Johnson put Jim in touch with Julie Brown, Deputy Director of the Northwest Area Health Center, who sent him a packet of information. Jim placed the Center on his list of organization prospects as well.

Jim found his information through his contacts. This is often the best way because a lot of barriers can be avoided by using this method. If Jim had not had his contacts, he could have sought information through a number of local sources including the United Way, the Better Business Bureau, or the local chapters of the National Society of Fund Raising Executives. He might also have contacted the American Society of Association Executives, the Points of Light Foundation's Volunteer Center, or a host of other organizations unique to each particular area of interest. In our present example, the local United Way and a health-related state association may have been the key to getting the information Jim Jones needed.

The information revealed under budget and financial condition tells an interesting story. While the American Health Association is in fine shape, the Northwest Area Health Center is running a deficit. The number of staff and the number of volunteers can assist you in determining the level of support volunteers may receive and which professional position may be assigned to support a particular volunteer position.

The information available today is overwhelming. In addition to the directories in your local library, local, regional, state, and national organizations are providing accessible information on the Internet with their own Web pages. The easiest way to obtain an Internet address is to call the appropriate organization directly. They will be happy to provide the information you need to access their Web page, if they have one.

James Jones' selection of the Southeastern Chapter of the American Health Association (AHA) and the Northwest Area Health Center (NAHC) are two interesting choices. AHA seems to have it all. Jim felt that he would be proud to be a volunteer with that organization. NAHC addressed his requirement of obtaining additional knowledge concerning individuals who are receiving health care but it does not have health insurance coverage.

1.5   LIST THE KNOWLEDGE, SKILLS, AND ABILITIES THAT CAN ASSIST YOU IN VOLUNTEERING

The last preparation before approaching a prospective not-for-profit organization is to list the knowledge, skills, and abilities that you feel you have acquired. This list can provide an array of selling points when you meet with not-for-profit representatives. Exhibit 1.4. provides an example of how James Jones measured his ability for a particular volunteer position.

(a) Personal Background

This will provide insight on who you are as a person and how it may relate to the volunteer position in question. James Jones has a volunteer background that relates to health-oriented activities. Exhibit 1.4 does not fully detail Jim's experiences but the actual document should.

EXHIBIT 1.4 A List of Knowledge, Skills, and Abilities for Volunteering

Name:	James Jones
Date:	12/4/97

Personal Background

I enjoy working with people to solve challenges. I began to volunteer as a teenager at the local hospital. In the past ten years I have volunteered for various not-for-profit activities that helped my community and assisted my children in their non-school activities.

Academic Background

I have a B.S. in health sciences and a M.S. in health administration. Although my career has taken me into health sales, I would like to use my academic background more in my volunteer activities.

Professional Background

Most of my professional positions have had a relationship with the health industry. My present position relates to health sales. My customer base consists of large hospitals and health networks. Here is a listing of my experiences. (List experiences or attach a biography.)

Other (List other knowledge, skills, and abilities that you feel would assist in future volunteer experiences.)

I came from a family rich in love but poor in worldly goods. Our family never had health insurance and we seldom saw a doctor.

(b)   Academic Background

This can help a great deal to illustrate an individual's knowledge based on a particular subject that can relate directly or indirectly to the volunteer position sought. In Jim's case, he has a degree that relates directly to the organizations for which he wants to volunteer.

(c)   Professional Background

This is the prime area that most not-for-profit volunteer recruiters seem to relate to. Although it should not be the only criteria, it is an important one. In Jim's case, his professional career has been spent in health-related industries which seems to fit well with the type of volunteer position that he seeks.

(d)   Other

This section deals with the skills and abilities that do not fit well in the other categories. Take the time to list these skills. The items listed here can hold the key to why you are seeking a particular volunteer position. In Jim's case, it is his background. His family was poor. They did not have health insurance and, therefore, they did not seek a health practitioner unless it was absolutely necessary. Jim may have been drawn to work in the health care industry due to his family situation. He may also be seeking a volunteer position to ensure that poor families, who do not have health insurance, continue to have an opportunity to receive quality health care.

1.6   DEVELOP A PLAN TO APPROACH AND TO GAIN ACCESS TO THE TOP NOT-FOR-PROFIT PROSPECTS

Now that you have completed your research and have determined the type of volunteer position you seek and the organizations that you would like to investigate, you are ready to approach and gain access to the not-for-profits that you have identified. Exhibit 1.5 can assist you in making these approaches successfully.

When you determine the not-for-profits that fulfill your requirements, list them in order of preference. This should be relatively easy based on your research. Seek the best person possible to gain access to. It may begin

EXHIBIT 1.5 A Plan to Approach and Gain Access to the Not-For-Profit Prospects

1. Determine the leading not-for-profit organizations that fulfill your requirement to volunteer;
2. Find out who the key volunteers and/or professionals are that lead the organization and are focused on the area(s) that interest you;
3. Review your network to determine if you have an individual that has the ability to approach any of the identified individuals;
4. If you can identify individuals who can help you to approach the leadership of not-for-profit organization, utilize them to "open the door;"
5. If you do not have someone in your network to "open the door," contact the highest individual that you have identified to gain access; and
6. Do not fully explain your wishes over the telephone. Your objective is to make an appointment to meet with the highest ranking individual possible. Note that you will need only a few minutes and that you wish to learn more about the organization to possibly participate and/or to contribute.

with a volunteer, but for the most part it will be a full-time professional within the organization who has knowledge of the various volunteer positions available. The key contact that you have developed for each not-for-profit prospect should be able to direct you to the best person within the organization, perhaps even the Chief Executive Officer (CEO). If that can be arranged, go for it. It will energize the process.

In Jim Jones's case, he was able to use the contacts he made through a client and a neighbor to obtain the best entry into the prospective organizations. Jim contacted the American Health Association through the operations director, Jack Thompson. This was due to the relationship that John Smith, Jim's client, had with Jack. Jim met with Jack at the organization's offices. Jack provided a wealth of information and a tour of the facilities. Jim Jones was also able to arrange an appointment with Julie Brown, Deputy Director of the Northwest Area Health Center. Although Julie had sent a packet of information, the meeting and the tour of the center helped Jim have a better understanding of the overall needs of the organization.

If you are unable to develop a key contact person, start by contacting the CEO of the organization directly. Call the organization to obtain the name of the current CEO. Then call again and ask for the CEO by name. In a number of cases, you will meet with another person but that is okay. You will have been referred to that person by the CEO and that will not go unnoticed.

The telephone call to the not-for-profit is one of the most important steps in the process. The call should be an inquiry call, not a call to volunteer. You are calling to inquire about the organization to possibly participate and/or consider making a contribution. If you performed well on the telephone call, you will increase the CEO's interest in meeting you. The CEO will ask questions that you need to be prepared to answer. Your research will help you answer the questions successfully. The CEO will want to know your background, your interests, and your abilities.

If you answer the questions well, you will have an opportunity for an appointment. If the CEO is not willing to meet with you, ask if you can meet with an associate. Most of the time, the CEO will refer you to a key person in the organization. When you call that person, be sure to tell them that you were referred to them by the CEO. If the CEO is not interested in helping you investigate the organization, then you should stop considering any position with that group. It is not an organization that seeks and welcomes volunteers and it is not an organization that will be eager to provide you with the return value that you seek.

At this point, you should have two to three not-for-profit prospects to investigate. This is an ideal grouping. It is always best to have multiple prospects to compare. This is not an exact science; do not be concerned if you end up with only one not-for-profit prospect. The process is still working even if you have eliminated organizations that do not fit your requirements.

1.7   CREATE AN AGENDA AND LIST OF OBJECTIVES THAT YOU CAN DISCUSS WHEN YOU INITIALLY MEET WITH THE NOT-FOR-PROFIT REPRESENTATIVE

It is now time to set up an appointment. Think of the initial meeting as a cultivation visit. It is a time to see the not-for-profit facility and its professionals first hand. It is also the time to acquire a sense of how the organization operates. The most important objective of the visit is to discover possible volunteer positions available and to begin to position yourself for the position desired.

Exhibit 1.6 provides a suggested agenda or list of objectives for the initial meeting. Note that the meeting has three parts: the pre-meeting, the meeting, and the post-meeting. Each of these areas requires your full attention to make the process successful.

Jim Jones made sure he followed the recommended steps. He developed an agenda that included the objectives that he wanted to accomplish. He knew that his objectives would have to be evaluated differently as he reviewed each prospective organization and that he would need to adapt

---

EXHIBIT 1.6 The Agenda and List of Objectives That You Can Discuss When You Initially Meet with the Not-For-Profit Representative

---

I. Pre-meeting(s)
  -Develop an agenda or list of objectives for the meeting;
  -Have a one page brief on the organization that you are seeing;
  -Determine, based on the information obtained, the area(s) that you would like to volunteer in; and
  -Send a short letter to the individual that you will be meeting to confirm the appointment.
II. The Meeting(s)
  -Open the meeting by complimenting the individual on the important role that their organization has played in the community;
  -Take the time to review your background;
  -Inquire what is currently occurring in the area that is of interest to you;
  -Determine the area(s) that you would like to volunteer in based on information gained before and during the meeting;
  -Suggest the area(s) that you would like to volunteer in and get a reaction to your request;
  -Based on the response, suggest that you would like to think a bit more about volunteering for the organization; and
  -Set the date for the next meeting.
III. Post-meeting(s)
  -Compare each of the visits to the not-for-profit prospects to determine if you wish to continue the process with one or more of them;
  -Send a letter to each of the not-for-profit representatives whose organizations you wish to continue the process with. Thank them for taking the time to visit with you and confirm the next meeting including date and time; and
  -Send a letter to each of the not-for-profits that you felt did not meet your requirements to cancel the next meeting and to note that you will be pursuing other volunteer opportunities.

---

to each group's unique culture. In preparing for the agenda Jim thought about:

1. How each organization functioned;
2. The relationship that the organization had with its volunteers;
3. The types of upper level volunteer positions that were available;
4. Who were some of the key volunteers;
5. The qualifications needed for these volunteer positions;

6. The time it would require to fulfill the role of each volunteer position; and
7. Whether or not the not-for-profit felt right for him.

(a)   The Pre-meeting

This is a time to develop the agenda and to list the objectives for the meeting. Exhibit 1.6 provides the outline but the details are unique and can only be developed by the person who wishes to volunteer. Be sure to take the time to list your objectives before the meeting. Also be sure to develop a one page brief on the not-for-profit organizations that you are meeting. Your research should be enough to complete this task.

Be prepared to take along the forms you developed on the types of volunteer experiences sought (based on Exhibit 1.2) and a listing of your knowledge, skills, and abilities for volunteering (based on Exhibit 1.4). Finally, once the appointment has been set by telephone, be sure to send a short letter confirming the appointment. This will illustrate to the organization's representative that you are serious about investigating the organization and it will ensure that the date, time, and place are correct.

(b)   The Meeting

This is the time to demonstrate that you are a rare find. Although you are there to learn, you need to take control of the meeting. In fact, you called the meeting and you are there to discover information and to make a decision that will directly affect your life.

Open the meeting by complimenting the representative on the quality of the organization. Illustrate this by reviewing the findings that you obtained about the organization. Take the time to review your background. Emphasize the areas in which you have an interest. Inquire if volunteer positions currently exist in the general areas that interest you. Let the representative provide you with information on current opportunities. Make a suggestion or two on positions that may interest you. If the volunteer positions presented do not interest you, then suggest a few positions that would interest you and see what kind of reaction you receive.

Tell the representative that you would like to think about the opportunities and compare them to the other volunteer opportunities that you are investigating. See what reaction this receives. Set a date to visit the not-for-profit representative before you leave the meeting. This will help keep the process moving and let the not-for-profit representative know that you are still serious.

(c)   The Post-meeting

This process should include a review of all the visits made to the competing not-for-profits. Compare each of them to the requirements that you placed on your Volunteer Benefits Requirements Form (based on Exhibit 1.1). Based on that evaluation, determine the organizations that you wish to continue to visit. Send a confirmation letter to them to verify the next meeting. If you have dropped any organizations from your prospect list, send a letter thanking them for their time and tell them that you will be pursuing other volunteer opportunities.

Now is the time to focus on the remaining not-for-profits.

1.8   DEVELOP A ONE PAGE BRIEF ON THE VOLUNTEER POSITION DESIRED

Exhibit 1.7 lists four areas to consider:

1. The requirements of the position;
2. Your qualifications;
3. The general, personal, and career requirements that this position fulfills; and
4. Any other areas that need to be addressed.

This one page brief provides the prospective volunteer with a powerful tool to sell the not-for-profit representative on providing a meaningful volunteer position. This can be prepared if a particular position was suggested or can be effectively used to sell a new or expanded volunteer role.

In Exhibit 1.7, James Jones prepared himself for the second round of meetings. He was told that only a few top level volunteer positions were available at the Northwest Area Health Center. The Chair of the Public Relations Committee was one of them. Jim's one page brief provided ample data to show that he was well-qualified for the position. Most of the data was obtained through the research process. Jim did add one stipulation under the "areas that need to be addressed" category, namely, that the organization must obtain liability insurance for its volunteers. He noted, however, that his company might be able to provide a donation to offset the cost. Jim was aware that although a number of state and federal governments have begun to offer liability protection to volunteers, volunteer leaders could still be subject to certain lawsuits. A basic liability policy would offer added protection.

EXHIBIT 1.7 The One Page Brief on the Volunteer Position Desired

Not-For-Profit Organization:	Northwest Area Health Center
Volunteer Position Desired:	Chair of the Public Relations Committee
Name:	James Jones

The Position in Brief

The position calls for an experienced public relations person with corporate contacts who can recruit qualified volunteers for the committee. Must be able to attend the monthly meetings of the committee and have the time between the meetings to perform the tasks outlined in the job description.

My Qualifications

I have had a great deal of experience in the fine art of public relations. Although my present position is not directly involved in the public relations field, I obtained training in college and spent the first seven years of my career working full-time as a public relations professional. My background has assisted me in attaining my current position and to become the manager of the sales force at my company. My public relations training continues to be used on a daily basis.

General, Personal, Career Requirements That This Position Meets

The committee chair seems to be a highly visible position, most of the meetings will be held near my office, Northwest Area Health Center is a well-known organization, and its mission is health-related. It seems that the duties of the position could be carried out primarily during business hours, that I could gain teamworking skills and meet new people. It would also help me to better understand the local health care needs in my community, I would meet and associate with a number of the key health leaders in the area, and I feel that the organization could benefit from a closer relationship with my company.

Areas to Address

The materials given to me to date have not mentioned if the organization has liability insurance for its volunteers. If it does not, then I would want to request that the organization obtain the coverage before I officially volunteer. My company may be able to financially assist.

I would also want to review the strategic plan to determine if the organization is addressing the documented financial needs. Again, my company may be able to assist.

1.9 CREATE AN AGENDA AND LIST OF OBJECTIVES THAT YOU CAN DISCUSS DURING THE SECOND MEETING WITH THE NOT-FOR-PROFIT REPRESENTATIVE

(a) The Pre-meeting

Preparation for the second encounter is similar to the initial meeting. You will need to develop an agenda or list of objectives (see Exhibit 1.8) and a one page brief on the volunteer position desired (see Exhibit 1.7).

EXHIBIT 1.8 The Agenda and List of Objectives That You Can Discuss During the Second Meeting with the Not-For-Profit Representative

---

I. Pre-meeting(s)
   -Develop an agenda or list of objectives for the meeting; and
   -Develop a one page brief on the volunteer position desired.
II. The Meeting(s)
   -Open the meeting by thanking the not-for-profit representative for taking the time to see you again;
   -Review the last meeting;
   -Suggest that you have given some thought to volunteering for the organization and would like to discuss the opportunity further;
   -Present the one page brief;
   -Let the not-for-profit representative respond to your request;
   -Be flexible. The exact volunteer opportunity may not be available but another position may be presented that is just as good;
   -If offered, review the position in detail to make sure that it fits your pre-determined needs;
   -State that you want to think about the volunteer opportunity offered and wish to meet one more time; and
   -Set the date for the next meeting.
III. Post-meeting(s)
   -Send a letter to thank the not-for-profit representative for taking the time to visit with you and confirm the final meeting's time and date

---

(b) The Meeting

This will tend to be more relaxed than the initial meeting. By now you have established a relationship with the not-for-profit representative. Take the time to review the last meeting to make sure that the representative fully recalls what took place and tell him or her that you have given some thought to volunteering for the organization.

Present the one page brief on the volunteer position desired and provide time for the representative to react to the brief. This is the time to be flexible. The exact volunteer position you want may or may not be available. If the position is available, you have made your best case. If the position is not available, perhaps another position of the same or higher quality can be arranged. If the position is offered, review it in detail to make sure that you understand the opportunity. Take detailed notes. Thank the not-for-profit representative for offering the position and indicate that you would like to think about it. Set up an appointment for the final meeting.

Jim Jones followed the suggested plan as outlined above. This helped him to focus more on the volunteer position that he desired. He was offered a key position in the Northwest Area Health Center as Chair of the Public Relations Committee. This was exactly what he had sought. While it was not the leading health group, it provided the best opportunity to fulfill his needs and to provide a quality service to the community. The American Health Association could not offer Jim a key spot right away.

(c) The Post-meeting

This consists of sending a confirmation letter thanking the not-for-profit representative for offering the position. Tell the representative that you look forward to meeting again to discuss the opportunity further.

1.10 THE VOLUNTEER AGREEMENT

Before you attend the final meeting, a key document, the volunteer agreement, needs to be prepared. This is a detailed agreement based on the data obtained from the second meeting. Exhibit 1.9 provides a suggested outline. This document should contain what you understand to be the duties of the position and what the not-for-profit will provide to maximize the return value to you.

The volunteer agreement should be prepared by the prospective volunteer to ensure that these provisions are met. The not-for-profit representa-

EXHIBIT 1.9 The Volunteer Agreement

Not-for-Profit Organization:	Northwest Area Health Center
Volunteer Position:	Chair of the Public Relations Committee
Name:	James Jones
Date:	1/7/98

After careful consideration based on the data I have obtained on my own and my information-gathering visits to Northwest Area Health Center, I have determined that volunteering for the position of Chair of the Public Relations Committee would provide a service that the center needs and would provide me with the volunteer experience that I have been seeking.

I understand that I will be asked to perform the following duties:
- Chair the Public Relations Committee;
- Recruit seven members of the committee who have media/communications background;
- Preside over the monthly meetings of the committee;
- Help to develop a marketing plan;
- Be a member of the board of directors;
- Be a member of the fund-raising committee; and
- Become a sustaining member of the center.

The center will assist me to be successful by:
- Providing an orientation meeting to review the duties of the position;
- Providing past meeting minutes for the public relations committee, board of directors, and fund-raising committee;
- Providing a list of the key volunteers with the center;
- Extending invitations to major meetings and social gatherings of the center; and
- Assigning a contact person at the center who understands my role and can assist in supporting my volunteer effort.

It is my understanding that this will be a two-year commitment. It is also my understanding that if my personal or professional schedule would make it impossible to continue prior to the end of two years that I would give sufficient notice for the center to find a new volunteer chair. It is my understanding that an evaluation component will be put in place which will provide regular review of this position and that the evaluation will be conducted as a team effort between myself and the Chair of the Board. Upon my official appointment I will become a sustaining member of the center for two years at $500 per year.

James Jones	Date	Not-for-Profit Representative	Date

tive may prepare a similar document as well but it may not contain all of the elements that you desire.

In Exhibit 1.9, James Jones has done his homework. His volunteer agreement contains all the elements that he understands he will be required to do, including becoming a sustaining member of the center. It also lists all of the requirements that the center will perform in order to ensure that his volunteer experience will be successful. Jim has also noted when he will volunteer and he has given himself an escape clause in case his job or personal circumstances make it impossible for him to continue as a volunteer for the center.

1.11 CREATE AN AGENDA AND LIST OF OBJECTIVES THAT YOU CAN DISCUSS AT THE FINAL MEETING WITH THE NOT-FOR-PROFIT REPRESENTATIVE

The final meeting as outlined in Exhibit 1.10 has as its major objective the completion of obtaining the desired volunteer position.

(a) The Pre-meeting

This calls for the development of the agenda and the list of objectives for the meeting and the creation of the volunteer agreement as outlined above and in Exhibit 1.9.

(b) The Meeting

This is quite casual, now having met twice before, and it is a meeting that can be accomplished quickly. This is the time to note that you are seriously thinking of volunteering for the position in question. Present the volunteer agreement that you have prepared. Let the not-for-profit representative respond. If the organization has a volunteer agreement of its own, be flexible. Offer to use their form but make sure that all of your requirements are contained in the combined volunteer agreement.

Jim Jones was well prepared for this final meeting. He had brought with him the volunteer agreement that he developed. In his case, the organization did not have an agreement so they used Jim's. He received just about everything he sought. The organization was delighted that Jim's

EXHIBIT 1.10 The Agenda and List of Objectives That You Can Discuss at the Final Meeting with the Not-For-Profit Representative

I. Pre-meeting(s)
   -Develop an agenda or list of objectives for the meeting; and
   -Create a one page volunteer agreement for presentation.

II. The Meeting(s)
   -Open the meeting by thanking the not-for-profit representative for meeting again;
   -Note that you want to seriously consider volunteering for the position;
   -Present the one page volunteer agreement;
   -Allow the not-for-profit representative to respond to the agreement;
   -The not-for-profit may have an agreement of its own. If so, agree to use their agreement and suggest that the essence of your request be placed in the document;
   -Ask for a packet of information on the duties of the volunteer position, the dates of meetings, and the names, addresses, and telephone numbers of the volunteers that will be involved with you;
   -Ask if you can have an orientation session to review the duties of the position prior to the first meeting or function that you will need to attend; and
   -Inquire about the evaluation process concerning your volunteer position.

III. Post-meeting(s)
   -Send a letter thanking the not-for-profit representative for the time that was spent and for helping to make the process of volunteering so enjoyable.

company would assist in helping to underwrite the cost of a liability insurance policy for volunteers at the center. This had been an area that the center had needed help with for some time.

Ask for a packet of materials on the position in question and set a date for an orientation meeting to fully discuss the position in detail. Also, inquire about the evaluation process and how it relates to the position in question. Make sure that you are a vital part of the evaluation process.

(c)   The Post-meeting

This consists of sending a thank you note to the not-for-profit representative to express your appreciation for the time spent and for making the process enjoyable.

1.12   CONCLUSION

James Jones succeeded in procuring a key volunteer position at the North-west Area Health Center. Although the center was number two on his list, it was his family background that convinced him to seriously review this volunteer opportunity. The combination of service to the community and the return value offered made the sale. The organization also took the time to work with Jim to discover the type of volunteer position that would best fit him both personally and professionally.

In short, the Center obtained a quality volunteer; the community and the clients at the Center will benefit from his volunteer work; Jim's employer will benefit from the positive community relations that will result; Jim will be a more educated and involved employee; and Jim will benefit in a number of other personal and professional ways.

Chapter 1 has outlined methods to seek volunteer opportunities that maximize the benefits to your community and to you. Chapter 2 will show the individual how to maximize the volunteer experience and receive return value. You are a valuable asset to your community. You can make a difference through volunteering and volunteering can make a difference in you.

APPENDIX

WORKSHEETS*

*These worksheets can also be found on the computer disk located at the back of the book.

The Volunteer Benefits Requirements Form

Name:
Type of Volunteer Experience Sought:
Date:

The following listing contains the benefits or "return value" that I wish to receive from my next volunteer experience. They represent both my personal desires/needs and the career enhancements I seek.

General Requirements

Personal Requirements

Career Requirements.

Types of Volunteer Experiences Sought

Name:

Date:

Volunteer experiences can vary. One not-for-profit can provide a wonderful experience at the committee level while another organization may offer an experience at the board level that is filled with problems and disappointments. That is why it is important to clearly articulate the type of experience that you seek.

Area Sought

Level of Responsibility Required

Description of the Type of Position Requested

Time and Location Sought

Other Areas *(List particular areas or concerns that you may have.)*

The Not-For-Profit Organization Prospects

Name:

Date:

Name/location:

Contact/referral:

Budget and financial condition:

Number of staff:

Number of volunteers:

Mission:

Programs:

Areas that fulfill my volunteer goals:

Other:

Name/location:

Contact/referral:

Budget and financial condition:

Number of staff:

Number of volunteers:

Mission:

Programs:

Areas that fulfill my volunteer goals:

Other:

Name/location:

Contact/referral:

Budget and financial condition:

Number of staff:

Number of volunteers:

Mission:

Programs:

Areas that fulfill my volunteer goals:

Other:

A List of Knowledge, Skills, and Abilities for Volunteering

Name:

Date:

Personal Background

Academic Background

Professional Background

Other (List other knowledge, skills, and abilities that you feel would assist in future volunteer experiences)

The One Page Brief on the Volunteer Position Desired

Not-For-Profit Organization:
Volunteer Position Desired:
Name:

The Position in Brief

My Qualifications

General, Personal, Career Requirements That This Position Meets

Areas to Address

The Volunteer Agreement

Not-for-Profit Organization:
Volunteer Position:
Name:
Date:

James Jones   Date   Not-for-Profit Representative   Date

▼2 What Is Return Value and How Can It Benefit You?

2.1 INTRODUCTION

You may be thinking of volunteering for the first time, or you may already be a volunteer, but would like to receive additional personal benefits from the experience.

Although the main benefit of volunteering is rendering help to another person, an entity, or community, this is not what we mean by return value. Return value is the overall benefit that an individual can receive from the volunteer experience. These benefits vary depending on the quality of the experience and the advance planning that takes place.

Through their time and money, volunteers have provided immense benefits to nearly one million not-for-profit organizations and to the millions of individuals that those entities serve. While providing these donated services, volunteers also received a great deal in return. Generally speaking, volunteers not only receive varied skill enhancements, they also receive leadership traits as well.[1]

2.2 TODAY'S VOLUNTEER PROSPECT

A profile of a volunteer prospect in today's environment differs a great deal from the typical profile of just a few decades ago. This change has tended to have an effect on the length and type of volunteer experiences that most individuals seek. Work habits, business travel, two-income families, financial stress, and a number of other factors have had a profound effect on the way individuals view volunteering. This has resulted in a general leveling off of the numbers of volunteers since 1993. In many cases, several volunteers are needed to meet the requirements that one volunteer fulfilled just a few years ago.

2.3　VOLUNTEERING'S ADAPTATION TO A CHANGING WORLD

Volunteering is in the process of transition. Just as the not-for-profit community is facing the new realities of change and the business community has adapted to a new global competitiveness, so must volunteering adapt to this changing environment.

Individuals do not have as much time or opportunities to volunteer as past generations have had. In addition, many individuals lack the background of volunteers from the past. This provides both a challenge and an opportunity for not-for-profits who seek quality volunteers. This transition can also provide an opening or a greater opportunity for individuals to seek and to obtain return value from the experience.

Individuals who wish to volunteer need to understand the changes that are taking place in the volunteer process. In addition, they also need to have an equal understanding of the methods in which to achieve the highest level of volunteer experience possible.

Finding a quality volunteer experience is not as easy as it used to be. The first-time adult volunteer, who may have had some experience volunteering as a youth, faces a real challenge in finding a quality opportunity. Recently, I was asked by an individual in her late twenties, "I want to become a volunteer but really don't know how to find a quality opportunity." This individual, who I will call Linda, was a college graduate, married, and held a research position at a national not-for-profit organization. She had recently moved from California to the Washington, D.C. area and did not have any real connections with the area. Linda's question is not that unusual.

What was Linda really asking when she said that she didn't know how to volunteer? Linda really wanted to know how she could find a quality volunteer opportunity that would fit her personal needs. She knew that she could volunteer for a number of organizations but what she was really seeking was return value from her volunteer experience.

We assume that everyone knows how to volunteer. This is simply not true. This is particularly apparent when the volunteer experience is not directly connected to benefiting a family member or friend, for example, volunteering to help your daughter's youth group. Yet, this is the ideal time to attract adults to volunteer.

We need to provide stronger bridges to adult volunteering through more organized youth volunteering programs. The Independent Sector's 1995 *Giving and Volunteering in America* report notes that individuals who volunteered in their youth tend to volunteer almost twice as much as adults.[2] Note Exhibit 2.1.

Volunteering needs to be a vital part of the lives of all young people. A number of school districts now have mandatory service requirements that must be fulfilled in order to graduate from high school. Students can choose the type of service that they want to perform, but it must meet established standards including a minimum number of hours.

While this increases awareness of the need to serve a community, it may not provide the essence of volunteering. In fact, it could do more harm than good if students view service or volunteering as a burden rather than an opportunity. That is why it is so important to develop volunteer programs with both the need and the person who will volunteer in mind.

Volunteering needs to be taught in all levels of academia as a natural thing to do. It should not be presented as just another requirement. A vol-

EXHIBIT 2.1 Differences between Volunteers and Non-Volunteers

	Volunteers	Non-Volunteers
When they were young, did some type of volunteer work	70.5%	37.5%
Believe volunteering is important because it "allows me to gain a new perspective on things"	77.9	49.7
Gave time in the past 12 months to help a needy friend or relative	80.8	54.3
Attend religious services weekly	50.3	28.5
When they were young, belonged to a youth group or similar organization	77.7	49.6
Believe that it is in their power to do things that improve the welfare of others	80.3	58.3

Source: *Giving and Volunteering in the United States*, Independent Sector- Gallup Survey, Washington, DC, 1996.

unteering curriculum needs to be integrated into elementary, middle, and high school courses. A college course on the universal benefits of volunteering should be available and encouraged for all students.

If you are a seasoned volunteer, you understand the important role that you play in not-for-profits. You have felt the joy of volunteering and you have seen the direct effect that you have made in helping others. It is a great feeling to help others and, if you are like most individuals who volunteer, you have received as much or more from the experience. A number of personal and career benefits that will be explored in this chapter may have been part of your past volunteer experiences. You have grown as an individual because of them. However, you may find that your future volunteer experiences will be even more satisfying by placing increased emphasis on return value.

2.4 THE PERSONAL BENEFITS OF VOLUNTEERING

When people are asked the number one reason that they volunteer, almost all individuals respond that it is the self-satisfaction of helping others. In *The National College Graduate Study on Volunteering*, conducted from 1990 to 1991, of the 1305 responses returned, 1094 or 83.82 percent noted that self-satisfaction/helping others was the primary reason why they volunteered. Exhibit 2.2 illustrates that no other response even came close. All other areas were less than one percent. The only area of any size was the non-responses. This is a wonderful showing of what individuals think about the volunteer process. It also shows that individuals not only take the role of volunteering seriously, they do so with eagerness and joy as well. Since the survey was administered, a number of changes have occurred. Our personal lives have become more complicated through increased stress, less job security, and a number of other factors. This has affected the levels of volunteering. Yet, it is volunteering that could provide what is now missing in many of our lives.

Steven J. Danish, Ph.D., Chairman of the Psychology Department at Virginia Commonwealth University, noted, in a Prevention Magazine Health Book series, that "people who help other people seem to get helped themselves at least as much as the people they help."[3] Dr. Danish and others in his field talk about the self-esteem, pride, and emotional benefits that come from volunteering.

I was, at one time, a CEO of a health federation. One of the ways that we promoted the organization was to establish "wellness" groups at work

EXHIBIT 2.2 Personal Benefits Received from Volunteering

Response	Total Number	Total Percentage
Self-Satisfaction/Helping Others	1094	83.82%
Family	1	0.08
Ego	3	0.22
Education	1	0.08
Fellowship	1	0.08
New Friends	1	0.08
Religion	1	0.08
Self-Esteem	1	0.08
Making a Contribution	1	0.08
Non Response	207	15.40
Total	1305	100.00

sites and to conduct health fairs at shopping malls. Through that process, I began to understand that good health is not only taking care of yourself, it also includes the socialization factor of helping others. The act of helping others can reduce stress and increase self-esteem.

Beyond better health, self-satisfaction, and helping others, are there additional personal benefits to be derived from volunteering? Absolutely. In fact we have only begun to scratch the surface. Volunteering is similar to any experience you may have—you get out of it what you put into it. Part of the magic of receiving return value from volunteering is how you approach the experience. This was discussed in more detail in chapter 1.

A partial list of personal benefits or skills that volunteering can provide include:

1. A better understanding of the art of group dynamics;
2. The ability to work efficiently in a team driven environment;
3. Increased written and verbal communications skills; and
4. An opportunity to increase your network of friends and business contacts.

The list can go on and on. The return value will depend on what you seek, how much you are willing to put into the experience, and the quality of the experience itself.

2.5 A BETTER UNDERSTANDING OF THE ART OF GROUP DYNAMICS

Group dynamics has been a part of the not-for-profit process from the very beginning. By group dynamics I mean the process or art of successfully working within a group environment to achieve individual and/or group objectives. While this process is a core part of the not-for-profit method of operation, it has not been a part of the for-profit organizational structure until recent. The skill of group dynamics is a needed commodity in today's work environment where team building and group decision making has become the norm. Individuals who understand and can successfully use the skill of group dynamics are a valuable asset to a for-profit organization.

2.6 THE ABILITY TO WORK EFFICIENTLY IN A TEAM DRIVEN ENVIRONMENT

Working in a team environment is part of the at-work environment in most of the leading companies throughout the world. This is a dramatic change from the leader/follower mind-set of a few years ago. All employees are expected to provide both skill and leadership to the projects they are assigned. Teams also cross over traditional department lines and levels of positions. The objective is to bring together the best people and resources to perform the task at hand. A team driven environment needs individuals who understand the process and have had experience working within a team. Volunteering within a not-for-profit environment can provide a wealth of experience in teamwork, that is, how to achieve an objective through motivating individuals to contribute to a group goal.

2.7 INCREASE WRITTEN AND VERBAL COMMUNICATIONS SKILLS

Written and verbal skills are high on any job description list. Employers seek employees who can communicate. Often, individuals do not have the opportunity to develop this skill in the workplace. Without practice individuals cannot gain the confidence and know-how to grow and succeed in their selected profession. Volunteering provides ample opportunity to use both written and oral communications skills. Not-for-profits continually need volunteers to assist in writing articles for newsletters and journals as well as with oral communications in the form of presentations and educational training opportunities. Volunteering provides a wonderful opportunity for individuals to increase their written and oral communications skills.

2.8 AN OPPORTUNITY TO INCREASE YOUR NETWORK OF FRIENDS AND BUSINESS CONTACTS

One of volunteering's major benefits is that a network of friends and business contacts can be made. This is one way in which many professionals seek contacts for their businesses. It is also a way to find friendships that can last a lifetime. Volunteering can also place you as a peer with key community leaders who would ordinarily be out of your reach. Imagine being a fellow committee member with a person that you would like to talk to about a major business opportunity. Well, it is happening every day and it can happen to you as well.

2.9 OTHER BENEFITS TO VOLUNTEERING

There are a number of other benefits to volunteering including the ability to work more effectively with committees and boards, developing a strong sense of personal mission, increasing strategic planning skills, working with different constituencies, understanding ethical and moral standards, feeling a sense of personal power, understanding social patterns, increased willingness to take risks, becoming more concerned about the future of society and, above all, the satisfaction of helping to provide a service to the needy.

Volunteering can be an individual experience but it tends to be much more of a group or partnership experience. Most individuals tend to volunteer with others and most liked to be asked to volunteer by others. Exhibit 2.3 outlines this phenomenon. It reveals an interesting story about how individuals volunteer.

2.10 THE CAREER BENEFITS OF VOLUNTEERING

Usually, when a review of the benefits of volunteering is concluded, career benefits are not among the list. This is an unfortunate oversight. Volunteering can have a profound effect on one's career. Exhibit 2.4 illustrates this point. The exhibit was taken from the study conducted from 1990 to

EXHIBIT 2.3 Characteristics of Volunteers

They volunteer . . .	
Alone and with family but not with friends	8%
With friends and family but not alone	2%
Alone and with both family and friends	40%
Alone and with friends but not with family	33%
Only alone	17%
	100%

They Volunteer . . .	
Both informally and through an organization	17%
Only through an organization	53%
Only informally	30%
	100%

Source: The Points of Light Foundation, Washington, D.C., in cooperation with the Gallup International Institute.

1991 titled *The National College Graduate Survey on Volunteering*. The study sampled alumni from eight higher education institutions from California to West Virginia who had graduated from their respective institutions 25 years ago. The range of responses varied, but the point is clear—these individuals felt that volunteering indeed provided an avenue to gain skills.

One of the known facts about volunteering and the one that scored the highest was the ability to make new contacts. Business leaders have been

EXHIBIT 2.4 Professional Benefits Gained through Volunteering

Made new contacts

Developed a strong sense of personal mission

Committee and board experience

Strategic planning

Ability to work with different constituencies

Better understanding of social patterns

Sense of personal power

Increased willingness to take risks

Opportunity to work with leaders and others in the community

Became more concerned about the future of society

Satisfaction of helping to provide a service to the needy

using volunteering as a way to meet prospective clients and to network with peers in the community for a long time. This is a technique that anyone can use. Whether you are just starting out in your career or whether you are a chief executive officer of a major company, volunteering can often open the doors that you need opened.

The astute person understands that developing a strong personal mission is the secret to success. Competition is strong and it is easy to focus on that rather than your personal vision. Successful people understand that they are not in competition with others but, rather, are in competition with themselves. Volunteering can provide a number of productive ways to meet and to exceed your personal mission or goals.

Here are just some of the wealth of career skills and contacts that volunteering can provide:

1. It can increase your ability to work with different constituencies. This could help you to gain market share locally and even globally;
2. It can provide an opportunity to work with leaders and other key contacts in your community. This is the opportunity to gain insight on management techniques as well as opening up key networks to increase business;
3. It can help you to become more visionary through an increased concern about the future of society;
4. It can increase your skills in taking calculated risks to move you far ahead of the pack;
5. It can refine your skills in working more productively with committees and gaining valuable board experience with leading business leaders; and
6. It can increase your awareness of the personal power that can be gained through becoming a positive force in your community.

To clarify, here's a fictional example. Janice Wilson is a great example of how these principles can work. Janice was a bright student who began to write for her school paper in high school. Three years later, she became the editor. The paper won a number of awards for its coverage of stories that affected students and the community.

When Janice began college, she knew what she wanted to do. Her dream was be a lead reporter for a well-known newspaper. While she was in college, she studied journalism and wrote feature articles for the school newspaper. In her senior year, Janice submitted her work to a number of major newspapers, but she was not hired.

When Janice graduated from college, she was determined to break into the journalism profession. She relocated to a major city but she was still unable to secure a position on a newspaper's staff. Janice had to settle for a job as a copy editor at a local advertising firm in order to make ends meet.

Janice began to get discouraged until she met a client who advised her to seek a volunteer position that could give her experience and a chance to demonstrate her talents. The client told her that the right volunteer position could sharpen her skills and open new avenues of finding her dream job.

Janice told the client that she did not know how to go about finding the right volunteer position. In response, the client recommended that she develop a brief profile similar to a resume that would spell out exactly what she could provide to a group seeking a volunteer. The client also advised her to prepare a list of the types of organizations that she might like to associate with.

Janice took the client's advice and listed a number of her talents and skills. She also identified the three causes that would interest her: health, youth, and womens' issues. After some research, Janice discovered two organizations in the area that could assist her in searching for the right position: the United Way and the local chamber of commerce.

Although seven not-for-profits were discovered through these organizations, only one seemed to fit Janice's needs: the Mason Health Clinic. The clinic is a leading health service for disadvantaged women in the area. As it turned out, the clinic needed a communications plan that would inform more women in the area about their services and attract additional financial resources.

Janice became the communications chair for the clinic and provided the assistance that they needed. The clinic was overwhelmingly grateful and they recognized Janice at a special event held for all of their volunteers. At the event, Janice was given an opportunity to express how much she had enjoyed her position as the communications chair.

During the social event following the ceremony, Janice was approached by several people who thanked her for the great job that she had done at the clinic. One person, named Bill, asked her a lot of questions including what she did as a profession and what her aspirations were. Janice told Bill that she wanted to be a reporter for the major newspaper in town.

After a few more minutes of small talk, Bill handed her a business card. When Janice looked at the card, she noticed that Bill was the managing editor of the major newspaper she wanted to work for. Bill told her to stop into his office on Monday and added that he would be interested in seeing her resume.

When Janice showed up on Monday, she learned that the newspaper had just started looking for a new reporter. She also found out that Bill had been very impressed with her communications plan and her other work at the clinic. Janice was hired on the spot and she achieved her goal of becoming a successful reporter. In a very short time, she was assigned a number of lead stories.

Janice's breakthrough came from the simple act of volunteering. Although her story is fictitious, the process is not. These stories happen every day and they can happen for anyone who volunteers. The return value that an individual receives from volunteering is immense. Volunteering should become a vital part of everyone's life.

In Janice's case, the experience of volunteering could have started a lot earlier. In high school, Janice could have gained valuable skills volunteering for a not-for-profit who needed its monthly newsletter edited. In college, Janice could have found a volunteer position in a not-for-profit as a reporter for a monthly journal. This experience would have given her the opportunity to network and she might have met the person who connected her with the dream job right out of college. When Janice relocated to the major city, she could have used the power of volunteering to establish an immediate network for fulfilling her dream.

Volunteering is not an exclusively adult activity. Instead, it should begin early in life. While volunteering can do good for needy people and for the community, it should also be viewed by volunteers as a way of improving themselves and can be used as an important tool by young people who want to gain skills; by young adults who want to establish themselves in the community and in their professions; by adults who want to maintain skills and give something back to society; and by senior citizens who want to contribute to society and feel that they are still vital and needed.

2.11   CONCLUSION

Volunteering's benefits to the community and to the world have been enormous. Yet individual acts of good work can assist individuals in growing and better understanding themselves.

Volunteering's effect on the individual who volunteers was not well documented until *The National College Graduate Study on Volunteering* was released in 1991. The study concluded that individuals do, in fact, receive return value from volunteering including a number of personal and career skills. The study also documented that individuals who actively volunteer gained leadership traits regardless of the type of volunteer experience or profession that they pursued.

Much is still to be learned from the simple act of volunteering, but one thing is for sure—the individual who volunteers can receive as much or more from the experience than the individual who is helped. Volunteering is truly a wonderful process.

ENDNOTES

[1]Pidgeon, Walter P., *Volunteering: The Leader's Competitive Edge,* The Union Institute, Cincinnati, OH, 1991, p. 1.

[2]*Giving and Volunteering in the United States,* Independent Sector, Washington, D.C., 1996.

[3]"Volunteerism: The Great Escape," 1988, *Prevention Magazine Health Books*, Rodale Press.

How Not-For-Profits Can Increase the Quality and Quantity of Volunteering

The not-for-profit organization finds its base or purpose through its volunteers. This concept may not be immediately apparent when you review the average sized not-for-profit. On the surface, the organization is being administered by a staff that seems to be in charge. This, however, is not the case.

Full-time professional staff at not-for-profits are, for the most part, dedicated individuals who ensure that the work of the not-for-profit is conducted well. They are the caretakers, the advisors, and, in many cases, the visible day-to-day leaders, but they are not the owners. No one really owns a not-for-profit. It is designed under the Internal Revenue Service to have no stock. A not-for-profit is required to have a meaningful mission that focuses on an identified need within a community. Therefore, it is the volunteer who sets the policy and governance of the not-for-profit.

The act of volunteering can be approached in a variety of ways by not-for-profit leaders. The approach, however, depends on the age, size, and culture of the organization in question. The age of the organization can provide a number of clues. Start-up not-for-profits are often exclusively volunteer-led. Usually, a group of individuals has come together to promote an idea or cause. To assist in this effort, they form a group, which is often loosely put together. As the group matures, the volunteers decide that they want to formalize the organization. They incorporate and apply for a 501(c) status under the Internal Revenue Code. The organization may continue to be led exclusively by volunteers.

The original group of volunteers who form a not-for-profit organization usually become the board. The exact name may vary from board of directors to trustees. Whatever the name, the function is the same. A board is organized to be the protector and authority of the group formed. As the group matures, committees will be created to perform needed tasks. Additional volunteers will be attracted to serve on these committees but it is the board who has the ultimate authority and responsibility for the health and vitality of the not-for-profit. All not-for-profits are required, under the Internal Revenue Code, to have volunteer boards. This is an important distinction. For it is the volunteer board who has the ultimate power in a not-for-profit. Professional staff including the chief executive officer and all other volunteer groups within a not-for-profit report to the board.

Most not-for-profits begin as a volunteer run organization—a small group of individuals who believe in the mission and are willing to volunteer to help achieve the initial goals and objects. As a not-for-profit matures, it reaches a point where the volunteers cannot continue to run the organization by themselves. At this juncture, they hire an individual, usually on a part-time basis, to handle the administrative duties. As the organization continues to mature, so do the day-to-day requirements. The volunteers now hire a full-time person who is given permission to hire additional staff.

The years go by and the organization grows. The staff of the organization also grows to meet the expanded need. The responsibility of the day-to-day operations of the organization has been entirely given over to a Chief Executive Officer who supervises a staff. The role of the volunteers of the not-for-profit organization has changed as it matured. Yet, volunteers still play a vital part in the organization. In the beginning, the volunteer did it all. Now the organization relies on professional guidance to do certain services that make it easier for volunteers to fulfill the original mission of the organization. The current organization performs at a level several times greater than the original group due to the partnership created between volunteers and professionals.

Not-for-profit professionals who work with volunteers need to understand the important role that the volunteers play in the success of an organization. Without volunteers, the vital work of a not-for-profit would not be fully accomplished. This includes administrative, programmatic, and funding requirements. The exact function and degree will depend on the culture of each individual organization. It is interesting to note, for example, that studies continue to document that individuals donate at higher levels when they are more directly involved with the organization.[1] The level of volunteering, therefore, has a direct correlation to the level of personal giving.

The recruitment and retention of volunteers is not as simple as it was in the past due to a number of factors. The lack of time seems to be the number one obstacle. To remain competitive in this changing volunteer market, not-for-profits must employ recruitment strategies that treat the process as a competitive issue that uses exchange theory and other marketing principles to gain the attention of potential volunteers.[2]

As the competition for an individual's time increases, not-for-profits need to provide new incentives for individuals and their employers to volunteer. These incentives need to be based on a measurable return value to the targeted individual or employer.

The exciting news is that volunteering can provide a number of benefits. Traditionally, volunteering provides a monumental service to the community and to scores of individuals who receive the services. Volunteering can also render return value to those who volunteer. Part I highlighted a review of the immense benefits that can be derived from the act of volunteering. A more in-depth review of these findings, taken from *The National College Graduate Survey on Volunteering* study conducted from 1990 to 1991, can be found on the computer disk on the inside back cover of this book.

Part II of this book will explore the important role that not-for-profits play in the attraction and retention of volunteers. This section will also encourage not-for-profits to create strategic plans that increase the emphasis on the total benefits that volunteering can provide to both the community and to the individual who volunteers.

Although volunteering is generally thought of as a positive force in our society, the percentage of individuals who volunteer has leveled off in the last decade. The world has changed dramatically during that time. These changes have had an effect on how individuals volunteer and if they volunteer at all. The process of attracting and retaining volunteers, therefore, must be adapted to meet these changes. Part of that adaptation needs to include the promotion and enhancement of the return value that the individual receives from the process.

ENDNOTES

[1]*Giving and Volunteering in the United States,* 1996, Independent Sector, Washington, D.C.

[2]Fisher, James C. and Kathleen M. Cole, *Leadership and Management of Volunteer Programs,* Jossey-Bass Publishers, San Francisco, CA, 1993, p. 82.

▼3 The Role of Return Value in a Not-For-Profit's Volunteer Recruitment Plan

3.1 INTRODUCTION

No matter what level of volunteer recruitment a not-for-profit organization has achieved through traditional methods of promotion or marketing, the introduction of, or increased emphasis on, return value can have a significant positive effect.

Not-for-profits tend to treat potential volunteers as givers rather than receivers of services. The theory behind return value changes the direction or the approach of attracting and retaining individuals who volunteer. It creates new insight on how to enhance the experience of volunteers and it provides an exciting way to attract individuals who wish to volunteer. It is a process that promotes the theory that potential volunteers are prospective consumers who require a tailored experience that meets their individual needs.[1]

3.2 VOLUNTEERING'S BENEFITS: A MAJOR TOOL IN RECRUITING VOLUNTEERS

As you have discovered in Part I, individuals who are interested in receiving return value from their volunteer experiences can do so if they develop a systematic way of approaching not-for-profits. Individuals have sought personal benefits from their volunteer experiences for some time. Yet, in many cases they have not achieved their full benefit or potential through the volunteer experience. Not-for-profits, on the other hand, have not fully used the marketing advantages that could be presented to prospective volunteers on the personal benefits received from the volunteering process.

Most not-for-profits seek volunteers on a regular basis. From the small organization to the large multi-faceted institution, there is a constant push to procure volunteers for numerous vacant positions. Most not-for-profits have a plan in place that outlines the methods and details the steps needed to recruit the volunteers that will be required for the institution. The focus, however, seems to be centered primarily on the current needs of the not-for-profit. The list can be endless and the need is constant. In most nonprofits, there is always a need, a position that needs to be filled. Yet, in some cases, volunteer positions are filled with well-meaning individuals who strive to do their best but are not the right choice for the position. In other cases, volunteer positions are "filled" with individuals who for some reason or another are not active at all. These failed volunteer experiences provide little or nothing to the community and they may turn off the individuals involved to the volunteer process altogether.

The management of the needs of the most vital element of a not-for-profit, the volunteer, has not been the top priority of a number of not-for-profits. Other challenges seem to take precedence, including funding, advocacy, and programmatic functions. The survival of a number of not-for-profits depends on ensuring that these functions are successfully administered. The art of recruiting and retaining volunteers is often given a lower priority.

The development and execution of a well-designed volunteer recruitment and retention program will take time and strategic thought. Yet, greater attention to the volunteer process could be a key to solving some of the more urgent needs of a not-for-profit. This section will focus on methods of breathing new life into a volunteer plan by increasing the opportunities to provide the prospective volunteers with the opportunity to receive additional value from the process.

As you review the opportunity to use return value, try to visualize a realistic way of bringing some of the methods suggested into your volunteer program. If you cannot envision how you would have the time to develop and execute an entire volunteer plan, perhaps you can focus on part of the concept and give it a try. Once you have seen the positive response that individuals will display when an individually tailored plan is available to meet their needs, you will be convinced that a successful volunteer program requires a major emphasis on the return value of volunteering.

Volunteering begins in two ways. An individual will ask or be asked to volunteer. Although Part I encouraged individuals to develop their own volunteer plan and to seek volunteer opportunities on their own, most volunteering is still accomplished by asking an individual to participate.

Individuals should take charge of their volunteering activities by seeking and finding the volunteer position that fulfills their requirements. When these individuals approach a not-for-profit to investigate the possible volunteer opportunities available, the not-for-profit representative should take the time required for that individual to fully investigate the possibilities at that institution, regardless of whether or not the not-for-profit representative contacted is a program officer or the CEO. If the not-for-profit welcomes inquiries and goes through the proper process, chances are good that the individual will become a volunteer and will be a valuable asset to that organization. In the meantime, the need for volunteers cannot be fulfilled unless not-for-profits seek qualified volunteers to fill vacant positions.

Most not-for-profits have a volunteer plan. It may be a formal document that fills a loose-leaf book or simply an unwritten command to seek and find individuals who can help. Both extremes may not be adequate for today's environment. The pool of volunteers has changed a great deal in the last ten years. Time is at a premium. Individuals need to see return value—the significant direct benefits they can receive from volunteering.

The 1991 *National College Graduate Survey on Volunteering* reported that individuals who actively volunteer gain leadership traits regardless of the type of volunteer experience or profession that they pursued. It also concluded that individuals recognized that they received many other values as well. (See Exhibit 2.4.)

It is interesting to note that the traditional motivation for individuals to volunteer (to help the needy and to gain satisfaction from the process) is still very strong among those surveyed. Yet, when compared to the professional benefits gained through volunteering, it ranked fourth.

Note what came in first. "Making new contacts" should not be a big surprise to not-for-profit executives who understand the significance of bringing together the power and dynamics of a community to further their institution.

The second benefit, the ability to work with different constituencies, is becoming a major way to attract volunteers as well. As the population continues to become more diverse, individuals are seeking ways to understand more fully the dynamic that is taking place. This can be a powerful incentive to motivate individuals to volunteer.

The third benefit provides additional insight as to why people spend their time volunteering. Note that it is the *opportunity* to work with leaders and others in the community. This is not merely networking but it is also the chance to see how influential people do things, an opportunity to learn from the masters how to be successful.

The fifth benefit is truly revealing. Although it ranks last on this list, it far outperformed a number of other benefits that would seem to be obvious winners, including committee and board experience and strategic planning. The benefit that scored lowest, a sense of personal power (29.86 percent), illustrates that individuals who volunteer are seeking to help others and themselves and are not eager to be involved in power issues.[2]

Prospective volunteers seek to give and to get value. Not-for-profits have been, for the most part, focusing on only one of these values, the giving part. In today's environment, not-for-profits who wish to recruit quality volunteers need to focus on the total value package that includes the value that the volunteer can provide to the not-for-profit and the return value that the volunteer can receive from the experience.

3.3   IN SEARCH OF VOLUNTEERS

The search for volunteers has traditionally been focused on a one-track system that included the need within the not-for-profit and the availability of volunteer talent in the community. If an organization needed a chair to run the annual fund drive, they would first review the volunteer pool in the not-for-profit and, if they determined that no one was available, they would begin the search in the community. The search would vary depending on the not-for-profit's culture or maturity. Typically, the volunteers and professionals of the organization would create a list of potential candidates and rank them in order of ease of approachability and how well they thought the person could perform the task.

The top candidate would be approached by a volunteer who was considered a peer to set up an appointment to discuss the volunteer opportunity. The meeting would take place with the candidate and the not-for-profit would be represented by the volunteer who called the meeting. A leading professional from the organization would also attend. The sell would take place and the individual would respond. Most of the time it was a positive response or, if it was a "no," it would be for good reasons and the individual would help the institution in some other way, perhaps through a donation. If the candidate did turn the opportunity down, then the group would approach the second prospect.

This process was quite successful within a given community since the volunteer prospect was known by the individuals who were the volunteers and professionals in the group. This process is still being used and is still having a fair success rate. What has occurred in the past decade, however, is that the playing field has begun to change. Not only is time away from work and family at an all-time premium, the individuals who would be traditional prospects are not as well known. Individuals are not living in the same area as long as they used to be and they do not have the same sense of community.

This provides a new challenge but also a real opportunity for the not-for-profit who understands the need to create a multi-level approach to attract and retain volunteers. Not-for-profits who are serious about "prospecting" for volunteers should look at the process from three vantage points:

1. The recruitment of volunteers on a one position, one search need;
2. Focusing on key employers within the community to encourage employee volunteering; and
3. Creating a community-wide effort to attract volunteers.

(a)   The Recruitment of Volunteers on a One Position, One Search Need

As long as there are not-for-profits, there will be a need for a singular recruiting program. Even if the other two areas are highly successful, certain positions cannot be filled unless direct attention is placed on matching qualified candidates to the needed volunteer position. These are often the top level positions of the organization.

This does not mean, however, that the full value of volunteering should not be explored. In this case, preparation before the task is most important. A full review of the person should be made. This can be done much more easily today with various services and access to Web pages on the Internet. However, do not overlook the valuable information that can be obtained from trusted individuals in the not-for-profit. The sell should include both the value that can be given to the community and the value that the individual will receive from the experience. Your research can help a great deal but be sure to ask the volunteer prospects themselves what return value they seek.

(b) Focusing on Key Employers Within the Community to Encourage Employee Volunteering

Although not-for-profits have recruited corporate leaders for key volunteer positions, most not- for-profits have not focused on the real potential that lies within the office buildings, factories, and industrial parks that span their communities. Potential volunteers exist to fill all the vacancies possible.

The key is to understand the needs of both the prospective volunteer and the employer who controls the employee at least 40 hours a week. This is where return value can really get the attention of both the employer and the employee alike. Volunteering has a lot to offer employers. A number of corporate leaders understand that employee volunteering can go well beyond the good will that the process provides. Astute employers understand that employees who volunteer can become more productive workers.

As Peter F. Drucker suggests, "America's third sector institutions are rapidly becoming creators of new bonds of community and a bridge across the widening gap between knowledge workers and the other half . . . In well run third sector organizations, there are no more volunteers, there are only unpaid staff . . . unpaid staff are thoroughly trained, and given a specific assignment with performance goals."

It is Drucker's opinion "that the third sector offers its volunteers a share of personal achievement in which the individual exercises influence, discharges responsibility, and makes decisions . . . . Increasingly, executives in business, especially people in middle management, are expected to serve in decision-making positions as board members of not-for-profit institutions . . . . They practice management by objectives, and more thoroughly than most businesses do."[3]

The key is to develop a close relationship with employers who have an interest in your not-for- profit. This can be accomplished by finding a link. Some links are obvious, for example, a health organization may find it appropriate to form a relationship with a health-related industry. Others can be more subtle, for example, a neighborhood center linking up with a local company to promote reading and math programs. The employer can help train current employees through volunteering while helping to train possible future employees within the community.

(c) Creating a Community-Wide Effort to Attract Volunteers

This final area provides an opportunity for the not-for-profit to create a more general and ongoing promotional effort that will assist in maintaining a high level of visibility to prospective volunteers. This increased exposure may help to close a number of volunteer sales for a not-for-profit. The community-wide effort can be a vital reinforcement of the first two parts of the plan and it may help to attract individuals who will approach your institution on their own as discussed in Part I.

While this part of the plan can be mostly promotional in nature, it should not exclude a direct recruitment campaign that will attract both individuals and groups to volunteer. The total value package should be emphasized, including the value that the community can gain and the return value that the individual can and should obtain. This is an opportunity to attract volunteers who can directly assist in various activities within an organization and to attract groups who can perform a service or hold events that can support your organization programmatically and financially.

(d)   Retooling for Today's Volunteer

The promotion of volunteering's total value is the key to attracting today's potential volunteer. This means that not-for-profit leaders need to rethink the way that they recruit and retain volunteers. This process will be fully explained in Chapter 6. It is a blend of what has been done in addition to a more focused approach that individualizes the method of attracting and retaining volunteers. Greater emphasis needs to be placed on the process of volunteering in not-for-profits. It is one of the most important functions of these institutions and one of the vital ways to meet the ever-increasing demands of the community.

3.4   CONCLUSION

The goal of this chapter is to "set the stage" for the rest of Part II which will discuss how not-for-profits can increase the quality and the quantity of volunteers. This can be accomplished through creating a process that encourages full value from the volunteer experience. This needs to include not only the dedicated services that individuals provide by volunteering for not-for-profits, it also needs to include greater emphasis on the return value that the individual can receive through volunteering.

This more focused approach will attract increased numbers of volunteers and, if it is administered properly, it will retain volunteers for longer periods of time. The net effect for not-for-profits who use these techniques will be an increased quality of service that they render to the community through more satisfied volunteers and the assurance that the individuals who volunteer will grow significantly through the process.

ENDNOTES

[1]Fisher James C. and Kathleen M. Cole, *Leadership and Management of Volunteer Programs,* Jossey - Bass Publishers, San Francisco, CA, 1993, p. 84.

[2]Pidgeon, Walter P., *Volunteering: The Leader's Competitive Edge,* The Union Institute, Cincinnati, OH, 1991, p. 127.

[3]Drucker, Peter F., *The New Realities,* Harper & Row, New York, NY, 1989, p. 203.

▼ 4 A Comprehensive Volunteer Strategic Plan for Not-For-Profits

4.1 INTRODUCTION

One of the most important activities of a not-for-profit is the attraction and retention of volunteers. This process seems endless because it really is. The process never stops, as volunteers are always needed. Organizations differ in how they involve volunteers. Some organizations have volunteers listed but are really run by the professional staff, while other not-for-profits work with multiple levels of volunteers that perform most of the work of the not-for-profit. Each organization must determine the role that volunteers will play based on the culture and needs of the institution. There are three ways to define the need for volunteers:

1. Determine how volunteers can help achieve organizational goals;
2. Assess the costs and benefits of having volunteers; and
3. Develop a plan for volunteer participation.[1]

Determining how volunteers can help achieve organizational goals is an important first step in creating a plan that will attract and retain quality people. Today's potential volunteer is interested in performing a task that is well defined, takes a limited period of time, and really accomplishes something. They are also interested in the return value that will be acquired in the process. Not-for-profits need to clearly identify areas where volunteers can provide service. This can be accomplished through a team effort between the volunteer leadership and the professional staff. The need should be based on the current strategic plan that outlines both traditional and new or expanded needs for the not-for-profit.

Potential volunteers have much to offer but what they offer varies from person to person. This is why it is important that not-for-profits have clearly defined needs that can be translated into both realistic and worthwhile experiences for individuals who wish to volunteer. Not all activities are suited for volunteers. Volunteer work needs to be packaged to fit the needs, desires, and time of today's busy volunteer.

Secondly, a not-for-profit must also assess the costs and benefits of having volunteers. In most cases volunteers save the organization money. However, this is not always the case. Volunteering must provide a benefit that is larger than the direct and indirect cost of operating a volunteer plan. Measuring the cost is not as easy as it sounds when volunteers cross through both programmatic and operational budgets. It can be accomplished if you develop a project by project cost analysis. The major cost is often the time it takes by the professional staff to administer the project, followed by the support resources needed. A quality volunteer program traditionally focuses on how to help the organization grow through memberships, fund-raising, educational activities, and influence.

The third and most important part of defining the need for volunteering is to develop a plan for volunteer participation. Professionals in the not-for-profit field understand that successful volunteer involvement involves a planning process. The plan often focuses on a need rather than the entire organization. Often, this leads to a panic recruitment of volunteers to solve an immediate need. This can be successful for the immediate need but it does not address the long-term reality. Long-term volunteer development will help to retain quality volunteers and attract new energized volunteers who have discovered that the organization in question provides a multi-valued volunteer experience.

Volunteer programs have tended to emphasize the needs of the not-for-profit and their mission to persuade individuals to donate their time. This has been an effective way to attract volunteers for most of this century. The trend is changing, however. Individuals today are faced with a number of distractions, specifically, less time and more demanding careers that prevent them from volunteering. A volunteer plan, in today's environment, needs to include value for not only the not-for-profit but for the volunteer as well.

The volunteer plan that will unfold in this chapter will emphasize value. It will illustrate how a not-for-profit can seek and obtain a full measure of commitment and work from a volunteer's standpoint. The process will also encourage not-for-profits to provide a full measure of return value for the individual who volunteers as well.

A case study will be used to illustrate the need for a value driven volunteer plan. The exhibits in this chapter have been completed to bring the plan alive. A number of the exhibits are planning forms. Blank forms are provided on the computer disk that can be found on the inside back cover of this book. They are there for your use.

The case study for this chapter is a not-for-profit called The Jacksonville Environmental Coalition. The Coalition is an active regional group that was incorporated in 1972. Its mission is "to improve the environment within the region, particularly focusing on the air and water." The Coalition has a current budget of $1.2 million, a staff of eight, and it recruits about 250 volunteers per year. The organization has quality leadership in both the Volunteer Chair, John Paul, a retired business executive, and Susan Wallace, the current Chief Executive Officer, who has an academic and professional background in environmental issues.

The organization continues to struggle in attracting and retaining volunteers. Funding is also a challenge—the organization depends solely on contributions. The Coalition has gone through a few maturity stages and it now is ready to seek a new level of excellence. The organization wishes to branch out to form new partnerships with other organizations and with businesses. It also wishes to focus on recruiting volunteers at all levels of its operations.

The Coalition's profile may sound familiar. Thousands of not-for-profits fit similar patterns. The question for the Coalition is: Can it find the volunteer talent and financial resources to help the organization grow? The answer may lie in achieving both goals simultaneously through a strategic volunteer plan.

In order to create a volunteer plan, a not-for-profit needs to create a systematic approach that will compliment the strategic plan of the organization. These two plans cannot be separate. The plan must address the focused needs of the not-for-profit. In the case of the Jacksonville Environmental Coalition, fund raising should be one of the chief needs. The Coalition needs financial stability and a reliable volunteer pool. Here are the recommended steps for forming such a strategy:

1. Determine the volunteer needs of the not-for-profit.
2. Identify the assets that the organization possesses.
3. Incorporate the volunteer strategy into the not-for-profit's strategic plan.
4. Develop a position profile for each volunteer need.
5. Establish opportunities for partnerships with outside sources.

6. Develop a volunteer marketing plan.
7. Determine which target markets to focus your volunteer plan on.
8. Create a volunteer agreement that is tailored to meet individual needs.
9. Educate new volunteers though an orientation session.
10. Establish and execute a volunteer recognition plan.
11. Implement a comprehensive volunteer evaluation plan.
12. Recycle the plan based on the data collected through the evaluation process.

4.2   DETERMINE THE VOLUNTEER NEEDS OF THE NOT-FOR-PROFIT

The first requirement is to establish a volunteer plan to determine the volunteer needs of the organization. The attraction and retention of volunteers to assist in expanding the organization into new and more strategic avenues of activities is critical. Making an assessment of your needs should include all current volunteer positions, anticipated positions, and even a wish list of volunteer positions. Each volunteer position is important. Each person who volunteers for those positions is important. The objective of the volunteer plan is to successfully match the right individual to the appropriate volunteer position.

Exhibit 4.1 provides an overview of the volunteer needs of the Jacksonville Environmental Coalition. The sample form provided includes the additional volunteer needs of the Coalition. The core volunteer needs are 230, and 165 have been attained to date. In reality, an entire review should also be developed within the volunteer needs list to make sure that all positions are filled.

For the most part, organizations have established a core group of volunteers and have recruited individuals for higher positions by promoting volunteers up through the ranks. This process opens up entry-level positions that need to be filled. It is important that the volunteers who are listed within the core group of volunteers are reviewed thoroughly as well. They need the same nurturing as the new volunteers do. This is the retention part of the volunteer process, a part that is often overlooked in the volunteer plan.

Out of the 165 core volunteers that the Coalition has identified as retained, there will be a few who will leave for personal reasons, a few who are dissatisfied, and a few who are bored with their position and want to change. Most volunteers will not tell you any of this. The need assessment process can reveal most of these situations and help the not-for-profit keep

EXHIBIT 4.1 The Volunteer Needs Assessment

Not-for-profit:	Jacksonville Environmental Coalition
Chief Executive Officer:	Susan Wallace
Volunteer Chair:	John Paul
Date:	December 10, 1997

Positions/ Description	Remarks	Retained	Old	New
		165		
Vice Chair of Board	Seasoned Administrator		1	
Fund-Raising Chair	Well known/ability to raise funds		1	
	"Phon-a-thon" Workers		15	15
	Major gifts solicitors			10
Water Environment Chair	Knowledge of issue		1	
Air Committee	Knowledge of issue		5	
Quality Water Project	Chair			1
	Committee			14
	Area volunteers			85
Clean Air Project	Chair		1	
	Government affairs		1	2
	Writers			2
Regional Coordinators	Able to promote issues at this level		10	10
Local Ambassadors	Able to promote issues in local areas		30	15
Sub-Totals		165	65	154
Total Recruitment Needs				219
Total Volunteer Needs				384

ahead of the process, so be sure to add all the volunteer positions into your volunteer plan because it will save time in the long run and pay dividends.

In the Coalition's case, for example, most of the hidden problems can be resolved. If a volunteer is given an opportunity to express dissatisfaction, often the problem can be fixed and the volunteer will stay. If the volunteer is bored, you need to find out what they would like to do and let them do it. This could be the very individual who creates a new and exciting opportunity for the organization.

The final and most difficult part of the volunteer needs assessment is the disposition of volunteers who have not performed to the standard set. The volunteer plan needs to have provisions for this problem. This will be detailed further in the chapter within the evaluation part of the volunteer plan. In most cases, volunteers who have not performed will be identified through that process and can be recycled into another position if they do not leave on their own.

The Jacksonville Environmental Coalition has reviewed their core volunteers and found 165 positions can be "retained." This was accomplished by working closely with the volunteer process to determine who wishes to continue and promoting proven volunteers to new leadership positions. This leaves 65 current positions that will need to be filled. The Coalition is also interested in expanding their operations and they have determined that 154 additional volunteer positions will be needed to achieve their goal. This means that the Coalition will have a "total recruitment need" of 219 volunteers for the coming year. This is a significant increase over last year's actual volunteer recruitment figures. In order to accomplish its goals, the Coalition needs to focus on filling both established and new positions. The traditional method of obtaining volunteers has been to promote volunteering at rallies and other events of the organization. It is clear that new methods are needed to achieve these challenging objectives.

4.3   IDENTIFY THE ASSETS THAT THE ORGANIZATION POSSESSES AND INVESTIGATE POSSIBLE PARTNERSHIPS

The Coalition needs to develop a new strategy to attract such a large volume of volunteers. To accomplish this, they need to discover the hidden assets that the group can promote. Not-for-profits tend to think that they do not have significant assets to market to the public. This is far from the truth. To accomplish this, review all functions of the not-for-profit. This should include both the traditional programs that are provided to the ideas or concepts that would be possible if volunteer assistance and/or funding was available. Take a look at the support function, i.e., the current facilities, etc. to determine the possible role of volunteers. This process should dwell on the volunteer opportunities that would attract individuals to become involved with your institution, not merely a manual labor position.

Most organizations have a great deal to offer. This includes both new and established not-for-profits. In most cases, the assets of a not-for-profit tend to be either hidden below the surface or so obvious that they are taken for granted. This is one of those cases in which a not-for-profit needs to think more like a traditional business—if my organization was a business and the future depended on attracting customers, who would use my services? What are the incentives for volunteers to be attracted to my shop?

For the most part, a not-for-profit should not look at its operations for all the answers. It is not the way we run our shops that attracts most of our volunteers; it is the products and services that we produce for the community that attracts interest. This is also the value that the volunteer receives from their relationship with the organization. If we focus on the volunteer more as a customer who is seeking return value from the services that they provide and that the volunteer may not continue to serve unless they receive these benefits, not-for-profit professionals may be more apt to customize the individual volunteer experience.

What are some of the common assets of a not-for-profit? The most obvious is its mission. This is the beacon that shines for all to see and draws the volunteers to you. Is your mission compelling? Can it be vocalized and put in print? Can it be instantly understood or is it three paragraphs in length, confusing, or, worst of all, dated? What programs do you provide to the community and how can they attract and retain volunteers? Who are your current volunteers? Can they attract other volunteers to assist? How does the organization relate to other organizations and the community? Can this attract others to volunteer? One of the positive parts of making an assessment of an organization is identifying the areas that are weak or noncompelling so that they can be refined. This will only strengthen the organization.

Take the time to review the core programs and activities of the not-for-profit to determine if they can be packaged and sold to volunteers. Often, the programs that we take for granted, the tried and true activities that define the group, can be revitalized to bring new excitement and, therefore, new attention. New programs and even "wish programs" should be packaged to attract volunteers and possible new funders. These are activities that have not stood the test of time but, in the judgment of the not-for-profit, are needed to further the mission of the organization. While traditional programs can document past achievements, new programs need to sell the vision of the organization. Both traditional and new activities are salable. The key is to personalize the packaging and the selling of these programs or activities to fit the needs of individuals who wish to volunteer.

Therefore, the key to selling volunteers, funding proposals, or baby ducks is to know your market. The concept is called market segmentation. The key is to research your field to find the niche. This can be accomplished by reviewing the competition. Discover the areas where other organizations are doing similar programs and the areas where your organization is doing unique programs. Then you should pursue the areas where your organization has a major market share as well as uniqueness. Once you have found it, develop a plan and capitalize on your competitive position. It is important to note that not-for-profits are not capable of penetrating all segments of the volunteer market nor should they. They must find the area that they can excel in and identify the potential volunteers that are available. If this is properly done, there will be plenty of potential volunteers to go around.[2]

The Jacksonville Environmental Coalition has identified five assets. See Exhibit 4.2. In reality, an organization could discover a lot more. The Coalition feels that its mission was a real asset. It is timely and the organization has received a great deal of positive press from it. The visibility that the Coalition has received will greatly assist in attracting volunteers to the organization. Often, organizations are doing great work but no one knows about it. No one will come to your door if they do not know that a worthwhile group exists.

Note that in Exhibit 4.2, the Coalition has identified a possible partnership with the Air First Corporation based on their mission alone. In our

EXHIBIT 4.2 The Identification of Not-For-Profit Assets

Not-for-Profit:	Jacksonville Environmental Coalition
Chief Executive Officer:	Susan Wallace
Volunteer Chair:	John Paul
Date:	December 10, 1997

Asset	Description	Partnership Opportunities
Mission	Timely issue that has positive press	The Air First Corporation
Volunteers	Several key leaders in the community	Harford Electric Co.
Good grassroots reach	Need for a number of local volunteers	Jacksonville Chamber of Commerce
Clear Air Project	Highly visible project	Clean Air Association
Quality Water Project	Highly visible project	Environmental Research Corporation

(List can be as long as the assets of the not-for-profit.)

example, the corporation can identify with the Coalition's mission because it reflects a number of core values in their corporate mission statement.

The role of partnerships with not-for-profits is gaining increased interest. Astute not-for-profit leaders understand that a number of internal objectives can be accomplished through working with other organizations to fulfill common goals. This not only includes policy questions but programatic functions as well. Funding sources are aware of the strength of partnerships and are more apt to fund a coalition of not-for-profits than a single group. They understand that a group of not-for-profits can make a greater impact and can be more successful than one not-for-profit. Partnerships do not end with not-for-profits, they can also be created with for-profits. This is an area that, if designed appropriately, can produce a lasting relationship which can have a positive effect on the area that the not-for-profit serves.

Such external entities can be allies in a number of ways. They can be asked to associate with the organization to simplify future mutual missions. The corporation may also have a volunteer employee program that can provide volunteer support and can also provide high level executive talent as well. They can also be potential partners in an arrangement that can include both volunteers and funding opportunities.

Note that the Coalition stated that its volunteers were an asset. The Coalition has been doing a good job of recruiting volunteers and several volunteers are prominent individuals in the community. The Coalition also has openings for volunteers at several levels. They have a reputation for providing volunteer recognition that is visible throughout the area.

The Coalition has selected the Harford Electric Company as a prospect. They feel that the electric company might have a volunteer interest in a number of opportunities both at the board or committee level and with the regional and local level programs. The Coalition feels that their grassroots reach has provided a strong network to accomplish the issues that the organization was founded upon.

The Jacksonville Area Chamber of Commerce was also identified as a partnership prospect. The Chamber has been in the press in the last few months for promoting the need for increased interest and support in the local recreational industry. The Coalition feels that one of their major issues, improving water and air quality, could make a natural partnership and, since the Chamber is a membership based organization, there may be ways to encourage their members to participate in Coalition activities.

The Coalition listed two projects: The Clean Air Project, which is more of an advocacy program, and the Quality Water Project, which will be an "in the field" endeavor that will require a number of volunteers. Projects are great ways to attract volunteers to an organization. The term "project" implies that it has a beginning and an end, although a large number do not. In the case of the Coalition, one project has an end and the other does not.

The Coalition's Clean Air Project is four years old. It is designed to keep state legislators aware of the need to pass legislation that offers incentives to businesses to comply with the clean air standard. The project has been successful due to the strategy of encouraging all sides of the debate to come to the table. The Coalition feels it is time to cash in on the positive role that they have played by developing closer ties with a national organization, the Clean Air Association. The association has a chapter in the state and represents a number of businesses in the state as well. A possible partnership arrangement with the Clean Air Association would include three parts or activities: advocacy opportunities, funding a visible effort together, and volunteer opportunities at the Coalition for business members of the State Clean Air Association and their employees.

The Quality Water Project is new. It is much more labor intensive and it will last for three years. The Coalition has received a small grant to develop the initial study but will need additional funds to conduct the monitoring of the study throughout the region. The Environmental Research Corporation was selected as a possible partner since it could provide the needed expertise and possible volunteer assistance and funding.

The Environmental Research Corporation has a small research lab in the region which employs 245 people who reside primarily in the area. They have a volunteer program and tend to take on group projects that require large numbers of their employees. The last volunteer activity they participated in required 87 employees and took eighteen months to complete. The corporation links their donation plan to employee involvement. They also have a matching gift program where employees who donate to a charity may request that the corporation match the gift up to one thousand dollars.

The Coalition has done its homework. They have identified the assets and they have linked these assets with possible partners. Later in this chapter, we will discuss the methods of gaining access to and selling a partnership.

4.4 INCORPORATING THE VOLUNTEER STRATEGY INTO THE NOT-FOR-PROFIT'S STRATEGIC PLAN

Note that the Coalition's volunteer plan strives to meet a number of important issues affecting the organization. A volunteer plan is a vital part of a not-for-profit's strategic plan. Volunteering is a core ingredient of the not-for-profit process. Yet, a number of not-for-profit strategic plans do not devote a great deal of time or space to volunteer initiatives. All not-for-profits need a strategic plan and all not-for-profit strategic plans need a detailed volunteer plan. The volunteer plan should outline the entire volunteer process including these three needs:

1. How to retain quality volunteers;
2. How to select individuals for existing positions; and
3. How to attract individuals for new volunteer opportunities.

The first and most important part of the process is the retention of volunteers who have provided a quality service. While this publication will not spend a great deal of time on the subject, it is important to state that retention of volunteers is the way to build quality programs and the way to retain volunteers is to provide a quality experience including as much return value as possible for those who volunteer.

The selection of individuals for existing volunteer opportunities that have been vacated by volunteers who have left or are promoted to new volunteer opportunities is a constant challenge. The advantage of these positions is that they are known experiences. Each activity has been documented and one can visualize the type of person needed to fill the position. The best way to fill a number of these positions is through your "farm club." Just like an athletic team, not-for-profits need to train volunteers for greater challenges. The development of top level volunteers through entry level volunteer positions can provide a strong senior volunteer team. If the farm club is in place, then the position can be easily filled. If it is not in place, then a search needs to be conducted to locate the proper candidate.

Attracting volunteers for new positions is not as easy. First of all, you may not have a clear picture of what the position will ultimately become. This means that you might not have a good idea of what kind of individual would best fit the position. While most positions are not unusual and a profile can be created, they tend to be developed as a work in progress due to a number of factors. Volunteers tend to do what needs to be done when they have the time to do it. Things tend to change. The culture of the organization is a factor and, no matter how well it is designed, the advance plan cannot possibly consider every variable.

The Jacksonville Environmental Coalition has integrated its volunteer plan into the organization's strategic plan. Exhibit 4.3 provides an outline of how they will ensure that the volunteer plan becomes a vital part of their organization's strategy. Note they have set an overall objective. The plan will include the necessary elements to attract and retain volunteers.

EXHIBIT 4.3 The Volunteer Section of the Strategic Plan

Taken from the Jacksonville Environmental Coalition's Strategic Plan, October 13, 1996.

The Volunteer Plan

Objective

The Jacksonville Environmental Coalition wishes to have an active volunteer recruitment plan that is value driven for both the coalition and for the individual who volunteers. The plan will include the necessary elements to attract and retain quality volunteers.

Phase One
> Goal One: Hiring a volunteer coordinator.
>> (List steps to accomplish goal.)
> Goal Two: Recruiting a volunteer committee.
> Goal Three: Create the plan.
> 1. Retention of volunteers;
> 2. One-on-one recruitment;
> 3. Community recruitment;
> 4. Attract the interest of other groups and not-for-profits; and
> 5. Form partnerships with for-profit entities.

Phase Two
> Goal One: Test marketing the five approaches of the plan.
> Goal Two: Evaluate the approaches.

Phase Three
> Goal One: Implementing the plan.
> Goal Two: Evaluating the results.

The Coalition has divided its plan into three phases. The timeline of the phases will vary depending on progress. The Coalition wisely states that the plan will unfold over a three-year period and does not state arbitrary due dates that may not be met. In reality, the plan should be much more detailed but the outline presented provides a good road map.

(a) Phase One, Goal One: Hiring a Volunteer Coordinator

This is a wise decision if you are serious about providing a well-designed volunteer program. In the case of the Coalition, as in a number of not-for-profits, funds are not available. So the plan will move on without one. Is this a good idea? There is no right or wrong answer to this question. Certainly, the addition of a full-time staff person would be an asset. A volunteer to act as volunteer coordinator could also be considered, if a volunteer with human resources experience could be located. In reality, most volunteer programs are successfully run with existing staff. Perhaps the Coalition can find the funds for the position in the future.

(b) Phase One, Goal Two: Recruiting a Volunteer Committee

The committee should oversee the full development of a sensible volunteer plan. The committee should do the following:

1. Act as a sounding board for ideas;
2. Assist in implementing part of the support need;
3. Recommend volunteers;
4. Take a leadership role in the recognition program; and
5. Help evaluate the plan itself.

To be successful, the committee needs direct advisory support and guidance from volunteer *and* professional leadership.

(c) Phase One, Goal Three: Creating a Plan

The Coalition's plan will focus on five areas:

1. Developing a retention plan to maintain quality volunteers;
2. Developing a plan that focuses on the top volunteer's needs and creating a one-on-one plan that will assist researching, cultivating, and asking key individuals to volunteer;
3. Focusing on a community-wide recruitment effort for volunteers;
4. Attracting interest in the Coalition's volunteer program from other groups; and
5. Forming partnerships with for-profit entities.

While the focus may vary from time to time, these five areas are generally core parts of a good volunteer plan. All five areas will need to rely on a solid plan to market the Coalition. The plan should include value to the organization and return value to the volunteer individual or entity.

(d)   Phase Two, Goal One: Test Marketing the Five Approaches of the Plan

This is an important step in the process. While some of the volunteer concepts of the plan have been used before, they should improve each year through the process. New ideas should always be tested. This process will ensure that the new parts of the volunteer plan are sound. It will also produce refinements. Test marketing helps to show that you are serious about providing a quality volunteer program.

(e)   Phase Two, Goal Two: Evaluating the Approaches

This will provide an ongoing test and it will bring home all that is being learned in the testing phase. It will also assist in marketing the plan. The evaluation process should be a continual part of the entire plan and it should be as flexible as possible in order to accommodate arising needs.

(f)   Phase Three, Goal One: Implementing the Plan

You should spell out the details of how the plan will be introduced and who the targeted individuals and entities will be. You should also specify the approach, sales tools, recognition process, and other items that will make the implementation of the plan a success.

(g)   Phase Three, Goal Two: Evaluating the Results

This will provide the final overview of the volunteer plan.

Exhibit 4.3 provides a skeleton outline of what a volunteer section of a not-for-profit strategic plan should contain. The volunteer goals should reflect and complement the other goals set in the document.

4.5   DEVELOPING A JOB PROFILE FOR EACH VOLUNTEER

Now that you have established your goals, discovered your assets, and integrated the volunteer plan into the strategic plan of your institution, it is appropriate to develop your first sales tool, a volunteer job profile. Basically, the job profile, as presented, is similar to a job description for each volunteer position. It may differ from the traditional volunteer job description in that it details the time, skills, and evaluation process needed to fulfill the position properly.

The profile is a document that will set the tone for the volunteer's role in the not-for-profit. It gives the volunteer all the basic information he or she needs to understand the position and its requirements. Nothing should be held back because the profile will be used to help the volunteer to make an educated decision about the position.

The Jacksonville Environmental Coalition prepared profiles for all of its positions. Exhibit 4.4 provides an example of one of the opportunities. This profile is for the Water Environment Chair's position. Note that the volunteer who takes this position will report to another volunteer. This should always be the case. The individual who the volunteer will report to at the Coalition is called a "guide," a name that came from the culture of the organization. This is a good way of describing the relationship since the guide will be responsible for helping the individual have a quality experience as a volunteer.

The profile should also list the number of individuals that the volunteer will supervise and play the guide role for. In the Coalition's case, it was twelve. Additional information should be available to highlight what the committee is expected to do. It should include a listing of existing committee members and their functions and the committee openings that need to be filled.

The duties of the position should be included and written clearly. Meeting requirements need to be included and should be as accurate as possible. Be honest about the requirements of the position. The volunteer will soon discover the real story and, if it is not what was agreed upon, you will have one less volunteer. If additional unscheduled obligations may occur, make reference to them.

Note that the example in Exhibit 4.4 indicates that the requirement will be 20 meetings per year, which is high. The time requirement needed to successfully conduct the volunteer role as Water Environment Chair is estimated at twenty hours per month, a time commitment that is at the high

EXHIBIT 4.4 The Volunteer Job Profile

The Jacksonville Environmental Coalition
Volunteer Position Standard
Water Environment Chair
December 5, 1997

Report to: Volunteer Chair, John Paul

Supervises: A committee of 12

Duties:

To develop and implement a regional public awareness program concerning the quality of water in the area's rivers and lakes.

Meeting requirements:

1. Hold a quarterly meeting of the Water Environment Committee;
2. Attend the monthly board meeting; and
3. Represent the Coalition at the Clean Air Association quarterly meeting.

Time requirements:

It is estimated that 20 hours a month will be needed to successfully perform this volunteer opportunity. The initial commitment for this position will be for one year.

Skills required:

Five years experience in water quality issues and a professional position that relates to the field.

Evaluation:

The position and committee progress will be evaluated quarterly through a team approach. The team will include the volunteer chair and the chair of the Water Environment Committee.

---

end of the individual volunteering commitment in today's market. It will take a dedicated volunteer to meet these standards.

The skills required section is an important part of the profile. It can help the Coalition focus on the type or quality of the person that should be sought. It may also help to eliminate inquiries from individuals who may want to seek an opportunity but are not qualified for the position.

The evaluation portion of the profile provides detailed information and ensures that an evaluation plan is in place. It also encourages a joint evaluation effort between the prospective volunteer and the volunteer guide. The volunteer job profile is a necessary tool in recruiting individuals to volunteer.

Not-for-profits must actively promote the concept of return value if they wish to increase the retention of existing volunteers and the attraction of new volunteers. Not-for-profits should develop forms that reveal exactly what kind of benefits individuals volunteering for their organizations want from their volunteer experiences. Exhibit 1.1 and Exhibit 1.2 should help in this process. Both forms can be easily adapted to fit an individual not-for-profit's needs.

The Coalition should develop this kind of form. For the purposes of our example, all future exhibits will be based on the fact that the Coalition's volunteer prospects have had the opportunity to express the needs they seek through volunteering.

4.6   ESTABLISHING OPPORTUNITIES FOR PARTNERSHIPS WITH OUTSIDE SOURCES

One of the most interesting parts of a creative volunteer plan is the development of new and exciting ways to approach and access external partners. In order to accomplish such a partnership, it is important to document and translate your assets into a practical package that will appeal to your target audience. These packages may take many forms but the important thing is that the initial document must be brief and to the point. Detailed documents can be developed at a later time. Most potential volunteer prospects do not want to be burdened with a huge document anyway; instead, they want basic information on the organization and the volunteer position in question.

The Jacksonville Environmental Coalition has provided the Quality Water Project as an example (see Exhibit 4.5). The document is short and to the point: it provides the name of the institution and the key person to contact, in this case, the Chief Executive Officer. It includes a description of the project. The actual document should also include the addresses and telephone numbers of everyone involved.

The next paragraph contains the "sell" of the project. The Coalition has titled this paragraph "Partnership Opportunity." It provides a soft sell and has a general overview. The detailed sale should take place when you meet the prospect or in a separate letter.

It is always best to provide a brief overview of the need. The Coalition has titled this paragraph "Project Need." Note that the need is really two requests. The first and main request is for volunteer assistance—a total of 100 volunteers are needed. The second request is for $200,000 in funding and a budget is attached to the document. If a budget is attached, it should be brief. A detailed budget can always be produced at the appropriate time.

EXHIBIT 4.5 Opportunities to Partner

The Quality Water Project

The Jacksonville Environmental Coalition
Susan Wallace, Chief Executive Officer

The Project

The Quality Water Project provides an opportunity to bring several elements of the community together to solve a common problem. Quality water is everyone's business. Water from our streams and lakes provides water to drink, assists in keeping our recreation industry productive, and attracts people and businesses to our community. The Quality Water Project will identify the areas that need improvement and will create the plan to ensure that the improvements are made.

Partnership Opportunity

The Quality Water Project will need to cross a number of sectors to be successful. Local, state, and federal governments will need to be involved. Businesses and the general public need to be part of the plan to be successful. In order to accomplish this coalition building, the Jacksonville Environmental Coalition will need to secure a business partner to bring greater strength to the project.

Project Need

The project will need both volunteer assistance and funding to be successful. It is estimated that over 100 volunteers who have the background and expertise in water quality will be needed. This will include:

- A volunteer chair to lead the effort. This person will need to be a recognized leader in water quality issues;   1
- A committee that spans the range of talent needed to develop the project; and   14
- Area volunteers to monitor progress   85
   Total   100

Funding requirements are estimated at $200,000 to develop the project. A budget is attached.

The packages or projects that are developed become the outgrowth or sales pieces of the organization. Packets should be developed for core projects, new or proposed projects, and wish lists. These should be kept handy and taken on cultivation calls—you never know when someone will mention an idea that fits well with a project you have on the back burner.

4.7 DEVELOPING A VOLUNTEER MARKETING PLAN

Developing a marketing plan for your organization's volunteer effort will help ensure success. Securing volunteers is a core part of the business of a not-for-profit. Competition for the time of potential volunteers has risen steadily each year. This includes both volunteers secured through work-related volunteer programs and traditional volunteer recruitment. Therefore, in order for your volunteer opportunities to gain interest, the marketing plan for securing volunteers has to be focused, flexible, and timely.

A not-for-profit should approach a volunteer marketing plan as an opportunity to increase the visibility of the organization. While the plan will often be focused on certain types of potential volunteers, it is an opportunity to increase the attention of the community towards the not-for-profit. Beyond following the volunteer marketing plan found in Exhibit 4.6, certain guidelines should be followed:

1. Be sure to provide full disclosure of the type of position in question and the time resources that are required by the potential volunteer;
2. Make sure that the not-for-profit's status is clearly stated, i.e., financial health, etc.;
3. Encourage potential volunteers to contact current volunteers, provide a list;
4. Be open to new ideas that potential volunteers may offer; and
5. Be prepared for a negative response. Do not force the issue. The potential volunteer may not be ready or suited for the position in question. The person may be a potential volunteer for the future and, if handled well, can be approached again.

The Jacksonville Environmental Coalition developed a ten step approach to secure volunteers for their organization. Their approach is basic and it can be adopted by any not-for-profit. Exhibit 4.6 illustrates the Coalition's plan in detail.

The first step in creating the marketing plan is determining the volunteer needs of the Coalition. In order to do this, the Coalition made a list of

EXHIBIT 4.6 The Volunteer Marketing Plan

The Jacksonville Environmental Coalition

Volunteer Marketing Plan

1. Determine the volunteer needs of the coalition;
2. Develop a task force made up of current volunteers, friends, and professionals and meet to review volunteer prospects to determine the appropriate volunteer position match;
3. Link volunteer needs to the appropriate individual, community group, business, or other group in the area;
4. Develop a cultivation plan on each individual and group targeted;
5. Find a key person to make the initial contact;
6. Have the key person contact the prospect by telephone to set the appointment;
7. Have the key person meet with the prospect and one or two additional people;
8. Determine interest and discover what the coalition can provide as return value. Schedule a second meeting with prospect;
9. Develop the volunteer agreement/brief proposal based on both the need of the coalition and the prospect's anticipated return value discovered during the first meeting; and
10. Meet with the prospect for the second time and present the volunteer agreement/proposal brief.

volunteer prospects that was compiled from several sources, including past prospect lists and survey questionnaires that were sent to key volunteers, friends, and Coalition professionals. The professional staff placed the prospect names into different categories, ensuring that each volunteer position had at least five or six prospects.

The Coalition's next step is to develop a task force made up of current volunteers, friends, and professionals which will meet to review the volunteer prospects and to determine the appropriate match for each volunteer position. This is the time to rank and rate the prospects. The proper mix of people at this meeting will help provide a fair and appropriate evaluation of the leading prospects. There should be at least three volunteer prospects for each position.

This can be an exciting meeting as well as a great opportunity to increase the volunteer worth of the organization. The Coalition will take full advantage of the meeting. They have invited a number of key outside friends to the gathering. These outsiders can provide a wealth of information including the names of additional prospects and inside information on current prospects and partnerships.

The Coalition should use the meeting to introduce the new volunteer plan that will increase the focus on the return value. If the Coalition focuses on these objectives, the meeting will be a huge success and, through a true community evaluation effort, they will be well on their way to making a giant leap forward simply by increasing the quality and quantity of their volunteers.

4.8   DETERMINING THE TARGET MARKETS ON WHICH TO FOCUS YOUR VOLUNTEER PLAN

Now it is time to link open volunteer positions to the appropriate individuals, groups, and businesses in the area. The Coalition has developed a form that will make it easier to compare and to match the identified target markets, volunteer opportunities, volunteer prospects, and volunteer's needs, as shown in Exhibit 4.7.

The Coalition has selected a number of targeted markets including the individual prospects, community groups, other groups, and businesses. The leading candidates are listed on the sheet. Each volunteer prospect is assigned to a team of two or three individuals who will oversee the marketing effort.

Each of the teams have met separately to develop the cultivation plan for each targeted individual or group. It is interesting to see how the groups have developed their plans. Some of the teams worked within the team to identify the key people who will approach the volunteer prospect. Other groups brought new players into the process who can add influence or gain access. In either case, a cultivation plan was developed. These plans have a higher chance of success because they are unique to each individual prospect. The plans will focus on the prospect's needs rather than the Coalition's requirements.

Each team has found the key people to make the initial contact. The objective is to use the *right* people; not the most *convenient* people. These key people contacted the prospect and set up an appointment. They were able to conduct the initial contacts in a casual way since, for the most part, the prospect knew and respected the person who was calling. When the meeting took place, the key person and the rest of the team of no more than three people attended the meeting with the prospect. The presentations were low-key.

EXHIBIT 4.7 Determining the Target Audiences on Which to Focus the Volunteer Plan

The Jacksonville Environmental Coalition

Volunteer Plan External Targets

Targeted Markets	Volunteer Opportunities	Volunteer Prospects	Total Need
Individual	Vice Chair of Board	Patricia Smith	1
	Fund- Raising Chair	Robert Whitney	1
	Water Environment Chair	Jane Weber	1
Community	Regional Coordinators	Local service clubs	20
	Local Ambassadors	Jacksonville Chamber	45
	Air Committee	General Public	5
Other Groups	Clean Air Project	Clean Air Association	6
Business	Quality Water Project	Environmental Research Corp.	100
	Fund-Raising Small Gifts	Harford Electric Co.	30
	Major Gift Solicitation	Air First Corporation	10
Total	10	10	219

Before the meetings began, however, the Coalition gave demonstrations on how to conduct the initial meetings. This was done at the task force meeting. At this time, the Coalition also suggested that its volunteer cultivation teams should fulfill six objectives at these meetings. These six basic objectives are:

1. Introducing each person and stating why they are at the meeting with the volunteer prospect;
2. Introducing the Coalition to the prospect;
3. Presenting the volunteer position;
4. Determining the prospect's interest;
5. Determining the return value that the prospect seeks and what the Coalition can provide for the prospect; and
6. Setting up a date for a second meeting.

The Coalition's volunteer team meetings went well and almost 85 percent of the candidates noted that they had an interest in the volunteer opportunities. The teams who received refusals started the process over again with the next volunteer prospect on their list.

4.9 CREATING A VOLUNTEER AGREEMENT THAT IS TAILORED TO MEET INDIVIDUAL NEEDS

Each team will begin to develop a volunteer agreement for each volunteer prospect. Exhibit 4.8 provides an overview of the agreement that was developed for Jane Weber who was asked to chair the Water Environment Committee. The document was created from the notes taken at the team meeting with Jane and from two additional calls clarifying the benefits that Jane wanted to get from the experience.

The team then met with Jane to review the volunteer agreement. The agreement notes that this is a highly visible position that needs someone who is willing to provide significant time and energy for the initial appointment of one year. The document provides a listing of the standards that the Coalition needs to abide by and it cites how the Coalition will assist in making Jane's volunteer experience successful. The plan provides the return value that she is seeking. The agreement also reviews the evaluation component and the role that Jane will play in fulfilling that requirement.

After some refinements, Jane signed the agreement and the team leader, Helen Brown, put her signature on it as well. Jane was warmly welcomed into the "Volunteer Class of 1997." She was given a packet of information on her new role which also contained the date for the new volunteer orientation meeting.

4.10 EDUCATING NEW VOLUNTEERS THROUGH AN ORIENTATION SESSION

Providing orientation programs for new volunteers is time well spent. New volunteers need to be assimilated into the not-for-profit as quickly as possible. They need to feel that they are welcomed and have an extensive value to the organization.

The best way of accomplishing this task is creating a way to bring them into the organization well versed on the role that they will play and feeling that they are part of a vital team in the community. They also need to build a bond with other new volunteers. All of this can be accomplished

EXHIBIT 4.8 The Volunteer Agreement

Not-For-Profit Organization:	Jacksonville Environmental Coalition
Volunteer Position:	Water Environment Chair
Name:	Jane Weber
Date:	2/9/98

It is our pleasure to offer you the opportunity to chair the Water Environment Committee. This decision was based on your past volunteer record and your professional interest in water quality. This is a highly visible position that will demand significant time and energy for you to succeed. It is my understanding that this is a position that you are seeking and that you will be able to commit at least one year to this important volunteer position.

In order to perform successfully, the following standards will need to be met:
- Act as the active Chair of the Water Environment Committee;
- Recruit 12 members of the committee who have a background and an interest in water quality;
- Preside over the quarterly meeting of the Water Environment Committee;
- Attend the monthly board meeting;
- Represent the Coalition at the Clean Air Association quarterly meeting; and
- Become a sustaining member of the Coalition.

The Coalition will help you to be successful by:
- Providing an orientation meeting to review the duties of the position;
- Providing past meeting and board minutes for the Water Environment Committee and the Clean Air Association;
- Providing a list of the key leaders of the Coalition;
- Providing an opportunity for you to represent the Coalition at the national meeting of CAA;
- Assisting your company, the Environment Research Corporation, to become an active partner in the Quality Water Project; and
- Assisting you to better understand the role of the board of directors.

The evaluation component will be conducted as a team effort between you and the Volunteer Chair. This process is designed to ensure that your volunteer experience has been productive for both you and the Coalition. Upon your official appointment, you are encouraged to make your sustaining membership commitment. Welcome to the volunteer leadership ranks of the Jacksonville Environmental Coalition. We are delighted to have you involved with our program and look forward to working together to improve our environment.

Jane Weber	Date	Helen Brown	Date

through a volunteer orientation session designed to build confidence in the organization. The new volunteers will also gain a few friends in the process.

The orientation session for the new volunteers at the Coalition is scheduled for three weeks after the major round of volunteer recruitments takes place. It will be held at the Coalition's office and the design of the meeting will be interactive and dynamic. See Exhibit 4.9.

John Paul, the Volunteer Chair, will open the meeting. He will present the new volunteers with "the Coalition volunteer pin." The pins will be put on each volunteer by the board members of the Coalition.

John will then introduce the new volunteers to April Gray, the 1997 Class Advisor. April was a new volunteer last year and was elected as the 1996 Class Chair. One of the duties of this elected position is to become the Class Advisor for the following year. This tradition has helped the Coalition in assimilating volunteers more successfully.

April will review her volunteer experiences from the previous year, discuss the overall history of the organization, review the volunteer structure, and demonstrate how the new volunteers will become involved in the organization. April will introduce the Chief Executive Officer of the

EXHIBIT 4.9 The Volunteer's Orientation Session

Opening	Conducted by the highest ranking volunteer available.
Introduction to Class Chair	Conducted by the highest ranking volunteer available.
History of the Organization	Class advisor.
Volunteer Structure	Class advisor.
Introduction to Professional	Class advisor.
Professional Structure	Conducted by the highest ranking professional available.
Introduction of Class Professional	Conducted by the highest ranking professional available.
The Return Value of Volunteering	Class professional.
Volunteer Needs	Class advisor.
Individual Volunteer Positions	Volunteer guides meet new volunteers in smaller groups.
Evaluation Process	Class advisor.
Induction into the Class	Class advisor/class professional.
Closing	Conducted by the highest ranking volunteer possible.

Coalition, Susan Wallace. Susan will review the professional structure of the organization and introduce the new volunteers to the 1997 Class Professional Advisor, Tom Terry.

Tom is assigned to the 1997 class and he will continue this job for the *full* year to ensure that the class receives the attention that they need to have a productive year. Tom will review, in detail, the Coalition's commitment to providing maximum return value to volunteers.

Volunteer guides will attend the meeting and they will sit down in small groups to review the positions of their volunteers. New volunteers will report to their volunteer guides on a regular basis. The process will be more of a mentoring activity; it will not be a traditional boss/employee relationship. By the time this brief initial meeting is over, there should be a bond between the volunteer guide and the new volunteer.

When the group comes back together, the class advisor will review the evaluation process. She will emphasize that the plan exists to ensure that the Coalition's activities are accomplished and that each volunteer receives the return value they desired.

Finally, each new volunteer will be inducted into the Class of 1997 by the class advisor and the class professional. They will be given a small gift or plaque that notes that they are a volunteer for the Coalition. The closing will be conducted by the Volunteer Chair, John Paul.

The orientation meeting at the Coalition does a lot more than simply provide information. It inspires, provides recognition, and makes each new volunteer feel that they have become involved with an organization that cares for the environment and for them as individuals. By the time the meeting is over, each volunteer will feel proud to be part of the organization.

The time and effort placed on the volunteer orientation can be paid back a hundredfold by what the volunteer will provide to the organization directly and the good will they will project to external audiences.

4.11   ESTABLISHING AND EXECUTING A VOLUNTEER RECOGNITION PLAN

A volunteer plan can make a significant difference in how an organization attracts volunteers. One of the necessary ingredients for retaining volunteers is a well-designed recognition program. Volunteer recognition has been part of not-for-profits for a long time. Traditionally, organizations have provided recognition for individuals' contribution of time, the most precious gift of all.

For the most part, however, these recognitions amounted to a certificate or a plaque and, maybe, an occasional listing in a noted publication.

While this kind of recognition has been beneficial and has contributed to thanking each individual, it is often not consistent with, and seldom is personalized enough to fit, the volunteer's needs or wishes.

A recognition program does not have to cost a fortune to be effective. Most volunteers understand that not-for-profits have limited funds for such activities. What the average volunteer seeks is a simple thank you and recognition in front of their peers. Mostly, however, volunteers seek return value and this can be incorporated into the recognition program.

The Jacksonville Environmental Coalition has made sure that a quality recognition plan is in place. Their recognition plan is divided into two parts:

1. The Individual Plan; and
2. The Group/Business Plan.

The Coalition realizes that the individuals and entities who help make the volunteer plan work want recognition. They also realize that the recognition needs to be provided differently than it has been in the past.

Exhibit 4.10 provides the details of the Coalition's plan. Note that the individual plan recognizes the volunteer for work that has been performed. This is a simple but profound statement. Recognition needs to be reserved for individuals who actually perform and it should have different degrees.

The Coalition has not settled the details of the overall recognitions because they vary each year. The Coalition provides an array of standard awards for volunteers each year that includes the volunteer pin given to each volunteer at the orientation meeting. Letters are sent out to all of the individuals who volunteered over the past year, thanking them for the contribution of their time and energy. The letters are signed individually by both the Volunteer Chair and the Chief Executive Officer. Personal messages are handwritten on the letters whenever possible.

Recognition is also given in a number of publications, in particular, the annual report. Certificates are given to all volunteers. Plaques are given to volunteer guides and special volunteer awards are reserved for the one or two volunteers who "go the extra mile." This special recognition is given out every year and it can be given to any volunteer in the Coalition, although it is often given to a volunteer who works at the regional or area level.

Volunteers are also recognized for their tenure at the Coalition. The Coalition has found that this helps to retain volunteers. Each individual is given a pin that is similar to the volunteer pin except that it displays the number of years that each volunteer has served. Volunteers are given this recognition after serving for one year.

The theory behind providing such an early recognition device was that most of the Coalition's volunteer losses occurred in the second year of

EXHIBIT 4.10 The Volunteer Recognition Plan

The Jacksonville Environmental Coalition

Volunteer Recognition Plan

<u>Individual Plan</u>

All individuals will receive recognition for the work that they have performed with the Coalition.

The recognitions will be provided in the following way;

1. Each volunteer will receive a letter thanking them for their valuable contribution;
2. Each volunteer will be recognized for their work in the annual report;
3. Individual recognition pieces will be provided based on volunteer work including:
   -Volunteer Pins/Certificates
   -Plaques
   -Other appropriate recognition pieces;
4. Volunteers will be recognized for tenure starting with the end of the first year:
   -Pins -Certificates
   -Lifetime volunteer achievement wall at Coalition office after five years + individual plaque; and
5. The annual evaluation of each volunteer will ensure that they have received the return value that they sought.

<u>Group/Business Plan</u>

All groups and businesses will receive recognition for the direct assistance they have provided to make the Coalition plan so successful. The recognitions will be provided in the following manner:

1. Each entity will receive a letter thanking them for their valuable contribution;
2. Each entity will be recognized for their work in the annual report;
3. Recognition pieces will be provided based on the level of involvement:
   -Certificates
   -Plaques
   -Other appropriate recognition pieces;
4. Entities will be recognized for tenure starting with the end of the first year:
   -Pins/Certificates
   -Verbal recognition at the annual meeting
   -Printed recognition on materials produced within the project
   -Lifetime volunteer achievement wall at Coalition office after five years + individual plaques
   -Use of the Coalition's partnership logo on appropriate materials; and
5. The annual evaluation of the involvement of entities in the volunteer plan of the Coalition will ensure that they have received the return value that they sought.

service. The Coalition felt that the early recognition would assist in lowering the rate of loss and it worked well enough that they began to give out certificates noting the tenure of each volunteer. The certificates, however, are given in five-year intervals and, thus, have more prestige.

The Lifetime Volunteer Achievement Wall provides a lasting recognition at the Coalition's office. Every individual who has volunteered for more than five years has their name placed on the wall. The wall is designed so that the names can be easily attached and can be moved up the wall as the tenure increases. It is a *living* wall of volunteering; not a *past* wall of volunteering. Volunteers who visit the office often take the time to view their progression and the progression of their peers. A Lifetime Volunteer Recognition Award is given out each time the volunteer's name moves up the wall.

The most unique part of the recognition plan takes place during evaluation of each volunteer at the end of the year. While the evaluation ensures that the standards of the Coalition are met, it also ensures that each volunteer receives the desired return value from their experience. During the evaluation, the volunteer and the guide discuss and agree on the return value that the individual has received from the process. Thus, the evaluation has become yet another recognition device.

The Coalition realizes that groups and businesses who help make the volunteer plan a success should be recognized. The Coalition also realizes that this recognition has to be different than individual recognitions. Groups and businesses have helped the Coalition conduct a successful volunteer plan in a variety of ways, including accessing and enticing executives to become key volunteers, opening the employee volunteer programs that encourage volunteering for the Coalition, and sponsoring projects that include funding and encouraging employee groups to volunteer.

Letters will be sent thanking these groups or businesses for the contributions that they have made. Each letter will describe the contribution and state how it made a difference. They will also be recognized in various Coalition publications including the annual report.

Recognition pieces will be given out to groups and businesses. This will follow a pattern similar to the individual awards. Certificates will be given to all groups and businesses. Plaques will be given to businesses that were heavily involved. A special award will be given if a group or business performs exceptionally well. This award will not be given out each year; only when the need arises.

Tenure recognition will be given to groups and businesses starting in the first year. The theory behind this is that if the group or business is recognized in the first year they may want to continue working with the Coalition in order to receive future tenure recognition. The tenure awards are designed to be given out in five-year intervals. These recognitions will include pins for the key players in the groups or businesses as well as certificates and verbal recognition at the annual meeting.

Many of the groups and businesses want visibility as a recognition and the Coalition is eager to oblige. Groups or businesses who are involved with any particular project will be recognized in all the printed materials pertaining to the project. Groups and businesses are also eligible for both the Lifetime Achievement Wall and the Contributions Recognition Wall. Both distinctions provide attractive wall plaques that can be placed in the group's or business's offices. Each plaque has a tenure and giving bar that can be replaced as the lifetime tenure and giving increases. The groups and business are permitted to make reference to their involvement with the Coalition and they can also use the Coalition's special partnership logo on stationery and other appropriate items.

The bulk of recognitions will be given to volunteers, groups, and businesses at a special recognition gathering that takes place at the annual meeting. This forum provides maximum visibility and the Coalition takes advantage of this by encouraging media coverage and by sending out press releases to local newspapers, industry trade publications, and any other publication that the volunteers and businesses suggest. The Coalition's recognition plan enhances the organization's image by placing the emphasis on the individuals, groups, and businesses who make the volunteer plan a success.

4.12   IMPLEMENTING A COMPREHENSIVE EVALUATION PLAN

A comprehensive evaluation plan plays an important role in the successful conclusion and recycling of the volunteer plan. The volunteer plan covers all of the activities of an organization and it involves all of the volunteers and professionals. A well-designed evaluation plan will reveal how this overall plan succeeded and it will uncover areas that need improvement. Most importantly, the evaluation plan will reveal whether or not the volunteers received the return value that they had expected.

The Jacksonville Environmental Coalition has linked the evaluation plan with its recognition plan. The leadership of the Coalition thinks that the evaluation plan is helpful in discovering and recognizing the needs of both the Coalition and the volunteers. This process will also ensure that volunteers receive the full return value that they deserve. The Coalition has developed ten steps to ensure that the evaluation plan is successful. These steps are discussed in Exhibit 4.11.

EXHIBIT 4.11 The Volunteer Evaluation Plan

The Jacksonville Environmental Coalition

Volunteer Evaluation Plan

1. Gather all data together including original individual volunteer agreements and general progress in all areas.
2. Volunteers who are guides meet with the volunteer chair and the chief executive officer to review the past year in general, and how volunteering contributed to the Coalition.
3. Volunteer guides review the progress that each volunteer made within the team and complete the volunteer evaluation form.
4. Each volunteer is asked to complete the volunteer evaluation form.
5. The volunteer guide meets with each volunteer to hold the evaluation meeting.
6. The final volunteer evaluation form is completed with the agreement of both parties.
7. The volunteer evaluation forms are sent to the volunteer chair for general review.
8. The Coalition volunteer evaluation report is created based on all the evaluation reports.
9. Recommendations are made to the board of the Coalition.
10. The Coalition's volunteer plan is developed for the next year.

The Coalition will gather data such as the original volunteer plan and reports on the general progress in various areas. Volunteers guides will meet with the Volunteer Chair and the Chief Executive Officer to review the past year; specifically, how volunteering contributed to the Coalition. Detailed notes will be kept to make sure that a permanent record is established for the year's activity. These materials will be refined and key parts will be used for various publications, future discussion, and promotional purposes.

Volunteer guides will be given evaluation forms for all the volunteers under their direction. The forms will be filled out and they will include appropriate information such as the name of each volunteer, the duties that the volunteer assumed, and the ways that the Coalition agreed to assist the volunteer. All of the information contained on the evaluation form will be taken from the volunteer agreement that the volunteer and the Coalition jointly developed at the beginning of the year.

Exhibit 4.12 illustrates the use of the form by showing how the volunteer guide completed this document for Jane Weber, Chair of the Water

EXHIBIT 4.12 The Volunteer Evaluation Form: Volunteer Guide's Responses

The Jacksonville Environmental Coalition

Volunteer Evaluation Form **Draft Form By:** <u>John Paul</u>
Volunteer: Jane Weber
Position: Water Environment Chair
Period of Time: 2/9/98 to 12/31/98
Volunteer Guide: John Paul

How the Evaluation Process Works

The following volunteer evaluation is designed to ensure that the Coalition and the volunteer received the maximum value from their association with each other. The Coalition's evaluation process is designed to be a positive process of exchange of ideas and thoughts to improve the volunteer program overall and to ensure that the experience of each individual is as rewarding as possible. The process has been made as simple as possible. Each volunteer is asked to complete the form and to meet with the volunteer guide. The volunteer guide will also complete a form on each volunteer in the team based on the agreed upon volunteer agreement. During the evaluation the ideas and thoughts of both parties are placed on the final evaluation form. The final evaluation form will be sent to the volunteer chair. The Coalition Volunteer Evaluation Report will be based on all of the evaluation forms. All volunteer evaluation forms will be kept confidential. Qualitative levels will be based on the opinion of each person, on a scale of 1 through 5 with 1 being the lowest and 5 being the highest. Qualitative measures will be based on actual numerical goals that were set, i.e., 5 committee members out of 8 would read 5 of 8. The Coalition appreciates your assistance in evaluating its volunteer program.

Actions That the Volunteer Agreed to Take	Qualitative	Quantitative
-Act as the active chair of the Water Environment Committee	5	
-Recruit 12 members of the committee		7 of 12
-Preside over the quarterly meeting of the WEC	3	
-Attend the monthly board meeting	4	
-Represent the Coalition at the CAA	4	
-Become a sustaining member of the Coalition	5	

Actions That the Coalition Agreed to Take	Qualitative	Quantitative
-Provide an orientation meeting	5	
-Provide past meeting minutes of WEC, board, and CAA	5	
-Provide a list of leaders	5	
-Provide opportunity to represent Coalition at nat'l. mtg. of CAA	5	

EXHIBIT 4.12 (Continued)

Actions That the Coalition Agreed to Take	Qualitative	Quantitative
-Assist your company, ERC, to become a partner in QWP	5	
-Assist to better understand the role of the board	1	

Additional Information

Overall, Jane Weber was a fine chair of the Water Environment Committee. She recruited seven committee members. Jane seems to really enjoy the role as chair. I am a bit concerned, however, that she was unable to make a number of the WEC meetings.

It seems that the Coalition has provided the agreed upon value to Jane. Jane's company seems to have enjoyed the volunteer and financial partner arrangement that was developed. Jane still needs to have a training session on the workings of the board.

I would recommend that Jane continue in the role as the chair of the Water Environment Committee for one more year. I also recommend that Jane be considered for a greater board role in the future.

Overall Evaluation:
Volunteer: 4
Coalition: 4

Jane Weber did well as the chair of the Water Environment Committee. Jane will be a key leader for the Coalition in the coming years.

The Coalition provided almost all of the requirements sought by Jane.

John Paul   Date
Volunteer Guide

Environment Committee. The original list of agreed items was completed at the beginning of the volunteer experience by Jane and by the Coalition.

The volunteer guide had an opportunity to provide both a qualitative and quantitative reply. With most volunteer positions, however, there are more qualitative than quantitative answers. The levels have been made flexible on purpose. The form is not designed as a rating instrument but, rather, as a way of documenting whether the Coalition's activities were accomplished and whether the volunteer received the appropriate return value.

There is also an area for additional comments and for an overall evaluation. This provides room for John Paul to explain his rating and to note any ways that the Coalition needs to assist Jane Weber. It also provides room to list recommendations.

When this is done, the Coalition will set up a volunteer guide's meeting. At this meeting, they will review the individual evaluation forms in detail and discuss the overall evaluation process. This meeting will instruct the guides on how to fill out the forms in a more uniform way.

In the case of Jane Weber, John Paul feels that she has done a wonderful job, but he is a little concerned she has not been making the committee meetings. He also thinks that the partnership agreement that Jane's company is conducting with the Coalition is going well.

John Paul was able to note all of these feelings on the evaluation form. He indicated that Jane still needed to have a training session on the workings of the board, but John recommended that Jane continue in her role as chair of the committee. He also recommended that Jane should be considered for a more important role on the board in the future. John indicated a rating of "4" for the role that Jane played as a volunteer and he gave the same rating for the quality of return value that the Coalition provided for Jane. Finally, John signed the document.

It is important to note that this document will not be given to the Coalition. It will only be used at the meeting with Jane Weber.

Jane received a blank evaluation form in the mail, as she expected. John Paul had called her to set up a meeting to develop the final evaluation form, which will be the one that is sent to the Coalition.

When John called Jane, he instructed her to fill the form out before their meeting. John indicated that he would do the same thing and that their meeting would concentrate on combining the two reports. Jane's volunteer evaluation form was accompanied by a letter from the volunteer chair.

Exhibit 4.13 shows Jane's ratings and concerns. Notice that Jane rated herself lower in a number of areas than John Paul did. This is not unusual. Most individuals are more critical of themselves than others are. Notice also that more volunteers were recruited than John Paul had figured.

Under "additional information," Jane indicated how much she had enjoyed being the chair of the Water Environment Committee and she explained why she was unable to attend many of the committee meetings. She suggested that she be reassigned to another position but she expressed an interest in continuing as chair for one more year and being given the new assignment in the third year. She indicated that she might be interested in an officer's position on the board.

Jane mentioned that she never received any training on the board's function and she indicated that she still needs minutes from some of the

EXHIBIT 4.13 The Volunteer Evaluation Form: Volunteer's Responses

The Jacksonville Environmental Coalition

Volunteer Evaluation Form   **Draft Form By:** <u>Jane Weber</u>
Volunteer: Jane Weber
Position: Water Environment Chair
Period of Time: 2/9/98 to 12/31/98
Volunteer Guide: John Paul

How the Evaluation Process Works

The following volunteer evaluation is designed to ensure that the Coalition and the volunteer received the maximum value from their association with each other. The Coalition's evaluation process is designed to be a positive process of exchange of ideas and thoughts to improve the volunteer program overall and to ensure that the experience of each individual is as rewarding as possible. The process has been made as simple as possible. Each volunteer is asked to complete the form and to meet with the volunteer guide. The volunteer guide will also complete a form on each volunteer in the team based on the agreed upon volunteer agreement. During the evaluation the ideas and thoughts of both parties are placed on the final evaluation form. The final evaluation form will be sent to the volunteer chair. The Coalition Volunteer Evaluation Report will be based on all of the evaluation forms. All volunteer evaluation forms will be kept confidential. Qualitative levels will be based on the opinion of each person, on a scale of 1 through 5 with 1 being the lowest and 5 being the highest. Qualitative measures will be based on actual numerical goals that were set, i.e., 5 committee members out of 8 would read 5 of 8. The Coalition appreciates your assistance in evaluating its volunteer program.

Actions That the Volunteer Agreed to Take	Qualitative	Quantitative
-Act as the active chair of the Water Environment Committee	4	
-Recruit 12 members of the committee		8 of 12
-Preside over the quarterly meeting of the WEC	2	
-Attend the monthly board meeting	3	
-Represent the Coalition at the CAA	5	
-Become a sustaining member of the Coalition	5	

Actions That the Coalition Agreed to Take	Qualitative	Quantitative
-Provide an orientation meeting	5	
-Provide past meeting minutes of WEC, board, and CAA	3	
-Provide a list of leaders	5	
-Provide opportunity to represent Coalition at nat'l. mtg. of CAA	5	(Continued)

EXHIBIT 4.13 (Continued)

Actions That the Coalition Agreed to Take	Qualitative	Quantitative
-Assist your company, ERC, to become a partner in QWP		4
-Assist to better understand the role of the board		1

Additional Information

Overall, I had a wonderful experience this year as Chair of the Water Environment Committee. Although I am still recruiting committee members, the current members are really making it happen. I really enjoyed my other experiences with the Coalition. I was unable to make most of the meetings with the WEC. The meeting dates often conflicted with my work schedule. I would suggest that I be reassigned to another function that I can attend.

I have been satisfied with the value that I have received personally from the experience. I still need to receive the past minutes from the CAA meetings however. My company seems to be satisfied with the partner arrangement but I feel that they should receive more visible recognition for the $100,000 grant that they made this autumn. I would still like to have a training session on the workings of the board. I attended three board meetings to date but am not sure of my overall role.

I would like to remain the Chair of the Water Environment Committee for one more year and would then like to take on a new assignment. Perhaps an officer's position on the board would be appropriate.

Overall Evaluation:
Volunteer: 3.5
Coalition: 3

Overall I felt that I performed well in my first year as the chair of the Water Environment Committee.

The Coalition, I felt, did a good job as well in providing me with the support and value that I sought from the experience.

Jane Weber   Date
Volunteer

meetings. Overall, Jane feels that her company is satisfied with the partnership arrangement but feels that they are a little disappointed with the amount of visible recognition they have received, particularly for their recent grant of $100,000. Jane ranked her performance a "3.5" while rating the performance of the Coalition as a "3." When she was done, Jane signed the document.

At this point, Jane Weber will meet with John Paul to hold the evaluation meeting. They will compare their notes and combine their individual documents into one.

Exhibit 4.14 provides the combined results of the evaluations that Jane and John prepared. Note that some changes occurred in the volunteer agreement section and that the proper number of volunteers recruited was recorded. Jane and John refined the qualitative numbers by using some of John's numbers and some of Jane's numbers. In the category, "represents the coalition members," they averaged their numbers and arrived at a rating of 4.5. The same process occurred in the Coalition portion of the evaluation.

The document looks completely different in the "additional information" and "overall evaluation" categories. Traditionally at the Coalition, the volunteer guide completes the "additional information" section. This gives the volunteer guide ample space to clarify the evaluation from the mentor's point of view. For example, John recommended that Jane continue in the chair position and be considered for a more important role in the future. Jane has the opportunity to express herself in the "overall evaluation" section.

The final evaluation resulted in a higher overall score. Again, it is important to remember that the evaluation is not a test; rather, it is an opportunity to ensure that Jane Weber's volunteer experience was as beneficial as possible. Both Jane and John signed and dated the Volunteer Evaluation Form when it was finished. John will make sure that Jane receives a copy of the final form and that the original is sent to the Coalition.

The Coalition keeps all individual volunteer evaluation forms confidential. The professional staff extracts information from these forms and compiles the data into the Volunteer Evaluation Report. Exhibit 4.15 provides a sample of the report that the Coalition developed.

If this was the actual report, the document would go well beyond the report format so that it could be used as a promotional piece. In this fashion, the report would be able to document past volunteer success and it could be used to attract new volunteers for the following year.

The report should include stories, photos, and quotes that will bring the volunteer experience to life. It should also put a positive spin on the wonderful contributions that volunteers have made and it should explain how the Coalition has consistently provided return value to its volunteers. The statistical summary of the report should bridge the past and look to

EXHIBIT 4.14 The Volunteer Evaluation Form

The Jacksonville Environmental Coalition

Volunteer Evaluation Form   **Final Form By:** Jane Weber
                                                              John Paul

Volunteer: Jane Weber
Position: Water Environment Chair
Period of Time: 2/9/98 to 12/31/98
Volunteer Guide: John Paul

How the Evaluation Process Works

The following volunteer evaluation is designed to ensure that the Coalition and the volunteer received the maximum value from their association with each other. The Coalition's evaluation process is designed to be a positive process of exchange of ideas and thoughts to improve the volunteer program overall and to ensure that the experience of each individual is as rewarding as possible. The process has been made as simple as possible. Each volunteer is asked to complete the form and to meet with the volunteer guide. The volunteer guide will also complete a form on each volunteer in the team based on the agreed upon volunteer agreement. During the evaluation the ideas and thoughts of both parties are placed on the final evaluation form. The final evaluation form will be sent to the volunteer chair. The Coalition Volunteer Evaluation Report will be based on all of the evaluation forms. All volunteer evaluation forms will be kept confidential. Qualitative levels will be based on the opinion of each person, on a scale of 1 through 5 with 1 being the lowest and 5 being the highest. Qualitative measures will be based on actual numerical goals that were set, i.e., 5 committee members out of 8 would read 5 of 8. The Coalition appreciates your assistance in evaluating its volunteer program.

Actions That the Volunteer Agreed to Take	Qualitative	Quantitative
-Act as the active chair of the Water Environment Committee	5	
-Recruit 12 members of the committee		8 of 12
-Preside over the quarterly meeting of the WEC	2	
-Attend the monthly board meeting	4	
-Represent the Coalition at the CAA	4.5	
-Become a sustaining member of the Coalition	5	

Actions That the Coalition Agreed to Take	Qualitative	Quantitative
-Provide an orientation meeting	5	
-Provide past meeting minutes of WEC, board, and CAA	3	
-Provide a list of leaders	5	

EXHIBIT 4.14 (Continued)

Actions That the Coalition Agreed to Take	Qualitative	Quantitative
-Provide opportunity to represent Coalition at nat'l. mtg. of CAA	5	
-Assist your company, ERC, to become a partner in QWP	4	
-Assist to better understand the role of the board	1	

Additional Information

Volunteer Guide's Report

Overall Jane Weber was a fine Chair of the Water Environment Committee. She recruited eight committee members who are doing a great job. Jane enjoys the role as chair. She is not able to make the WEC meetings due to a conflict with her job. I recommend that Jane be reassigned to another function.

The Coalition has provided most of the agreed upon value to Jane. Jane still needs the past minutes from the CAA meetings, however. Jane's company seems to have really enjoyed both the volunteer and financial partnership arrangement that was developed. Additional recognition would be recommended for her company's recent financial support of $100,000. Jane still needs to have a training session on the workings of the board.

I would recommend that Jane continue in the role as the chair of the Water Environment Committee for one more year. I would also recommend that Jane be considered for a greater board role in the future.

Overall Evaluation:
Volunteer: 4
Coalition: 4

Volunteer's Report:

I enjoyed my role as the chair of the Water Environment Committee. I would like to be a key leader for the Coalition in the coming years.

The Coalition provided almost all of the requirements I sought in my volunteer experience.

Jane Weber	Date	John Paul	Date
Volunteer		Volunteer Guide	

EXHIBIT 4.15 The Volunteer Evaluation Report

The Jacksonville Environmental Coalition

Volunteer Evaluation Report for 1998

Volunteer Chair:	John Paul
Chief Executive Officer:	Susan Wallace
Date:	March 1, 1999

I am delighted to report that the Jacksonville Environmental Coalition volunteer plan was a monumental success. This has been due to both the volunteer guides who acted as mentors and the volunteers themselves who gave one hundred percent to the effort. This report is a reflection of the dedication and enthusiasm of everyone who was involved in the volunteer effort in 1998.

John Paul
Volunteer Chair

Statistical Summary

Market	Participants	1996	1997	1998	1999 Goal
Individual	Number of Volunteers	194	230	384	400
	Volunteers Retained	54%	71%	75%	77%
	Number of New Volunteers	97	105	219	212
Community	Number of Organizations	1	3	5	7
	Number of Organizations Retained	0	1	2	4
	Number of New Organizations	1	2	3	3
Other Groups	Number of Groups	0	1	2	3
	Number of Groups Retained	0	0	1	1
	Number of New Groups	0	0	1	2
Business	Number of Businesses	0	1	3	5
	Number of Businesses Retained	0	0	1	2
	Number of New Businesses	0	1	2	3

Additional copy should be added to support the findings, including success stories. This document can be used to provide both recognition for those who have participated and for marketing the next year's plan. The final piece should include photos that depict involvement and testimony from all four focus areas.

the future. In the Coalition's case, the reader can see real progress over the past three years and they can expect growth well into the future.

The volunteer committee should review the final report, approve it, and send it to the board for final approval. The volunteer committee should send a list of recommendations to the board regarding the approval. These recommendations should come from a number of different sources, including the volunteer evaluation forms.

4.13 RECYCLING THE PLAN BASED ON THE DATA COLLECTED THROUGH THE EVALUATION PROCESS

The final part of the evaluation plan is to develop a volunteer plan for the next year. This can be accomplished if the volunteer plan followed the recommended steps and if the evaluation process provides the needed information to make educated decisions for the following year.

In the case of the Jacksonville Environmental Coalition, they have followed the plan. Their plan was flexible enough to be adapted throughout the course of the year. This was a great help in adjusting the plan during the year and it improved the plan on a continual basis. Finally, the volunteer committee made additional refinements for next year based on the recommendations provided by volunteers, friends, and professionals. The Coalition is ready to do it all over again.

4.14 CONCLUSION

The most important element for real change and progress in a not-for-profit organization is volunteers. They are the leaders. They are the organization.

Not-for-profit organizations need to pay more attention to their volunteers and they need to be concerned about their needs and desires. The competition for an individual's time is fierce. Individuals have ample opportunities to spend their free time with their family, on recreational pursuits, at work, and, even, by volunteering at another not-for-profit.

Not-for-profits need to spend a little more time on volunteers' needs because they can get a whole lot more back in return. Not-for-profits can provide individuals with a real purpose in life. They can render personal recognition at a level that is rarely provided. They can inspire. They can train. Finally, they can produce leaders who will continue to volunteer and will make a real difference in the not-for-profit and the community that the institution serves.

All of this can be accomplished by creating a volunteer job profile that the volunteer is asked to meet. In return, the profile must serve as a promise by the not-for-profit to serve the volunteer. This service must include return value that the volunteer needs to make their volunteer experience beneficial.

Is all of this worth it? It is if a not-for-profit wishes to retain quality volunteers and to gain the reputation that will attract additional volunteers. Volunteering has leveled off and competition is fierce. Not-for-profits must use their own initiative to gain additional volunteer support. When this is achieved, the organization will flourish and additional financial resources will be easier to obtain.

ENDNOTES

[1]Unger, Janet L., "Volunteer Development: Individual and Organizational Considerations," *The Nonprofit Management Handbook,* John Wiley & Sons, Inc., NY, 1993, pp. 256–259.

[2]Fisher, James C. and Kathleen M. Cole, *Leadership and Management of Volunteer Programs,* Jossey - Bass Publishers, San Francisco, CA, 1993, pp. 86–87.

APPENDIX

WORKSHEETS*

*These worksheets can also be found on the computer disk located at the back of the book.

The Volunteer Needs Assessment

Not-for-profit:
Chief Executive Officer:
Volunteer Chair:
Date:

Positions/ Description	Remarks	Retained	Old	New

Sub-Totals
Total Recruitment Needs
Total Volunteer Needs

The Identification of Not-For-Profit Assets

Not-for-Profit:
Chief Executive Officer:
Volunteer Chair:
Date:

Asset	Description	Partnership Opportunities

The Volunteer Section of the Strategic Plan

The Volunteer Plan

Objective

The Volunteer Job Profile

Report to:

Supervises:

Duties:

Meeting requirements:

Time requirements:

Skills required:

Evaluation:

Opportunities to Partner

The Project

Partnership Opportunity

Project Need

The Volunteer Marketing Plan

1.

2.

3.

4.

5.

6.

7.

8.

9.

10.

Determining the Target Audiences on Which to Focus the Volunteer Plan

Targeted Markets	Volunteer Opportunities	Volunteer Prospects	Total Need

Total

The Volunteer Agreement

Not-For-Profit Organization:
Volunteer Position:
Name:
Date:

_____   _____
Date   Date

The Volunteer's Orientation Session

Opening	Conducted by the highest ranking volunteer available.
Introduction to Class Chair	Conducted by the highest ranking volunteer available.
History of the Organization	Class advisor.
Volunteer Structure	Class advisor.
Introduction to Professional	Class advisor.
Professional Structure	Conducted by the highest ranking professional available.
Introduction of Class Professional	Conducted by the highest ranking professional available.
The Return Value of Volunteering	Class professional.
Volunteer Needs	Class advisor.
Individual Volunteer Positions	Volunteer guides meet new volunteers in smaller groups.
Evaluation Process	Class advisor.
Induction into the Class	Class advisor/class professional.
Closing	Conducted by the highest ranking volunteer possible.

The Volunteer Recognition Plan

The Volunteer Evaluation Plan

The Volunteer Evaluation Form: Volunteer Guide's Responses

Volunteer Evaluation Form
Volunteer:
Position:
Period of Time:
Volunteer Guide:

How the Evaluation Process Works

The following volunteer evaluation is designed to ensure that the Coalition and the volunteer received the maximum value from their association with each other. The Coalition's evaluation process is designed to be a positive process of exchange of ideas and thoughts to improve the volunteer program overall and to ensure that the experience of each individual is as rewarding as possible. The process has been made as simple as possible. Each volunteer is asked to complete the form and to meet with the volunteer guide. The volunteer guide will also complete a form on each volunteer in the team based on the agreed upon volunteer agreement. During the evaluation the ideas and thoughts of both parties are placed on the final evaluation form. The final evaluation form will be sent to the volunteer chair. The Coalition Volunteer Evaluation Report will be based on all of the evaluation forms. All volunteer evaluation forms will be kept confidential. Qualitative levels will be based on the opinion of each person, on a scale of 1 through 5 with 1 being the lowest and 5 being the highest. Qualitative measures will be based on actual numerical goals that were set, i.e., 5 committee members out of 8 would read 5 of 8. The Coalition appreciates your assistance in evaluating its volunteer program.

Actions That the Volunteer Agreed To Take   **Qualitative**   **Quantitative**

Actions That the Coalition Agreed To Take   **Qualitative**   **Quantitative**

Additional Information

Overall Evaluation:
Volunteer:
Coalition:

Date

The Volunteer Evaluation Report

Volunteer Evaluation Report for 1998
Volunteer Chair:
Chief Executive Officer:
Date:

Statistical Summary

Market	Participants	1996	1997	1998	1999 Goal
Individual	Number of Volunteers				
	Volunteers Retained				
	Number of New Volunteers				
Community	Number of Organizations				
	Number of Organizations Retained				
	Number of New Organizations				
Other Groups	Number of Groups				
	Number of Groups Retained				
	Number of New Groups				
Business	Number of Businesses				
	Number of Businesses Retained				
	Number of New Businesses				

Additional copy should be added to support the findings, including success stories. This document can be used to provide both recognition for those who have participated and for marketing the next year's plan. The final piece should include photos that depict involvement and testimony from all four focus areas.

▼5 Using the Return Value of Volunteering to Strengthen Fund Raising

5.1   INTRODUCTION

Fund raising is a vital part of all not-for-profits. Not-for-profits procure funds through a number of methods, including government funding, grants from foundations, business contributions, special events, sponsorships, project sales, sales of products or services, and gifts-in-kind.

Like volunteering, the ways in which not-for-profits procure funds is in transition. Government funding is decreasing and the competition for foundation and business donations is higher than ever. In the future, the key to the financial stability of not-for-profits will not be the external gifts that have sustained them over the past several decades. Instead, the key will be individual gifts that come from people that have a vested interest in the organization. Organizations that are not nurturing individual donors to provide immediate and lifetime gifts will be in deep trouble in the years ahead.

Another area that will sustain the not-for-profit will be the development of meaningful partnerships with businesses that have a logical relationship to the not-for-profit. As we will discuss in chapter 6, businesses are becoming more selective in how they donate funds because they, too, seek return value from their investments.

5.2 VOLUNTEERING'S ROLE IN STABILIZING THE FINANCIAL NEEDS OF NOT-FOR-PROFITS

Studies show that the more deeply involved individuals become with a not-for-profit, the more apt they are to support its causes. Large, lifetime gifts have been made by individuals who had been volunteers years before and who had been totally forgotten by the not-for-profit. These individuals typically had fond memories of their volunteer experiences and wanted to ensure that the institution would continue its service to the community well into the future.

One of the more emotional expressions of giving that I experienced started when I began to unearth a listing of past volunteers of the organization. At the time I was the Director of Communications and Fund Development at the Valley Forge Council, Boy Scouts of America, Valley Forge, PA. I started to cultivate the individuals on this list by simply sending each person a personal letter and the organization's newsletter. I continued the process, on a quarterly basis, for one year.

On December 26th, I opened a small envelope that was addressed to me and marked confidential. It contained a short message that noted how much the individual really enjoyed receiving the newsletters that I had sent. Apparently, they had brought back a flood of memories. The individual also stated that he was ninety-three years old and had decided that he would give his wealth away while he could still enjoy it. Inside the envelope was a personal check for $144,000. His signature was a mere scribble. When I called the gentleman to verify the gift, I discovered that he had died on Christmas day. His son told me that the donation had given him the greatest joy.

The power of volunteering is immense.

A quality volunteering plan can provide increased service potential to your not-for-profit and it can also provide an opportunity to begin a cultivation process that can result in annual or, even, lifetime giving for your institution. Once an individual volunteers for an institution, he or she should always be considered a potential giver. The process of giving may start with the annual campaign and it may gradually move into more long-term opportunities.

During the active volunteer cycle, the not-for-profit should provide a full value experience. This should include meaningful volunteer experiences, ample recognition, and as much return value as possible.

Most individuals who volunteer go through a cycle that includes one or more experiences at the not-for-profit. At some time the individual will express a desire to move on to another interest. This can happen at a variety of times in any volunteer's life. The individual may be young, middle-aged, or elderly. They may have spent two years or forty years as a volunteer with the institution. All too often, these individuals are given a certificate and immediately forgotten. This valuable resource has been lost by thousands of not-for-profits.

If your institution has created and maintained a volunteer alumni list, you are fortunate. If you are not that lucky, then you need to create one. The important thing is to have a process in place that keeps your institution in contact with your past volunteer leaders. The plan can focus differently on the past volunteers and can be as simple as a mailing program. The important thing is to keep past volunteers informed. They hold the potential for gift giving at its highest levels.

5.3   VOLUNTEERING'S ROLE IN ATTRACTING EXTERNAL FUNDING

A well-designed volunteer plan can hold the key to external funding. Successful not-for-profits have traditionally identified and secured influential people for key volunteer positions in their organizations. This helps in gaining access to funding sources that other not-for-profits cannot procure.

It is still a good strategy for organizations to bring in outside volunteers for key leadership roles within the institution. For organizations that have not had the ability to attract such individuals, there is another way to achieve this objective. Businesses have been gradually combining their employee volunteering and contributions programs. The reason for this trend is that employers want to exploit the combined strength of a coordinated employee volunteer program and an employer contributions plan.

This has had significant success for for-profits in fulfilling a number of human resource goals. Not-for-profits who can understand and take advantage of this strategy have also been quite successful.

In order for not-for-profits to take advantage of this trend, however, they need to be prepared to offer the benefits that businesses are seeking. Businesses want personalized volunteer plans that assist them in achieving both general and individual employee goals. If your not-for-profit is developing a full value volunteer strategy that includes return value, for-profits will be interested in doing meaningful business with you.

5.4 INTEGRATING FUND DEVELOPMENT INTO YOUR VOLUNTEER PLAN

A not-for-profit volunteer plan should include a fund development component. The fund development component should include leadership, alumni, and business partnerships. It should also spell out the role that new and current volunteers will play in the fund development process. Individuals who volunteer should understand that they will be asked to contribute to the not-for-profit and that they will be asked to cultivate others to contribute as well. Most volunteers understand that they should contribute to the not-for-profit since they are the key people involved and they will set an example to others to give as well.

It is the second area, the actual "asking" for the solicitation of gifts from others that causes a number of volunteers to pause. Not all volunteers are willing or able to ask for donations successfully. This, however, does not mean that they should not be considered part of the fund development team. Individuals who do not wish to ask for donations can assist the fund development team in a number of ways, including the traditional methods of support, materials development, and mailings.

Of course, do not overlook the basic needs of a successful development plan including prospect research data on *existing* donor prospects. And, by all means remember that some of the most revealing data can be obtained through word of mouth.

One of the more exciting areas to involve volunteers in is the discovery of potential new donors and, especially, in obtaining important new information that will assist in approaching, cultivating, and securing new gifts. Volunteers who are willing to cultivate and solicit prospective donors can provide a rich pool of people that can sell a prospective donor on the genuine needs of the institution.

Volunteers need to be made aware of the important role that philanthropy plays in the health and vitality of the not-for-profit. The orientation plan should be in place for all new volunteers and should include time set aside to discuss how the organization's finances work. Part of the training needs to show how all volunteers take part in the process. It is recommended that the training include:

1. An overview of the methods of fund raising;
2. The importance of volunteer participation in giving to the institution; and
3. The role of volunteers to attract funding sources.

5.5 AN OVERVIEW OF THE METHODS OF FUND RAISING

Not-for-profits approach fund raising in a slightly different way. It is, therefore, important for the incoming volunteer to be aware of the ways in which the organization raises funds. The methods generally include an annual campaign that focuses on individual small gifts and a project sales program to fulfill program funding beyond the traditional areas of the budget. More mature organizations may have a major gift and/or planned giving programs. Larger institutions may also have a capital campaign underway to fund building projects or to increase their endowments. The volunteer may not know any of this. If the volunteer is not brought up to speed, they will not be able to assist and could even be a negative force in the campaign. The volunteer should be briefed on all the aspects of the fund-raising effort and encouraged to present ideas to make the effort successful. For the most part, volunteers want to know all aspect of the organization that they have chosen to work at and are willing to help to ensure the financial success as well.

5.6 THE IMPORTANCE OF VOLUNTEER PARTICIPATION IN GIVING TO THE INSTITUTION

It is important for volunteers to provide financial support to the not-for-profit. Organizations depend on these funds to provide the base in which to work. It is also important for the community to know that the institution's volunteers have provided a high level of support as well. Volunteers should understand, right from the moment they begin their volunteer experience, that they will be asked to contribute to the institution. In most cases volunteers understand this important role and need only be asked in an appropriate way.

5.7 THE ROLE OF VOLUNTEERS TO ATTRACT FUNDING SOURCES

A vital role for the volunteer is to help identify and solicit potential donors for the institution. This has been said to be the highest level of commitment of a volunteer when they will ask others to give to the organization in which they are involved. Procuring funds, particularly major gifts, cannot be accomplished without the direct role of volunteers who assist in gaining access to the donor and who ask as a peer for the level of funds that are needed. Fund raising is a group activity that involves both the not-for-profit professional providing the support and the volunteer providing the leadership to secure the funds.

5.8   CONCLUSION

The functions of volunteering and fund development have a close relationship with each other in the not-for-profit institution. Individuals who volunteer are more closely related to the organization than any other group of individuals. They are a logical group to rely on for contributions while they are actively volunteering or when they become part of the volunteer alumni group. Volunteers can provide access to a number of external sources that can provide funding for an institution. Not-for-profits should take full advantage of this.

Volunteers should anticipate being asked to give and to recommend prospective donors. They should also be encouraged to cultivate and solicit other individuals for funds. Volunteering for an organization has an important responsibility that includes ensuring that the organization is financially sound. In return, the not-for-profit has the responsibility of ensuring that each person who volunteers receives the maximum return value from the experience.

▼6 Creative Partnerships with For-Profits Increase Volunteering

6.1 INTRODUCTION

The role of the not-for-profit and the for-profit sectors seems far apart. The not-for-profit sector traditionally exists to encourage the development of organizations that can provide vital services to the community that may not be available by any other means. The for-profit sector, on the other hand, produces the basic commodities that sustain humankind while offering opportunities for individuals to earn income by working and holding stock. The public sector, which includes government, functions to assist the community with essential services that the other sectors, for the most part, cannot provide.

In the past, not-for-profits received a majority of their money through federal funding in a number of different forms. It was not unusual for some not-for-profits to receive nearly half of their funds from government sources. This funding provided a false sense of security and, as a result, some organizations abandoned the traditional methods of fund raising. The not-for-profits that fit this profile came from all areas of the sector.

Unfortunately for many not-for-profits, the dam began to break when the federal deficit started to get out of hand. Congress sought ways to reduce the budget and, as a result, began to drop federally funded programs. The federal government sources sent warnings indicating that the not-for-profit sector would need to pick up the slack.

While not-for-profits saw major funding sources disappear, the new competitive market sent a wake-up call to the business community that companies who were not willing to change would not be around for long. To increase their competitiveness, companies began to cut the fat. Downsizing quickly became a buzzword and the workforce witnessed a new way of doing business that included more team decisions and less authority at the top. Middle managers became an endangered species. In short, the workplace began to change to meet the new challenges that they faced.

The not-for-profit and for-profit sectors began to seek guidance and assistance from each other. As each sector looked at the other, they discovered that they had a number of common interests and had resources that could be valuable assets to the other sector. The next logical step was to form partnerships.

6.2   ARE PARTNERSHIPS POSSIBLE?

A simple answer to that question is yes. For-profits have formed partnerships with not-for-profits through sponsorships, affinity marketing programs, and educational endeavors. Larger corporations have volunteer programs that are helping both their employees and the company to achieve pre-determined goals and objectives. Part III will review this phenomenon in more detail.

It is fitting, therefore, that not-for-profits begin to play the game in a fashion similar to their for-profit counterparts. To be fully prepared to accomplish this task, not-for-profits need to know the leading questions and the needs of for-profits in order to market and sell partnership opportunities.

Some of the leading questions that need to be answered are:

1. What do not-for-profits have to offer to for-profits?
2. What do for-profits have to offer that not-for-profits need?
3. What do for-profits want from not-for-profits?
4. Can not-for-profits deliver the goods?

Partnerships between not-for-profits and for-profits are a positive reaction to the need of both sectors to explore, teach, and learn from each other.

6.3   WHAT DO NOT-FOR-PROFITS HAVE TO OFFER TO FOR-PROFITS?

Not-for-profits have real value to offer for-profits. One of the most important and basic values that can be offered is the "business" environment of not-for-profits. Businesses today can learn a great deal from how not-for-profits conduct their operations. Not-for-profits work in teams, build consensus, have the ability to work within a restricted budget, they network, and they give recognition when it is earned.

Working within a not-for-profit environment provides a value that is hard to describe but seems to be what most individuals seek. It is the feeling or sense of belonging that is being lost in the shuffle of constantly reinventing ourselves and our businesses. It is as Peter F. Drucker notes, "A social mobility that threatens to become rootlessness, with its "other half," its dissolution of the ties of farm and small town and their narrow horizons—needs community, freely chosen yet acting as a bond. It needs a sphere where the individual can become a master through serving."[1]

The most valuable asset of a not-for-profit is the ability to provide an instant "community" for those who participate. This is an immense value to employees who find themselves relocating every three to five years due to job changes or downsizing. Employers benefit from employee involvement as well. The fact that employees can become quickly involved in local activities and assimilate smoothly into the community assists in a quicker transition at the job as well as reducing stress and stimulating higher productivity. The sense of community can be a real asset to the workplace where the enhancement of a teamwork environment is needed more than ever.

Exhibit 2.4 illustrated the professional benefits that individuals surveyed felt they received from volunteering. A sampling of the benefits listed in the survey includes: making new contacts; the ability to work with different constituencies; the opportunity to work with leaders and others in the community; the satisfaction of helping to provide a service to the needy; the development of a strong sense of personal mission; the ability to plan strategically; and the gaining of committee and board experience.

The not-for-profit experience, through volunteering, can have a profound effect on those who participate. It offers an employer the opportunity to expose employees to an environment that provides both emotional and professional benefits. Most importantly, this can happen without the employer having to incur any direct costs. Most of the indirect costs are minimal and some are even optional. These costs may include expenses such as the administrative overhead of the employee volunteer program or targeted donations to select not-for-profits.

6.4 WHAT DO FOR-PROFITS HAVE TO OFFER THAT NOT-FOR-PROFITS NEED?

Obviously, the first thing that comes to mind is financial resources. Financial considerations are high on the list and the for-profit needs to expect that money will be a part of any package or partnership consideration. For-profits simply need to understand that not-for-profits cannot exist without ongoing funding.

However, you can be creative when you present your package of needs. This should not be a traditional approach for funding. First of all, it should be an approach to seek volunteer assistance. That is the area to focus on and, if funding is part of the package, let it underwrite the cost of the volunteer plan for the for-profit's employees.

Recently, a vice president of a large internationally known hotel chain was approached during the process of cultivation for a large gift. This company, like a number of other for-profits, had been positioning itself to be more competitive and it would take some time before it was open to solicitations by not-for-profits. The vice president commented that astute companies recognize that government funding of not-for-profits has been cut dramatically and that the government anticipates and welcomes increased financial commitments to not-for-profits. He added that business leaders are quite aware of the situation that a number of not-for-profits find themselves in as government funding decreases. They also see a direct benefit in a smaller federal government, namely less government intervention in their affairs. This is an opportunity for both not-for-profit and for-profits to form partnerships that can provide a new level of commitment and service to the community.

Beyond the financial resources of businesses, for-profits can offer the most important resource of all: people. The collective talent that business can provide can assist in solving most, if not all, of the volunteer needs of a not-for-profit. This resource is becoming available as companies begin to realize the potential benefit that volunteering can provide to their businesses.

The Points of Light Foundation (through its affiliation with nearly 400 local volunteer centers and over 70 corporate volunteer councils) and the New York City-based Conference Board (whose mission is to improve the business enterprise system and to enhance the contribution of business to society) co-sponsored a study in 1993 titled *Corporate Volunteer Programs: Benefits to Business*. The study concluded that corporate volunteer programs are increasingly valued for their role in meeting strategic business goals, in helping to build a quality work force, and in continuing to provide public and community relations benefits. They are also surviving restructuring and downsizing and they are targeting educational programs as their top priority.[2] This is evidence of the importance that quality for-profits place on the role that volunteering plays within their companies and through their employees.

6.5 WHAT ARE THE WAYS IN WHICH NOT-FOR-PROFITS AND FOR-PROFITS CAN WORK TOGETHER?

While Part III will detail the for-profit side of the volunteer process, it is important that not-for-profit leaders understand that creating lasting partnerships with for-profits can provide a mutual benefit to both parties. There are a host of ways that this can occur, including volunteering. Not-for-profits need volunteers and for-profits need quality employees. Partnerships can be formed to achieve both goals.

The following example helps to fully explain the mutual need between not-for-profits and for-profits. The Jarrettsville Youth League sponsors a number of sports activities in the area and needed volunteers to perform a number of vital functions as well as funds to run their programs. Traditionally, a call for volunteers had been made through the parents of the participants, signs in local stores, and by word of mouth. Sponsorships are traditionally procured by approaching local stores and businesses to ask for donations. Each year, the league recruited the volunteers needed and secured the funds required.

What if the Jarrettsville Youth League needed more than the basics one year? Say, for example, they needed to refurbish three baseball fields and construct two new fields, at a cost of $150,000. The additional expense cannot be raised by using the traditional methods. A partnership activity with a for-profit could be the answer. I have lived in areas where it would be easy to identify a corporate sponsor. For example, when I lived in Wilmington, Delaware, I was the only non-DuPont employee in my neighborhood. However, Jarrettsville is a rural community and it is not as easy to focus on any particular employer.

The answer to this problem may lie in conducting a survey of who currently participates in the league to determine the relationship of area employers to the participating adults and youth. This model produces a variety of choices. In our example, it was determined that it would take multiple business participants to be successful. Volunteer and professional individuals who are associated with the league will need to meet to determine the top businesses to contact, the best sale to make, and who should make the sale.

The case that should be sold to area businesses should go beyond the fact that the Jarrettsville Youth League needs funds to refurbish and construct new fields. The case should highlight the league's important role of building character, fostering teamwork, and providing opportunities for leadership training for area youth *and* for the volunteers involved. Utilization of a summary report of league participants that documents the employee participation of the targeted companies provides added support and strength to the sell. The League may even want to add comments from participants documenting the value that league activities provided to their personal and professional life, including skills that have adapted well at the workplace.

The proposal should reflect a continued involvement of their employees as volunteers and a full community-wide recognition plan for financial commitment that the business would make to the league. The recognition process will help to strengthen the ties between the company, the employees, and the league. Ongoing reinforcement of the partnership is a must if the arrangement is to continue.

This is a very basic example. The process can be as complex as either party wishes. The important thing to realize is that for-profits are now seeking such arrangements and not-for-profits should encourage the process.

6.6   WHAT DO FOR-PROFITS REALLY WANT FROM NOT-FOR-PROFITS?

This can be answered in three words: education, visibility, and recognition. For-profits have come to realize that their association with not-for-profits can be much broader than an occasional donation or recommending a manager to volunteer for a local group.

Education can be a powerful incentive for for-profits to enter into a partnership arrangement with a not-for-profit. This is not as well known as other incentives but once the for-profit understands the potential bottom line benefits, it can be a vital part of a comprehensive partnership.

Visibility can take many forms for a for-profit. Visibility may mean that the company's name is mentioned at a public gathering or it may mean that the business wishes to gain access to your members. Whatever the visibility that the for-profit may wish, it needs to be within the Internal Revenue Service's guidelines to ensure that it is both proper and legal.

Recognition is by far the easiest part of the process and, unfortunately, the most neglected. In our example, the League may want to name their baseball fields after the businesses that supported the refurbishing and development of each particular field. They might also give the businesses free space for advertisements on the fences or backstops. A business might even want to adopt a field to provide a more ongoing effort while receiving recognition at the same time. Recognition can take many forms; it is not merely a plaque.

The not-for-profit should be prepared to provide a wide variety of recognition. It is best to discuss the recognition options with the for-profit because the recognition will be much more meaningful if it fulfills the needs of the business.

6.7   CAN NOT-FOR-PROFITS DELIVER THE GOODS?

Most for-profits will naturally ask this question. Indeed, it is a logical question since, in many cases, for-profits are not accustomed to a not-for-profit providing any return on their charitable investment.

It is important to remind for-profits that they have received returns on their investments with not-for-profits since the beginning; they just have not realized it. Often, return value has consisted of community good will, recognition, and name identity. These have been good returns for past investments.

In today's business environment, for-profits want even more return value. Creative packaging of the benefits that a not-for-profit can provide that is tailored to meet individual business needs can sell well. Not-for-profits have the capability to deliver well beyond the expectations of for-profit needs while ensuring that the partnership will provide a new level of service to its mission.

For example, there was a firm that has been an active contributor to a national organization. The firm and its partners have given to the annual campaign for a number of years. They have also been active in sponsoring various activities, taking out ads in the not-for-profit's publications, and buying a trade show booth at the annual exposition. They were even involved at a similar level with several of the organization's local affiliates.

The leadership of the firm felt that they were not receiving full recognition for their efforts, and were wary when approached for a major gift. In the end, a plan was created to recognize all past and future philanthropic giving and various other activities. This was accomplished through a packaged recognition plan that would add additional value along with the major gift recognition plan. The plan included a number of ways to recognize the donor:

1. All traditional recognition programs were provided. This included both individual and group recognition pieces, invitations to receptions, and recognition in the annual report, etc.;

2. The organization was recognized as a sponsor of a major function at the annual conference;
3. A special recognition award was provided to the organization; and
4. The participants of the not-for-profit were made aware of the gift through a special article in the not-for-profit's newsletter.

The concept was incorporated into the organization's overall recognition program. This would not have been possible if the for-profit's leadership did not understand the worth of return value to the company and if the not-for-profit did not understand the immense value that focused recognition and other return value principles play in attracting and retaining quality volunteers and a sound donor base.

6.8   CONCLUSION

Creative partnerships between not-for-profits and for-profits can and should be pursued. Partnerships are already in place between hundreds of not-for-profits and for-profits and these partnerships are growing every day. They have been born out of necessity on both sides.

Both sectors recognize the fact that they need each other more than ever. It is this new mutual dependence that has opened new avenues of service and value to individuals, not-for-profits, for-profits, and the community.

Volunteer partnership plans are one of the key benefits that have been created by a number of astute for-profit and not-for-profit institutions. This has led to increasing the quality and quantity of volunteers who serve in those communities. Additional not-for-profit organizational benefits include increased funding by businesses through volunteer-driven projects. Partnership plans between not-for-profit and for-profit entities make sound strategic sense for both sides.

ENDNOTES

[1]Drucker, Peter F., *The New Realities,* Harper & Row, New York, NY, 1989, p. 206.

[2]*Corporate Volunteer Programs: Benefits to Business,* The Conference Board, Inc., New York, NY, 1993, p. 7.

The Important Role That Volunteering Can Play in a For-Profit Business

As the business world continues to change, businesses are seeking ways to remain competitive. Flexibility and teamwork are being heralded as ways of achieving global success in the years ahead. The workforce is rapidly adapting to these new methods. Companies are dividing workers into self-managed teams that provide employees with new freedoms and give management a new set of rules. Employees are being asked to do more and to work at a faster rate. All of this, of course, must be done with less resources and with fewer workers.[1]

The transition of the workplace has had a dramatic effect on how employees are perceived. Past systems focused on the control at the top, with several layers being placed between the top and the bottom. Often, the layers would be filled with managers who were given areas to control to make the business more profitable.

These models are gone. Many new systems have no borders; workers are assigned tasks that may fall into several departments. Other models have brought all of the product decisions into one sphere so that several workers may contribute their wisdom and leadership to making the venture a success.

Business leaders have sought to find ways to ensure that these changes are successfully implemented. They want to educate their workforce on how to cope and thrive in the new environment. Many corporations have the resources to hire consultants to evaluate their operations and to train their employees either on-site or through external educational opportunities. Most employers, however, do not have this luxury.

Today, employees in for-profits and not-for-profits are being asked to be team players and to possess a wide range of skills that will help facilitate organizational change.[2] For-profits leaders need to understand that their employees are the core of their enterprises. Therefore, it is important that employees' needs are not swept aside with the sweeping changes that are occurring at the workplace. For-profits must address three key areas of transition:

1. Changes in the workplace and changes in the organization's unwritten rules of the game;
2. Adjustments and pressures in employees' personal lives; and
3. The need for employees to re-evaluate their roles and responsibilities with regard to organizations and emerging markets.

While the for-profit and not-for-profit sectors each face significant challenges, they also have a number of opportunities, many of which lie in the two sectors working together, to seek answers and resources that each sector can provide to the other. For-profits have a wealth of knowledge, people, and resources that can assist not-for-profits in succeeding. Not-for-profits have an environment that can teach teamwork and group dynamics. They also have an enormous customer base. The key is to form partnerships that are mutually beneficial.

Part III of this book will provide an overview and suggest direct methods of helping for-profits and not-for-profits form significant working relationships through existing programs in either sector. The process will include traditional relationships such as volunteering and funding. It will also include new areas such as employee training, increasing visibility, networking, and enhancing a corporation's image.

The worth of the not-for-profit community can be measured in many ways. Perhaps the most significant way is in the worth of its people. According to the Independent Sector's 1996 *Giving and Volunteering in the United States* report, if no one volunteered in 1995, it would have cost tax payers $201.5 billion to supply the talent and the expertise that volunteering provided.

Cooperation between departments and within industries has yielded great success. The new level of team playing, however, is a truly exciting phenomenon. This new level involves cooperation between two entirely different sectors and it gives a whole new meaning to the word "change."

ENDNOTES

[1]Lublin, Joann S., "My Colleague, My Boss," *The Wall Street Journal*, New York, NY, April 12, 1995, p. R4.

[2]Kolozsvary, Laszlo, "Don't Forget People," *Beyond Computing*, New York, NY, October, 1996, p. 40.

▼7 Building Partnerships in a Changing World

7.1   INTRODUCTION

Change cannot be stopped, and those who try will simply be left behind. No one can make it alone in the present economy. It does not matter whether you are an employee, a volunteer, a sole proprietor, or a large multi-national corporation. At some point, you will need to seek partnerships or work together with other people to achieve your goals.

The need to work together for the common good or partner with other entities is not new. It has been part of business vocabulary and has been practiced since business began. What is new, however, are the kinds of partners that it will take to remain competitive.

The traditional methods of business have been discarded in favor of new techniques. The workplace is changing in reaction to the current and ever-emerging global market. For-profits have trimmed overhead, downsized the workforce, and changed their style of operations. They have also begun to seek new customers in a new environment that is shaping the way business is being conducted. The traditional division of workers and management has yielded to a whole new workforce that is led not by one, but by many. The traditional skills of leadership are not enough in the new environment. New skills such as team building, group dynamics, consensus building, and human relations skills are needed to conceptualize, research, test, produce, market, sell, and evaluate any given product or service.

Employees have been the biggest victims in the transformation of the workplace. They have been downsized, demoted, transferred, and given more work. Often, they are confused and stressed, wondering what will come next. "Will I be able to handle it? Will I even be here at all?" Managers, of course, have many of the same concerns.

One of the partnerships that for-profits should consider is a partnership across two completely different sectors, a bridge between the for-profit and the not-for-profit worlds. The for-profit sector has had an influence in the not-for-profit sector for some time. Traditionally, they have provided volunteer assistance and resources to not-for-profits in order to maintain a standard that would improve the community where the business was located. This was considered a "community service" and it projected a "good citizen" image to customers, stockholders, and the general public. Top executives volunteered for leading charities for similar reasons and, through that process, networked with the key players in the community.

As the transition in the business community began to occur, businesses had to look within to solve core operational problems and to question the traditional roles of business leaders and supporting charities. Businesses began to ponder the relationship they had with the not-for-profit community. They questioned if it was wise to continue and, more importantly, if such a continued relationship would be good for business.

Sharp companies realized that they were not the only entities facing new challenges. They were also aware of the challenges that communities near their facilities faced. These communities were dealing with serious problems such as illiteracy, drug and alcohol abuse, teen pregnancy, crime, homelessness, and poverty. Other community problems such as the quality of public schools, a shortage of trained employees, and spiraling health care costs had a direct effect in diminishing the ability of companies to compete in the global marketplace. Businesses realized that the government had a role in solving these problems but they understood that they could not do it alone. They realized that the government had actually transferred a number of these responsibilities to the not-for-profit sector due to budgetary concerns and the realization that the not-for-profit sector could perform these functions better and at less cost.

Business leaders knew that it would take quality people to meet these challenges. According to a Points of Light publication titled *Principles of Excellence in Community Service: A Message to America's Business Leaders*, it would take "[m]ore people than any government can pay. People who care enough to work at solving these problems, one step and one person at a time. People working in their own communities. Volunteers who rebuild lives and care for others."[1] Yet, companies were faced with other mounting problems within their organizations. How could businesses possibly provide direct assistance in the form of employee volunteering and financial resources at a time of reduced employee levels, tight budgets, and an eye to keeping as competitive as possible?

The answer is in the very thing that is driving both the sectors to rethink the way they are operating—survival. The role that each sector played in their interrelationship in the past was proper and adequate for the time, but times have changed. The current environment demands a whole new relationship. The new roles are challenging, but there are a number of fascinating opportunities for everyone to take advantage of.

Wayne Hedien, Chairman and Chief Executive Officer of Allstate Insurance, noted that "[o]ne of the best things that's happened in my business lifetime is a shift in attitudes about corporations and society. Today, it's clear that our stockholders and customers not only want us to be involved with the community. They expect us to be."[2]

7.2   WHAT CAN FOR-PROFITS GAIN FROM AN ASSOCIATION WITH NOT-FOR-PROFITS?

The Conference Board is a leading global business membership organization that enables senior executives from all industries to explore and exchange ideas that impact business policy. In 1993, they conducted a joint study with the Points of Light Foundation, an independent and nonpartisan organization whose goal is to motivate leaders to mobilize individuals for community service. The joint report, titled *Corporate Volunteer Programs: Benefits to Business,* found that corporate volunteer programs:

1. Are increasingly valued for their role in meeting strategic business goals;
2. Help to build a quality work force;
3. Continue to provide public and community relations benefits;
4. Are surviving restructuring and downsizing; and
5. Target education programs as their top priority.[3]

Notice that this list includes a mix of both traditional benefits and newer, more exciting benefits. These can all increase the bottom line of a business.

A 1991 study presented at the IBM Worldwide Responsibility Conference examined 188 American companies and discovered a strong connection between volunteer programs and return on company assets and investments. It included factors that directly affect profitability, such as improved employee morale, better teamwork skills, and increased productivity. The study concluded that "neglecting the company's responsibility to society threatens the health of the corporation."[4]

Both of these studies prove the growing notion that volunteering is an important part of a strategic plan of a for-profit concern. Volunteering can provide the first link to the not-for-profit sector and it can lead to additional partnership opportunities. These partnerships can make the relationship between for-profit and not-for-profit entities even more valuable. A for-profit can encourage volunteering in four ways:

1. The employee volunteers and informs the company;
2. The company provides a list of volunteer opportunities that an employee notices and reacts to;
3. The not-for-profit approaches a for-profit requesting volunteer assistance; or
4. The for-profit markets an individual employee or group of employees to a not-for-profit.

Company volunteer coordinators often have lists of not-for-profits in the community that are available to the employee. A good coordinator should know which organizations are quality groups and they should counsel employees before they accept any volunteer positions.

Often, a not-for-profit leader will approach a for-profit entity to seek a particular individual volunteer or certain groups of volunteers for a project or activity. This is a great compliment and a wonderful opportunity.

On occasion, for-profits will contact not-for-profits to place employees or groups of employees who have requested assistance. Taking the initiative in this way is often an advantage because the for-profit can seek exactly what it is looking for and it has more control of the process.

All of these methods are good ways to encourage volunteering. They are excellent first steps in helping employees plan volunteer work and in beginning to develop relationships with not-for-profit institutions.

The partnership between a for-profit and a not-for-profit can and should be a lot more than this, however. Chapter 9 will show why volunteering is the key to forming lasting relationships with not-for-profits.

7.3 WHAT DO NOT-FOR-PROFITS WANT FROM FOR-PROFITS?

It is always important to know what the other side wants when you sit down at the table. Not-for-profits are in need of a number of benefits that for-profits can provide. Obviously, the first thing that comes to mind is financial resources. While this is certainly important, particularly with the cutbacks in traditional areas of funding, it is just one item on the list.

Not-for-profits need for-profit expertise. This includes everything from answers to operational questions to marketing strategies. The reason for this is that not-for-profits have limited funds and cannot hire an expert every time there is a need for it. Usually, they rely on volunteers to fill this gap.

The need for not-for-profits to market themselves is really important. The conventional view is that not-for-profits are constantly promoting themselves and that they have a marketing plan in place to ensure that they gain market share. While some do, the vast majority of not-for-profits do not. In the current market, even a not-for-profit needs to be market-wise. Competition for volunteers, funding, and visibility is fierce. Not-for-profits who cannot aggressively market themselves will not survive.

Not-for-profits also need contacts to open doors for them. Just like for-profit leaders, not-for-profit leaders need to be able to reach key people that can help further the missions of their institutions. Not-for-profits need to reach key people for advocacy, volunteering, funding, and programmatic purposes. This is a major asset that for-profits have and can offer to not-for-profits.

Technology is also on the list. Not-for-profits need to have up-to-date operations as much as for-profits do. The technology needed may or may not equal the technology that your for-profit possesses, but it should be adequate enough to support the mission that the not-for-profit is pursuing. For-profits can provide a wealth of knowledge and gifts-in-kind and they can donate equipment that is still useful.

The most valuable resource that for-profits can offer is people. This can include the vice president taking the lead in launching a major capital drive for the local symphony or a group of 25 office workers assisting in building homes for the homeless. Both volunteer acts have enormous value for the community.

Then, of course, there is money. Not-for profits face an uncertain future with major declines in government funding and individual donations. Not-for-profits are adapting to this change, however. Increased emphasis is being placed on major gifts and lifetime giving, but this will not be enough to fund the programs that are being discarded by the government and meeting the ever-increasing needs that are felt throughout our communities.

These needs and challenges can become opportunities to help increase the numbers and kinds of relationships between the for-profit and not-for-profit sectors.

7.4 A CASE FOR A COMPREHENSIVE STRATEGIC PLAN THAT INCLUDES VOLUNTEERING

Notice that the title of this section is not "volunteer strategic plans" but, rather, strategic plans that *include* volunteering. For-profits who are seeking new partnerships with not-for-profits are developing a complete package of opportunities that will involve volunteering *and* other areas. These areas include contributions, memberships, sponsorships, trade show fees, and anything else that is needed.

For-profits are increasingly linking the plan to corporate goals and developing teams of employees who have different skills such as community relations, marketing, or sales. These plans are providing greater value to both for-profits and not-for-profits because they meet needs and they possess measurable worth.

The plan should also have the goal of providing return value to the for-profit. Return value is what the volunteer, whether an individual or an entity, wants out of the relationship. Return value has always been a part of the process of volunteering. Volunteers have always sought benefits from volunteering such as the satisfaction of helping others or networking.

Astute for-profits are looking for creative new ways to increase return value. For example, a for-profit that has an employee who needs better public speaking skills might encourage that employee to volunteer for a position in a not-for-profit that involves making public presentations.

Partnership agreements can help increase the value of the arrangement for both sides. They can also provide a way to fulfill significant goals and win new allies.

7.5 HOW TO CEMENT A RELATIONSHIP

It is important for a for-profit business to know how to approach and how to make an offer to a not-for-profit. It is equally important to know what to ask for and who should be asked.

The relationship between a for-profit company and one or more not-for-profit organizations can be developed in a number of ways. The relationship is best for the for-profit if it starts in a pro-active way. This may take the form of a donation or an offer of volunteers that fulfills one of the not-for-profit's needs. These are also great ways to get the attention of the key leaders in the not-for-profit. The initial approach should be part of the overall plan that fosters an ongoing partnership arrangement.

Not-for-profit leaders are continuingly searching for new arrangements that will further their organization's mission. They will certainly welcome calls from a for-profit representative to discuss mutual goals and opportunities for partnerships.

7.6　USING NOT-FOR-PROFIT LEADERS TO ENHANCE A FOR-PROFIT

Business leaders involved with not-for-profits appreciate the talent that many not-for-profit professionals possess. Many of these skills can be used to further a for-profit operation. Not-for-profit leaders can assist in training for-profit employees on the new workplace skills of teamwork and group dynamics. They can also be of great assistance in developing or revamping your strategic plan. Not-for-profit professionals are increasingly serving on for-profit boards where they assist in ensuring that the organizational policy is pro-active and bottom line oriented. Remember, not-for-profit professionals need to accomplish a lot of the same duties as their for-profit counterparts and they do so with significantly lower budgets.

7.7　CONCLUSION

Partnerships between for-profits and not-for-profits are growing because they are a necessity. Astute for-profits have taken advantage of this opportunity to assist the community, enhance their operations, and increase their bottom line all at the same time.

The new era of partnerships goes well beyond the traditional roles of the past, such as donations to charities. The new, comprehensive approach offers a number of services and funds to not-for-profits and, at the same time, encourages return value for the for-profit.

These new relationships are not temporary; they are ongoing and growing. They are relationships that advance the goals of both the for-profit and the not-for-profit. They are simply an arrangement whose time has come.

ENDNOTES

[1]*Principles of Excellence in Community Service: A Message to America's Business Leaders,* The Points of Light Foundation, Washington, D.C., 1992, p. 6.

[2]Ibid., p. 1.

[3]*Corporate Volunteer Programs: Benefits to Business,* The Conference Board, New York, NY, 1993, p. 8.

[4]Ibid.

▼8 Volunteering's Return Value to the Business World

8.1   INTRODUCTION

This chapter will focus on the direct return value that volunteering provides for a business. It is important, however, not to overlook the indirect benefits that volunteering provides, because these, too, accrue to the benefit of an employer. These benefits generally encompass quality of life issues within the community in which the business and its workers reside. Things like clean parks, neighborhood patrols, and athletic groups attract people to communities where they can become employees and they encourage employees to stay.

In 1993, *The Wall Street Journal* published an article titled, "Nonprofit Training For Profitable Careers" by Howard Isenberg, General Manager of CCL Custom Manufacturing in Niles, Illinois. Mr. Isenberg noted that, "Corporations interested in accelerating the education of their most promising managers would do well to look not at the nation's business schools but at what might seem an unlikely place: America's nonprofit organizations."[1] Howard Isenberg was referring to the enormous return value that volunteering can offer to employees who are encouraged to donate their time.

Carefully selected volunteering experiences can actually accelerate potential managers. Volunteering can be both a training ground and a proving ground for a for-profit's best people. Howard Isenberg's article states that "[t]hree to five years of volunteer work can provide management experience most corporations couldn't provide over 20 years, if it came at all."[2]

Volunteering, therefore, has return value that can benefit employees directly and benefit employers indirectly. A sampling of benefits include:

1. The encouragement of individual empowerment through teamwork;
2. Becoming creative and visionary;
3. The fostering of leadership and management skills;
4. Developing a strong sense of self;
5. Learning the strategic planning process through direct involvement;
6. The experience of working with diverse groups of individuals; and
7. An increased willingness to take risks.

8.2 THE ENCOURAGEMENT OF INDIVIDUAL EMPOWERMENT THROUGH TEAMWORK

The benefits of volunteering compare well with what business leaders think are the primary skills needed in the workplace. Robert Eaton, Chief Executive Officer of the Chrysler Corporation, was once asked to explain the huge success of his company. His one word answer was, "empowerment."

When Chrysler develops a new model or revamps an old one, it forms a team. The team is a "self-contained, multi-disciplinary group" of employees from engineering, design, manufacturing, marketing, and finance who work together to produce a quality product.[3]

Team building skills are a basic component of most volunteer experiences and they have been from the very beginning. Working as a team member is different than being directed by a manager. The team member can provide an equal share of input, advice, and expertise. A concept or idea can be developed and improved at a much higher rate through this process.

Companies like Chrysler have realized that empowered people are more productive. Volunteering can expose employees to the art of teamwork in a number of ways that can be adapted to a for-profit business setting. Committee and board work in not-for-profits provides valuable lessons for everyone involved. This is teamwork at its most formal level. The art of consensus building, negotiation, compromise, and arriving at a quality decision can be easily acquired in a not-for-profit setting.

Volunteering provides an opportunity to deliver products through the programmatic side of operations. In not-for-profits, the product is often a service, an intangible commodity that is at the heart of the fastest growing segment of business, the service industry. Volunteers who master the art of marketing and providing these services have acquired skills that can be valuable in today's service-driven economy.

According to a study titled, *Yours, Mine, and Ours: Facilitating Group Productivity Though the Integration of Individuals and Group Goals,* "the performance of work teams that were given both group and 'groupcentric' individual goals was 36 percent higher than teams that were given only group goals." Volunteering can train individuals to understand that individual goals and production can make the team goal a reality.[4]

8.3   BEING MORE CREATIVE AND VISIONARY

In the search to remain competitive, business leaders have come to realize that creativity is a major key to success. Creativity costs nothing to produce and can do more for less. Employees need to be encouraged to be creative in the workforce.

This is not as easy as it sounds, however. In the current work environment, employees are given little time to visualize what could or could not be. So the question is, where can employees find the time, energy, and environment to let their creative juices flow?

Volunteering can be the answer. Not-for-profits are in the business of creativity and visions. Well-run organizations really have no choice. If they want to survive, they must find ways to find enough volunteers, financial resources, and public support to fulfill their mission. Creativity and vision run rampant from new not-for-profits that need to open the door to $1 billion dollar campaigns at well-known institutions.

For-profit leaders can use this expertise by encouraging employees to become involved with not-for-profits who have mastered these skills. Employees who volunteer for such institutions and become actively involved can acquire skills that translate perfectly into their careers.

8.4   FOSTERING LEADERSHIP
AND MANAGEMENT SKILLS

When Howard Isenberg was president of the Barr Division of the Pittway Corporation, he had a chemist working for him who clearly had potential for more management responsibility. This individual knew all the basics, but lacked broader management experience. He counseled the chemist to volunteer on his own time without pay for a Chicago organization that specialized in helping unemployable men and women learn the work habits and the social skills necessary to find and to hold a job.

The Barr Division had a policy that employees should be encouraged to volunteer, but only if they believed in what the not-for-profit group was doing and felt comfortable in making a major commitment. The chemist took Isenberg's advice and quickly moved up through several volunteer positions to became a member of the board of directors of the organization.

Along the way, the chemist gained a number of experiences that he would not have gained at his regular job. One of his volunteer positions involved fund raising. This position assisted in increasing his interpersonal and social skills. As a member of the board, he called on corporate leaders to persuade them to hire clients of the not-for-profit. The quiet chemist had become a salesperson.

This experience helped the not-for-profit fulfill its mission, it helped the chemist grow personally, and it helped the employer because they now had a more experienced employee. All of this was made possible because a not-for-profit and for-profit formed a strategic alliance that addressed each other's needs.[5]

The not-for-profit can be an informal school that teaches individuals the art of leadership and management. Volunteering can easily demonstrate the truism that individuals who are managers are not necessarily leaders, while true leaders understand the art of people management. There are many managers who still do not understand that the traditional role of manager is passé in the current work environment.

A true leader, however, is sought more than ever. A leader who has the insight to understand the important role of teamwork and a leader who can envision the appropriate road to take to achieve the specific objectives has a grand future in the for-profit world.

The National College Survey on Volunteering substantiated a number of benefits that volunteering provides, but the most significant new finding was that individuals who actively volunteer gain leadership traits regardless of the type of volunteer experience or profession that they pursued.[6]

Businesses that provide an opportunity and encourage employees to volunteer will create a unique opportunity for them to engage in an activity that will help others. Most importantly for businesses, however, these opportunities will help themselves and their employees.

8.5   DEVELOPING A STRONG SENSE OF SELF

A strong sense of self may seem far removed from the needs of the workplace but it really is not. The re-engineering and refining of the workplace has taken its toll on the people who are the core of the business, employees.

Companies must invest as deeply in employees as they do in technology. According to Charles D. Winslow and William L. Bramer, however, this can only happen if they speak of "future work" not by measuring how well an employee carries out an assigned task but, rather, by redefining their employees' jobs so that everything they do is fulfilling the broad mission of the company.[7]

This broader view is not the method of operation within traditional business models but it has been the traditional model at most not-for-profits. Peter F. Drucker notes that, "successful and growing non-profit third-sector organizations also apply management internally . . . they practice management by objectives, more thoroughly than most businesses do. Staff members, whether paid or unpaid, are expected . . . to define the performance and contribution for which they are to be held accountable."[8]

Volunteering can have a powerful influence on employees and how they perceive themselves. The return value that is brought back to the workplace can provide tangible and intangible benefits for both the employee and the employer.

One of the intangible benefits that can be produced is a reduction in stress as a result of the "self spirituality" that comes from the volunteer process. This is not necessarily a religious experience, rather, it is a sense that the individual's functions can have a profound positive effect on the lives of others. It can produce both an inner peace and a clearer perspective on how an individual fits into life and his or her surroundings.

A March 1, 1995 *Wall Street Journal* article titled "In Re-engineering What Really Matters Are Worker's Lives" confirmed that corporate re-engineering is continuing to have an adverse effect on employees and their families. The cited survey noted that a dozen anonymous large employers documented that two-thirds of responding employees used flexible schedules and that personal leave remained flat or falling. The study noted that workers are stretched so thin that "no one is asking for anything." The result has been for creative companies, such as Merck and Xerox, to develop new ways to encourage employees to work smarter and to condense time. This was accomplished through the direct involvement of employees who wanted to find ways to have more time for work and family matters.[9]

The work overload and the stress that is produced in the current work environment is not healthy for employees or their families and it can even have an adverse effect on the employer as well. People cannot function well when they lose their direction or purpose. This can happen when too much is expected by employers or when employees try to keep up with impossible goals.

Volunteering can assist in solving this problem by showing individuals how to perform multiple tasks in a systematic way. This can be done without losing any satisfaction from the work or the benefits that it is providing to the community.

One of the more exciting ways that employee volunteer programs have addressed this issue is the development of family volunteer programs. This has helped to bring the employee's entire family into the volunteer process. It has also helped to attract volunteers and it has had a positive effect on the families and their relationship to the company. Companies with a large, diverse employee base like Dayton Hudson (Target Stores) and Federated Department Stores agree that family volunteer programs may be able to address a number of issues that families face in the current economy that dictates that most adult family members will have to work outside the home.

8.6 DIRECT INVOLVEMENT IN THE STRATEGIC PLANNING PROCESS

Another exciting benefit that volunteering can provide is an opportunity to observe the method in which a not-for-profit conducts its business. These observations can greatly assist an individual professionally.

A well-run not-for-profit conducts its affairs in a fashion similar to a well-run for-profit. Volunteers can contribute their expertise to solving business-related situations within the not-for-profit and they can discover the strategic thinking process that not-for-profits have developed to service the needs of their constituents.

Although there are many similarities to the for-profit model, not-for-profit strategic thinking has to be much more customer-driven because its products and services are usually intangible. Also, success is measured in different ways than traditional for-profits, yet a number of these measurements can be easily translated to for-profits who seek teamwork-driven and customer-driven operations. The following two examples illustrate this concept.

First, not-for profits rely on volunteers from diverse backgrounds who usually do not know each other prior to working together in teams to fulfill a goal within a pre-determined amount of time. The team determines how to accomplish the goal and who will do what. The decision is based on an individual's background and experience. The team members place peer pressure on each other to accomplish the individual tasks so the team goal can be accomplished on time.

Second, not-for-profits serve a variety of customers, yet they all possess common traits. All customers seek a solution to a problem that they cannot solve by themselves. Not-for-profits strive to produce a quality service using volunteers. This can be accomplished through securing funding from sources that, for the most part, do not expect a return on their investment.

Thinking in for-profit terms, it is amazing what it has taken not-for-profits to achieve these two basic concepts because neither can happen without strategic thinking. The process starts with a vision of where the entire organization should be within a given time. The plan is broken down into key components and issues that will be addressed by a team approach.

In the first example, individuals are matched by skills and placed into teams with individuals that they do not know. They are expected to develop a plan to reach a goal. Somehow, the individuals emerge with both the skills and leadership required to perform the task. Although it happens thousands of times a day in thousands of not-for-profits, it is still amazing to experience. This could not happen without a strategic plan that provides the necessary direction, leadership, and resources.

The second example is just as amazing. Imagine a for-profit asking its employees to work for free while various institutions and individuals willingly underwrite the cost of doing business for the company, expecting no monetary return on the investment. That is exactly what not-for-profits must convince the public to do every day. Not-for-profit institutions cannot be successful unless they develop a strategic plan that includes a marketing component that volunteers and funding sources will respond to. To accomplish this, not-for-profits hire professionals who have the talent to attract these two important groups.

For-profits that wish to examine and adapt to these principles can do so by encouraging their employees to volunteer within their community. Chapter 9 will discuss methods of encouraging employees to volunteer.

8.7 WORKING WITH DIVERSE GROUPS OF INDIVIDUALS

One of the most dramatic changes in the workforce today is an ever-increasing diversity of workers. This is a healthy trend for business because the supply of quality people is more plentiful than ever and people are the most valuable resource a business has. The current pool of workers possesses more talent than ever before and they are ready to take on the new work environment. The challenge lies in whether or not business leaders can adapt to understanding and supporting the needs of this new workforce.

The not-for-profit community has been involved in meeting the needs of diverse populations for a long time. They have set an example by encouraging a diverse volunteer and professional approach. If employees and managers want to experience the breakthroughs that a diverse team of individuals can achieve in solving important issues, the volunteer environment of a not-for-profit is the perfect place to go.

An almost forgotten methodology that is of great assistance in getting employees to appreciate the important role of a diverse workplace is a mentoring program. A number of not-for-profits use the mentoring concept to assimilate new volunteers into their organizations. Although mentoring is not as popular as it once was in the corporate community, it is still a viable way to train and inspire capable people to do their best. It can also provide an avenue of determining whether or not an individual has the potential to do greater things.[10]

8.8   AN INCREASED WILLINGNESS TO TAKE RISKS

The current workplace environment does not encourage most employees to take risks. In fact, many workers are happy to hold on to their current position and many are instructed not to make any waves.

Unfortunately, this is not the way a business or not-for-profit grows. Businesses that want to assume a leadership position in their field need to take calculated risks. A calculated risk is one that has been strategically thought out and has a genuine link to the mission or vision of the business.

Risk taking does not occur in a vacuum. Employees need to be a part of the process to ensure success and avoid " betting the farm." The only way to encourage risk taking is to build a culture that encourages positive change. Such a culture breeds excitement in the workplace. It creates the desire to arrive early and to stay late. It produces positive change. In this kind of environment, a business strives to re-invent itself on a planned basis—new products are developed, existing products are refined, and obsolete products are dropped.[11]

The not-for-profit community is a leader in the role of change. They adapt on an almost daily basis to community needs, funding availability, and people requirements. Volunteering can provide a wonderful learning experience for individuals who wish to experience the art of risk taking. Most of the functions within the average not-for-profit have an element of risk.

Funding is a great example of the kind of risk that a not-for-profit faces daily. What happens to programs and to not-for-profits who cannot secure the funding they need to keep the door open? They go out of business. This is not all that bad. Like businesses that fold, if not-for-profits cannot secure sufficient funds, perhaps they should not remain in business.

There are, however, a number of worthy organizations that get into financial trouble and need professional guidance to stay in business. This is where volunteers can be very helpful. Volunteers can assist in bringing these organizations back to life. In the process, they can learn a great deal about the nature of risk taking and how it relates to success and failure.

8.9   CONCLUSION

Volunteering can provide enormous value to the individual who gives time and energy freely. These benefits can help the individual both personally and professionally. They can also help anyone who has an association with the individual who volunteers, including family, friends, professional associates, and employers. Indeed, the return value of volunteering can have a profound effect on an individual's work performance and, therefore, on the bottom line of the business that employs that person.

It is logical for employers to encourage employees to volunteer for meaningful positions that will fulfill the need of helping others and provide direct benefits to the individual who volunteers. Volunteering can provide an array of return value if the person who volunteers understands the process and takes advantage of all that it can offer. Volunteering is one of the most important ways to educate employees on community, teamworking skills, diversity, strategic planning, and a number of other areas that are required in the new workplace. Volunteering and support for the not-for-profit sector are a key part of a successful business plan in for-profits.

ENDNOTES

[1]Isenberg, Howard, "Nonprofit Training for Profitable Careers," *The Wall Street Journal*, New York, NY, August 23, 1993.

[2]Ibid.

[3]Gunn, Eileen P., "Empowerment That Pays Off," *Fortune*, New York, NY, March 20, 1995, p. 145.

[4]Hein, Kenneth, "Why Teams Fail," *Incentive*, December, 1996, p. 11.

[5]Isenberg, Howard, "Nonprofit Training for Profitable Careers," *The Wall Street Journal*, New York, NY, August, 1993.

[6]Pidgeon, Walter P., *Volunteering: The Leaders's Competitive Edge*, The Union Institute, Cincinnati, OH, 1991, p. 126.

[7]Corcoran, Elizabeth, Redefining the Tools, Redefining the Job, *The Washington Post*, Washington, D.C., January 15, 1995, p. H4.

[8]Drucker, Peter F., *The New Realities,* Harper & Row Publishers, New York, NY, 1989, p. 202.

[9]Shellenbarger, Sue, In Re-Engineering What Really Matters Are Worker's Lives, *The Wall Street Journal,* New York, NY, March 1, 1995.

[10]Reynolds, Kenneth, The Importance of Mentoring, *CFO,* February, 1995, p. 76.

[11]Covey, Stephen, Making Change Count, *Incentive,* December, 1996, p. 21.

APPENDIX

VOLUNTEER INFORMATION: EXAMPLES FROM THE FOR-PROFIT SECTOR

During the research phase of this book I came across a number of businesses that were providing their employees with the opportunity to experience the full benefits of volunteering through quality employee volunteer programs. Some of these companies went far beyond the norm to provide their employees the maximum benefits of the volunteer experience. This Appendix provides a sampling of the programs and materials that these companies provided. These are fine examples of what can be accomplished through a partnership of individual employees, the business community, and the for-profit sector. The businesses highlighted are: Aid Association for Lutherans, Bank of America, EDS (Electronic Data Systems), Federated Department Stores, General Mills, and Pillsbury.

EXHIBIT A.1 Aid Association for Lutherans*

- Corporate Public Involvement Philosophy

- Executive Bulletin

- AAL ICT Information

- AAL ICT Application for Group Projects

---

*Reprinted with permission by the Aid Association for Lutherans, Appleton, WI.

AAL Corporate Public INVOLVEMENT program PHILOSOPHY

AAL's RESPONSIBILITIES AND OBLIGATIONS as a corporate citizen are fulfilled primarily through its corporate public involvement program. AAL takes seriously these responsibilities and obligations. • AAL's program focuses on its headquarters community of the Fox River Valley and extends to the state of Wisconsin and to other areas where AAL has a business presence. • As one of the largest businesses and employers in the Fox Valley, AAL is expected to be and desires to be a major influence in determining what the Fox Valley is and can become. AAL wants to lead in helping the underprivileged, in promoting a healthy and vibrant business climate and in enriching the quality of life for employees, friends and neighbors. • In meeting its corporate citizen responsibilities and obligations, AAL will lead rather than push and urge rather than force. In keeping with its pledge to preserve and protect members' assets, AAL will make an appropriate portion of employees, facilities and financial resources available to meet its responsibilities and obligations as a business and corporate citizen.

EXECUTIVE BULLETIN
PERSONNEL AND OFFICE PRACTICES

Distribution: Code A

P.O.P. Number: 219

Effective Date: Sept. 13, 1983

AAL INVOLVEMENT CORPS TEAM (AAL-ICT)

The AAL Involvement Corp Team (AAL-ICT) was organized in 1980 to promote voluntarism among AAL employees by matching employee talents with community needs. The program is in keeping with the United States President's call for more volunteer effort from the private sector.

AAL-ICT enables employees to assist worthwhile community activities, helps them develop leadership talents and gives them visibility and recognition for their volunteer efforts, in addition to helping them achieve corporate goals of improving AAL visibility, image and public understanding of AAL.

Employee participation in AAL-ICT and its projects is voluntary and under most circumstances does not involve use of company time or resources. However, since planning for some AAL-ICT projects may require some work time, employees interested in serving on the ICT are to obtain prior approval of their operating unit heads. Managers should consider the impact of ICT projects on corporate community relations when determining whether ICT participants should be allowed away from their work stations when ICT activities must be conducted during normal work hours.

AAL-ICT accepts project requests from employees and the community at large at least once annually. AAL-ICT considers the needs of each project and the skills available within the AAL employee family before selecting projects to be completed that year. Only not-for-profit organizations qualify for AAL-ICT assistance.

Corporate relations is responsible for the AAL-ICT program and final approval of AAL-ICT projects.

SUPERSEDES   None

CORRELATION   Human Resources Division
Law and Corporate Relations Department

E. James Dreyer
Vice President, Corporate
Relations and Communications

Source: Communications Division

Issue Date: Sept. 13, 1983

AID ASSOCIATION FOR LUTHERANS

INVOLVEMENT CORPS TEAM

Statement of Purpose

The Aid Association for Lutherans Involvement Corps Team (AAL ICT) was organized to promote volunteerism among AAL employees by matching employee talents with community needs. Established in 1980, the ICT serves as a liaison between home office employees and community organizations to encourage employee volunteerism within the community. This will help AAL carry out its responsibilities as a good corporate citizen and enhance AAL's image in the community.

Membership

Membership in the ICT is voluntary and on a yearly basis. Employees interested in becoming ICT members must have approval of their supervisors. Supervisors should be aware that ICT is a corporately backed program and that some work time probably will be required on ICT projects. The organizational structure and procedures of ICT are documented in the AAL P.O.P bulletin.

Meetings and Reports

ICT committee members will be required to attend a minimum number of meetings each year. Meetings will be held once a month for about one hour in the late afternoon near the end of the work day.

Each committee member is expected to be the leader of at least two projects during the year he or she serves. ICT meetings will be reporting sessions from the project leaders. Project planning should be done at sub-committee meetings of the employee volunteers. Upon completion of a project, the leader will complete a report of the project detailing time involved, name of employees participating and recommendations and comments on the project.

Recruiting Volunteers

Project leaders should recruit AAL employees to help with their project. This can be done personally, through *The Daily* or by any other method.

Application for Group Project To AAL Involvement Corps Team

Complete this application and return to Joanie Johnson, Aid Association for Lutherans, Appleton, WI 54919. If you have any questions, contact the Involvement Corps Team at (414) 734-5721, ext. 3210.

Note: This application can be used for **evening** and **weekend** opportunities for groups (2 or more), or one-on-one opportunities.

Agency Information

Name of agency/organization

Telephone number

Street address or R.R. and box number

City

State

ZIP Code

Contact person

Location of project

Statement of Need

Purpose of this project

People served by this project

Number of people impacted by this project

Project Description

Description of volunteer group project

Skills needed by volunteers

EXHIBIT A.2 Bank America*

- Service Learning Overview

- Skills Matrix 💾

- How to Document 💾

- Event Summary 💾

- Project Proposal 💾

- Employee Development Worksheet 💾

- Skills Checklist 💾

*Reprinted with permission by Bank of America, San Francisco, CA.

SERVICE LEARNING OVERVIEW

Service Learning is a hand-on approach to human resources development that identifies skills gained through volunteer services as an officer or leader in BA Club.

Service Learning takes place when employees learn, develop and demonstrate skills and gain work experience not formally associated with their regular job duties. This added experience serves to qualify employees for greater opportunities for personal and professional growth and development.

Program Benefits

- Formally recognize the value of business skills gained through service as a leader in BA Club.
- Transfer practical skills from Club Leadership experience to the job.
- Provide manager and employees with alternative ways to develop business skills.
- Provide a low-risk learning experience for both the individual and the bank.
- Allow employees to demonstrate skill competencies outside their present job.
- Contribute to the betterment of the bank and our communities.

Program Elements

Learning Objective—Challenges employees to learn and develop hands-on work experience through their active, volunteer participation as a club officer or leader.

Skill Development—Experience gained as club officer becomes a part of the employee's performance profile and can be documented through the RON system. Managers will be encouraged to consider this experience when evaluating and considering candidates for job opportunities.

Service outcome—Employees can provide a valued service to the company, and co-workers, as well as serve the needs of communities where we do business.

Club experience can in some cases replace training that is helpful but often not available to employees in any other way. In addition, employees gain valuable and practical experience in a variety of functions critical to success in today's business world.

SKILLS MATRIX

Following is a list of skills/knowledge/abilities that are inherent in volunteer service as an officer in the BankAmerica Club. Club service offers employees opportunities to gain experience and demonstrate proficiency in skills that enhance personal and professional development.

Skill	Ways to Practice	Reference
Assertiveness	• Serve as a fund raiser • Solicit pledges or support • Participate in event sign up drives • Be a recruiter	1, 2, 3, 4, 5, 6, 7, 8, 9, 10, 11, 12, 13, 17
Budget Management	• Chair an event with a budget • Chair a finance committee • Volunteer for a board position with finance responsibility • Plan an event within a budget	1, 2, 3, 4, 5, 6, 7, 8, 9, 10, 11, 12, 13
Change Management	• Do strategic planning • Help write group bylaws • Participate in a focus group • Be an active participant in a changing organization	1, 17
Conflict Resolution	• Serve on a board • Negotiate contracts with vendors • Chair a function or event • Participate in the planning/execution of a multi-committee event	1, 2, 3, 4, 5, 17
Creativity	• Chair a multi-sponsor, multi-committee event • Develop events to meet a variety of employee needs and interests • Plan strategic marketing and promotional event	1, 2, 3, 4, 5, 6, 7, 8, 9, 13, 15
Cultural Awareness	• Chair a Diversity Network • Volunteer in an activity that works closely with people unlike yourself • Serve in locations dissimilar to your own • Be a tutor or mentor • Make presentations to diverse audiences	1, 3, 7, 11, 15, 17
Decision Making	• Plan an event • Participate in a committee	1, 13, 17
Delegating	• Chair a committee • Assume a leadership role in an organization or event • Coordinate an activity or event	1, 2, 3, 4, 5, 10, 11, 12, 13

Skill	Ways to Practice	Reference
Event Planning	• Develop a marketing plan • Create advertisement materials • Negotiate contracts • Coordinate volunteers • Serve on a strategic planning committee	1, 2, 3, 4, 5, 6, 7, 8, 9, 10, 11, 12, 13
Flexibility	• Volunteer for any service involving children, elderly, or physically challenged • Coordinate other volunteers • Work on an outdoor event	1, 2, 3, 4, 5
Interpersonal Skills	• Become part of a speakers bureau • Be the public relations chair for an event or chapter • Recruit volunteers • Do fundraising • Volunteer to answer calls for a Hot Line • Serve as a tutor/mentor with young people	1, 2, 3, 4, 5, 6, 7, 8, 9, 10, 11, 12, 13, 17
Leadership	• Serve as the Chair of a committee or event • Supervise volunteers • Be the spokesperson for a group or organization • Work with young people as a tutor/mentor	1, 2, 3, 4, 5
Listening Skills	• Volunteer to answer calls for a Hot Line • Serve as a tutor/mentor • Provide crisis intervention counseling • Be a counselor • Work with sick people	1, 2, 3, 4, 5, 17
Managing People	• Manage volunteers • Establish procedures for an event or activity • Coordinate an event • Volunteer to be a facilitator	1, 2, 3, 4, 5, 10, 11, 12, 13, 17
Motivating Others	• Be a tutor • Work in fund-raising activities • Serve in a mentoring capacity • Chair a committee • Be a Walk team captain • Promote an event or organization	1, 2, 3, 4, 5, 17

(continued)

Skill	Ways to Practice	Reference
Needs analysis	• Develop strategic plans for an organization • Volunteer at a school • Develop surveys • Organize the acquisition and distribution of resources • Serve on a Finance committee • Volunteer as a counselor	1, 2, 3, 4, 5, 14, 17
Negotiating Skills	• Acquire resources for an event or organization • Provide leadership in a changing organization	1, 2, 3, 4, 5, 6, 7, 8, 9, 10, 11, 12, 13
Networking	• Edit a newsletter • Do public relations work • Acquire resources • Conduct surveys • Solicit funds or participation • Recruit volunteers or members • Serve on not-for-profit boards • Meet new people	All Positions
Organizational Skills	• Plan a multi-committee event • Edit a newsletter • Coordinate a large or multi-sponsored event	1, 2, 3, 4, 5, 6, 7, 8, 9, 10, 11, 12, 13, 15
Presentation Skills	• Become part of a speaking club • Be a spokesperson • Be the ToastMaster or master of ceremonies	1, 2, 3, 4, 5, 8, 12
Problem Solving	• Answer calls for a Hot Line • Plan an event • Be the on-site manager for a large event	All Positions
Project Management	• Plan an event • Be a chapter newsletter editor	1, 2, 3, 4, 5, 6, 7, 8, 9, 10, 11, 12, 13, 15
Recruitment; personnel evaluation and selection	• Plan an event which needs volunteers • Participate in the chapter's succession plan development	1, 2, 3, 4, 5, 6, 7, 8, 9
Risk Taking	• Evaluate potential events, make recommendations • Coordinate volunteers • Get involved in a new activity	1, 2, 3, 4, 5

Skill	Ways to Practice	Reference
Teamwork	• Coordinate a multi-committee event • Be a coach • Plan/coordinate an event	1, 2, 3, 4, 5, 6, 7, 8, 9, 10, 11, 12, 13, 17
Time Management- Prioritizing	• Manage resources • Manage an event within an established timeline • Facilitate meetings	1, 2, 3, 4, 5
Verbal Communication Skills	• Be a Toastmaster or master of ceremonies • Be a spokesperson	1, 2, 3, 4, 5, 8, 12, 17
Written Communication Skills	• Write for the chapter newsletter • Be the chapter newsletter editor • Develop letters • Serve as secretary—take minutes for the chapter meetings • Write proposals	1, 5, 15, 16

HOW TO DOCUMENT

Following is a list of ways to record newly developed skills/knowledge/abilities.

<u>WITH YOUR MANAGER</u>

- Document experience during a Career Counseling session.
-

<u>ON THE "RON" SYSTEM</u>

-

<u>ON YOUR PERSONAL RESUME</u>

-
-

<u>ON YOUR PERMANENT EMPLOYMENT RECORD</u>

-

TEAM AMERICA

Bank of America's Volunteer Network

EVENT SUMMARY

Please type or print.

EVENT Name _____ PROJECT # _____

TEAM LEADER Name _____ Unit # _____ PHONE (BANet) ____

TeamAmerica is a volunteer community service organization for employees and retirees of BankAmerica Corporation, its affiliates and subsidiaries.

Brief description of Project: _____

_____

_____

_____

What did TeamAmerica provide? _____

_____

_____

_____

What other materials or resources were required? _____

_____

_____

_____

VOLUNTEER HOURS:	Number of Volunteers	Number of Hours:Minutes	PROJECT SUCCESS *(Please Check One)*
Preparation Time— Team Leader(s)			☐ SUCCESSFUL
Employees + Retirees + Guests =			☐ AVERAGE
Totals:			☐ FAILURE

Did we achieve our goals? _____

_____

_____

Do you think TeamAmerica should undertake this project again? _____ Why? _____

_____

_____

Recommendations: _____

_____

_____

Thanks for your volunteer efforts and for completing this form.

Please attach all documentation (flyers, pictures, media coverage) and mail to TeamAmerica #03130.

TEAM AMERICA
★
Bank of America's Volunteer Network

EVENT SUMMARY
Please type or print.
EVENT Name   PROJECT #

TEAM LEADER Name   Unit #   PHONE (BANet)

TeamAmerica is a volunteer community service organization for employees and retirees of BankAmerica Corporation, its affiliates and subsidiaries.

NAME OF NON-PROFIT ORGANIZATION   TAXPAYER IDENTIFICATION NO. (TIN)

ADDRESS   (Number & Street)   (City)   (State)   (Zip)

EXECUTIVE DIRECTOR   CONTACT AT ORGANIZATION   TELEPHONE (   )

ORGANIZATION/AGENCY FOCUS:

☐ EDUCATION   ☐ CIVIC   ☐ FUND RAISER   ☐ BLOOD DRIVE

☐ ENVIRONMENT   ☐ HUMAN SERVICES   ☐ ARTS/CULTURE   ☐ OTHER:

NAME OF PROJECT

GOAL OF PROJECT   PROPER ATTIRE

DATE(S) OF PROJECT   TIME(S) (Specify AM or PM)

LOCATION OF PROJECT   (Address)   (City)   (Zip)

DESCRIBE TEAMAMERICA'S INVOLVEMENT (be specific)

NUMBER OF TEAMAMERICA VOLUNTEERS REQUESTED:	MINIMUM AGE FOR VOLUNTEERS (if any):	HAS TEAMAMERICA DONE THIS PROJECT IN PREVIOUS YEAR(S)? ☐ Yes ☐ No

SUGGESTED TEAM LEADER   MAIL CODE/UNIT #   TELEPHONE (BANet)
                                                                      (   )

SIGNATURE OF TEAMAMERICA DIRECTOR
                                              **Please send completed Proposal to
                                              TeamAmerica #03130**

(This section to be completed by TeamAmerica Manager)
Proposal reviewed and ☐ APPROVED ☐ DECLINED (reason: _____

MANAGER SIGNATURE: NOTIFICATION DATE: **PROJECT NUMBER**

EMPLOYEE DEVELOPMENT WORKSHEET

NAME: _____ TODAY'S DATE: _____

The purpose of this form is to help you identify areas where you could benefit from developmental opportunities. You and your supervisor can use this information to create a developmental plan. Your plan may include such things as training courses, on-the-job assignments or cross-training opportunities. Other development opportunities exist through volunteer service with a variety of organizations, including BankAmerica Club.

What do you see as your talents that help you do your job well? _____
_____
_____

What types of tasks best utilize these talents? _____
_____
_____

What do you see as your greatest development needs and/or skill gaps? _____
_____
_____

When do these development needs and/or skill gaps show the most on the job?
_____
_____

Is there any area where you think you need additional technical or skill training?
_____

If so, what skill or technical area? _____

What type of job do you see yourself doing five years from now? _____
_____
_____

What kind of training do you think you would need to reach that goal? _____
_____
_____

List any specific past projects or tasks that you would have been interested in doing but you were not a part of: _____

List any types of projects or tasks that you would be interested in doing: _____
_____
_____

SKILLS CHECKLIST

Following is a list of skills. Check those areas that you believe would help you most in the performance of your job and/or some other aspect of your personal development.

- ☐ Assertiveness
- ☐ Budget management
- ☐ Change management
- ☐ Conflict resolution
- ☐ Creativity
- ☐ Cultural awareness
- ☐ Decision making
- ☐ Delegating
- ☐ Event planning
- ☐ Flexibility
- ☐ Interpersonal skills
- ☐ Leadership
- ☐ Listening skills
- ☐ Managing people
- ☐ Motivating others
- ☐ Needs analysis

- ☐ Negotiating skills
- ☐ Networking
- ☐ Organizational skills
- ☐ Presentation skills
- ☐ Problem solving
- ☐ Project management
- ☐ Recruitment; personnel evaluation and selection
- ☐ Risk taking
- ☐ Teamwork
- ☐ Time management/ prioritizing
- ☐ Verbal communication skills
- ☐ Written communication skills
- ☐ _____
- ☐ _____
- ☐ _____

EXHIBIT A.3 Electronic Data Systems*

- EDS Community Affairs Overview

- Global Volunteer Day 1996 Executive Summary

- Choosing a Project, Contacting the Recipient Organization and Recruiting Volunteers

- Preproject Information Checklist

- Volunteer Recognition

- Recipient Organization Recognition

*Reprinted with permission by Electronic Data Systems, Plano, TX.

EDS COMMUNITY AFFAIRS OVERVIEW

EDS believes that everyone benefits when we shape our communities' environment in a positive way. EDS' Community Affairs program reflects that concept by combining cash and in-kind contributions and extensive employee participation to contribute to civic, charitable, educational and cultural organizations around the world. The commitment begins with the understanding that EDS is an integral part of the communities in which our employees live and work.

Corporate Contributions
In 1996, EDS provided cash contributions to **hundreds** of organizations worldwide. Our giving program strategically mirrors the company's business directives of cultural diversity, education, and technology as well as supports an improved quality of life.

Volunteerism
By placing less of an emphasis on monetary power and more on employee contributions, EDS is able to provide creative and personal solutions to the problems that plague our societies. One can find our employees worldwide volunteering in schools, giving blood, painting and rebuilding neighborhoods or raising money for nonprofit organizations. In 1995, **tens of thousands** of EDS employees volunteered throughout EDS locations in **30** countries around the globe.

Highlights:

- **EDS Global Volunteer Day**-Tens of thousands of EDS employees, family members, customers, and friends in 29 countries participated in more than 350 volunteer projects in their local communities.
- **March of Dimes**-In 1996, about 2,500 employees raised more than $244,000 for the March of Dimes. EDS ranked 21st in the nation. Since 1987, EDS employees and customers have raised well over $1,500,000 to improve the health and survival of babies, ranking EDS employees as a top fund-raiser, nationally and locally.
- **United Way**-Employee participation in local United Way campaigns is one way to improve the quality of life in our communities. EDS believes in working side-by-side with our neighbors to help make a difference. Our employees get involved through local volunteer projects, year-round educational programs, pledge campaigns, and leadership opportunities.
- EDS offices around the world partner with thousands of organizations in their own communities year-round, addressing local issues

Education Outreach

Employee volunteer efforts also extend into classrooms around the world. From Ireland to New Zealand, more than **5,000** volunteers serve **125** school partnerships in **31** states and **nine** countries. From mentoring, curriculum and career enrichment, and technical consulting and support to working with parents and school staff, they effect tomorrow's future today!

Highlights:

- Calumet Community Center-Dallas, TX
- Christian Brothers School-Dublin, Ireland
- Stockley Park School-UK

Loaned Executives

An extension of employee involvement is our loaned executive program. While remaining on EDS' payroll, these employees are staff members of nonprofit organizations, thus using their areas of expertise to meet the specific needs of the respective nonprofit.

Highlights:

- Advancing Minorities' Interest in Engineering-Baltimore, MD
- Paul Quinn College-Dallas, TX
- Phoenix Symphony-Phoenix, AZ

Information Technology Support

EDS is also able to uniquely capitalize on our expertise in the field of information technology to reach out to the global community.

Highlights:

- **Boys & Girls Clubs**-EDS developed and implemented computer centers in 7 clubs to be used by more than 9,000 student club members.
- **EDS Technology Grant Program**-This program awards monies to public elementary school teachers for information technology services and products based on their current applications of technology and plans for future classroom enhancements. Grant applications are made available to interested teachers through their school districts and the Internet.
- **In Touch**-An information system developed by EDS and donated to The Friends of the Vietnam Veterans Memorial facilitates the search for information about combat veterans.
- **JASON**-This year-round project includes a comprehensive and extensive school curriculum; a full program of teacher training; exercises designed for Internet; pre-produced programming on educational television; and two weeks of live on-site broadcasts—reaching a total of more than 33 million students, teachers and members of the business community. As the information technology provider and founding sponsor of the program, EDS fuses a whole cast of advanced technologies from robotics to telepresence to satellite communications with the sole purpose of introducing children to the adventures of science and technology.

Global Volunteer Day
1996 Executive Summary

A Quick Look at the Results
- **Tens of thousands** of employees teamed with family members, friends, customers, community leaders, employees from other area business, vendors, and many of the recipients themselves
  - from **29** countries
    - in at least **220** locations
      - serving more than **47,125** hours
        - in **381** projects
          - benefiting **4 million** children

Global Volunteer Day Objectives

- Celebrate EDS employees' **year-round commitment to community service** around the world
- Provide **team-building**, leadership development, and personal fulfillment opportunities for employees
- Establish a positive image for EDS as a **good corporate citizen** and team with customers to strengthen those relationships

Measurement Against the Objectives

How Did GVD Help Celebrate Year-Round Community Involvement?
EDS employees around the world are serving their communities all year in unique and creative ways. Global Volunteer Day is a one-day celebration of those employees' year-round commitment to their communities. The objective is to **promote ongoing,** successful **relationships** with organizations and **mobilize new volunteers.** How well does GVD accomplish this objective?

- Project coordinators reported that **88 percent** of the projects prompted their team to continue volunteering.
- **108** of the projects were managed by teams who had not participated in community activities before GVD.
- **76 percent** of the projects reported management participation as opposed to 65 percent last year.

Recipient organization and employee comments are one of the best ways to measure this objective.

Tell a Story of Success!

Every project was a winner for the recipients as well as the volunteers. However, the following projects were remarkable for different reasons.

India

Although the **EDS presence in India is small**—three expatriates and three local employees—that didn't stop those individuals from generating vendor support and successfully completing four projects in four different locations. In all, **77** volunteers spent **428** hours on the following projects:

- Naya Prayas shelter, New Delhi—Took the children to the park and to see a movie, providing lunch and games. Most of these **children had never had a soft drink before; none of them had experienced air-conditioning.**
- House of Kindness home for abandoned children, Andheri Bombay—Treated the children to a buffet in the park, a lion safari, and a mini-train ride.
- Temple of Love orphanage, Pune—Played with the children and donated shoes, food, and crayons
- Ministry of God home for abandoned children, Bahadurdally Village—Planted trees around the campus, played games and fed snacks to the children.

Beijing, China

In Beijing, **73** employees, family members, and friends spent **219** hours being the **first American company ever to volunteer their time at the Great Wall of China,** which, according to project coordinator Donna Lynn Allen, is "a real breakthrough for EDS China and for the Chinese/American relationship." They cleaned the Great Wall Museum, trimmed trees, picked up trash, and watered trees, plants, and flowers. The children volunteers learned the importance of caring for the environment and how to work as a team to accomplish goals.

Grand Rapids, Michigan, USA

This project, benefiting the St. Francis Xavier inner-city school, was a **truly global effort,** involving volunteers from Plano, Texas; Troy, Lansing, Auburn Hills, and Grand Rapids, Michigan: Charlotte, North Carolina, and even Australia. Almost **180** employees, family members, and other community volunteers completed five projects for this school, spending **647** hours doing it:

- Playground upgrade, including a fund-raiser that collected $2,250 and a **playground constructed** from its skeleton **in one day.**
- PC lab upgrade with PC donations from Purchasing in Troy and Plano, and PCs, printers, and modems from Operations in Auburn Hills. As a result, each child will have his or her own PC during computer class.
- School wish list was completed with 21 boxes of office supplies, books, learning aids, arts and crafts supplies, science class supplies, and toys.
- A party and picnic for the kids including poster painting, ring toss, relay races and more.
- Landscaping included planting flowers along the front of the school.

CHOOSING A PROJECT, CONTACTING THE RECIPIENT ORGANIZATION AND RECRUITING VOLUNTEERS

The first step in organizing a project is deciding what sort of volunteer project is appropriate for your location and your potential volunteers. This year, Global Volunteer Day has a special focus on children, the future of our world. Many children's organizations need volunteer help. Some volunteer opportunities with children involve interaction with the kids, while others do not. Choose a project that meets the needs of your community and your volunteers.

Note: *If your team has a commitment to an organization that does not directly benefit children, continue to support that organization. Involve children in the activity, if feasible, and you will be affirming the importance of helping others, thereby developing future volunteers.*

Project Ideas
Following are some national and global organizations benefiting children:

- Orphanages and children's homes
- Schools, preschools and partnership schools
- Abused children's shelters
- Day care and after-school centers
- CARE
- Children's hospitals
- Children's Educational Fund
- Children's Organ Transplant Association (COTA)
- Communities in Schools
- Big Brother/Big Sister
- Boy Scouts and Girl Scouts
- Boys & Girls Clubs
- Girls Inc.
- Junior Achievement

- Make-A-Wish Foundation
- March of Dimes
- Ronald McDonald houses
- Special Olympics
- UNICEF
- YMCA and YWCA

Depending on the interests of your volunteers and the needs in your community, your project could center around a school or day care cleanup; a food, toy or clothing drive; a fund-raiser; computer donations; donations of technical expertise; sporting or recreational activities; shelter visits; renovating or building homes for families; teaching kids to swim; or countless other activities.

Some Suggestions for Planning
- Half-day activities are best.
- Morning projects tend to get a higher attendance rate.
- Plan a rain-or-shine event; if your project is outdoors, have backup plans indoors or under cover.
- Don't commit to a project unless you are sure of your capabilities and those of your EDS volunteers.
- On average, **only 85 percent of employees who sign up for an activity will actually show up.**
- Use the project as a team-building and family event. Invite customers and their families.
- Emphasize that EDS employees and friends are the primary resource being donated.

Projects should be low-cost or without cost to both planners and participants. Many nonprofit organizations will help you identify community and volunteer needs. Contact the local branch of any available nonprofit organization. Following are some examples:

- Business in the Community—Europe
- Center for Better Corporate Citizenship—Japan
- Red Cross
- Rotary Club
- United Way—United States
- International Association of Volunteer Efforts

(continued)

- Local office of highest elected city or community leader—United States
- Any volunteer center

If there are no pressing needs in your immediate community, look beyond borders and identify resources and needs in a neighboring community or country.

The Initial Encounter

Before settling on a specific volunteer project, contact the prospective recipient organization to make sure there is a need for your services. If the organization can use you and your EDS team, this is an excellent time to begin planning and confirming the following details:

- Type of project
- Date (June 8—remember, the date cannot be changed)
- Time
- Location
- Number of volunteers needed and suitable age ranges
- Types of jobs to be performed
- Costs and supplies associated with project, if any, and who is responsible for costs
- Checklist #1 (page 16)

A successful, smoothly run project is more likely if roles and responsibilities of both EDS and the recipient organization are defined up front. Be sure to match the needed number of volunteers to the jobs defined. **Make sure all your volunteers have something meaningful to do.**

A tip for recruiting: **You might want to recruit 15 percent more people than you need to make up for potential no-shows.**

> **Note:** *Be aware that the actions of you and your group will reflect on all EDS employees, as well as on the corporation's business reputation and objectives. Please keep this in mind when dealing with the recipient organization. You may be the first and last EDS employee these people will meet. Also consider the possibility of a continuing relationship with this organization throughout the year*

Recruiting Volunteers

> *"Most people don't volunteer unless they are asked."*
> —Peter Lynch, retired mutual funds investment manager and seasoned volunteer

Who should participate in Global Volunteer Day?

EVERYONE! When recruiting volunteers for your event, include your leadership, family members, EDS customers, multiple EDS accounts, vendors—anyone and everyone you interact and work with. No matter how large or small your particular organization, you can make a momentous impact on your community. Don't feel that your organization is too small. Even one person can make a difference by visiting a sick child in the hospital. Plan an activity that your group can handle, and make it the best it can possibly be!

Inform colleagues about the project. Consider the following methods:

- Account and group newsletters
- Department and team meetings
- Office memos—see sample, page 12
- Special announcement flyer posted in your area—Information Kit cover
- Global Volunteer Day poster

Encourage your colleagues to volunteer. Consider the following strategies when recruiting volunteers:

- Gentle persuasion—never browbeat fellow employees into volunteering. A volunteer who is pressured into participating is not a "volunteer."
- Make your colleagues feel as good as possible about volunteering. Point out who will benefit and how. Emphasize the difference that can be made in the community and at EDS through their participation. Also emphasize fun and team-building opportunities.
- Ask your local leadership to send an endorsement and recruiting letter to your team and customers. Their support and participation can make a world of difference for employees.
- Promote the event as a family project among EDS employees and leadership as well as customers.

(continued)

Sustaining volunteers' interest and keeping them motivated is another important step to a successful project. The following tips offer suggestions for keeping the excitement building:

• Show the 1995 Global Volunteer Day video included with this kit. Or, you may borrow one by calling (+1) (214) 605-6782 [8-835]. Please state the format you require: NTSC, PAL, or Secam.
• Send periodic pre-event updates to your volunteer force with event details, names of volunteers signed up so far, total number of volunteers participating and so forth. Creative reminders, such as inexpensive plastic paintbrushes to teams who are going to paint a school, help build excitement.

Once your volunteers have had a rewarding and satisfying experience, they become ambassadors for EDS' volunteer program. In turn, they can help recruit new volunteers for your account's next project.

CHECKLIST #1

_____ Decide on project type through consultation with fellow employees.

_____ Review the Legal Regulations—Staying Safe and Secure section (page 14) before making a commitment to the organization.

_____ Contact organization(s) to make sure your services are needed.

_____ Determine project details, including time, location, number of volunteers needed and types of jobs.

_____ Present project concept via letter or presentation to supervisor or account manager involved in approving the volunteer project.

_____ Publicize event to interested employees. Use enclosed poster and duplications of black-and-white flyer for promotions in your area (see back of kit).

_____ Send confirmation letter to organization (see sample, page 17), and schedule meeting to review details of event.

_____ Determine costs, if any, and who will be responsible.

Complete and return Preproject Information Sheet (page 18) to David Vineyard no later than April 15.

PREPROJECT INFORMATION SHEET

Note: *This information is due **Monday, April 15, 1996**. All the information requested on this form must be provided. Fill out duplicates of this form for each individual project if your location is participating in more than one activity. This information will be used for reporting results to senior leadership. If you do not submit this form, your project will not be included on leadership reports. This form is also available on-line in OfficeVision. Type "GVDPREP" on the command line. Complete the form and press PF6 to send.*

I. Volunteer Coordinator Information

Thank you for agreeing to be a volunteer coordinator for the Global Volunteer Day project. We need accurate information to communicate with you. Please put your full work address, not a postal box number.

Name _____

Work address _____

City _____ State _____ Country _____ ZIP _____

Telephone number _____ Fax Number _____

Account name _____

SU name _____ SU leader name _____

II. Global Volunteer Day Project Information

Project description _____

_____

Name of recipient organization _____

Describe the general audience that this organization helps (for example, orphans, sick children, abused children, teenagers) _____

III. Involvement

How many EDS volunteers do you expect to participate in your project? _____

Are you partnering with an EDS customer(s)?   ☐ Yes   ☐ No

Note: *If you are interested in local media coverage for your event, refer to the press kit included with this Information Kit.*

Please return this Preproject Information Sheet by close of business **Monday, April 15,** to David Vineyard, EDS Community Affairs, 5400 Legacy Drive, H3-6F-47, Plano, Texas 75024; fax number (+1) (214) 605-8625 [8-835].

CHECKLIST #4

Day of the Event

_____ Arrive at least 45 minutes early so you can register volunteers and direct them to appropriate locations. Call volunteers by name and introduce them to one another to inspire camaraderie. Have leadership personally thank everyone.

_____ Use complimentary buttons as name tags and recognition for volunteers. We recommend writing volunteers' names with a fine-point permanent marker.

_____ If your local account has EDS banners or signs, hang them at the event.

_____ Continuously acknowledge and thank volunteers for their assistance. Try to visit all volunteers at least once or twice, and compliment them on their skills, involvement and spirit to make them feel good about contributing.

_____ If possible, have photos or video taken of volunteers in action throughout the day. Send copies to: EDS Community Affairs, Attn: Jamie Shinneman, 5400 Legacy Drive, H3-6F-47, Plano, Texas 75024 USA. These photos and videos cannot be returned. YOU MUST HAVE A SIGNED APPEARANCE RELEASE FROM ANY NON-EDS PARTICIPANTS. Photos and videos picturing non-EDS employees WILL NOT be used in Global Volunteer Day promotional material unless they are accompanied by a signed Appearance Release (see page 15). See photography and videography tips, page 20.

_____ Have drawing paper and colored pens or markers available for children at the recipient organization to draw a picture of their day with EDS volunteers. Make copies of page 28 for parents or guardians to sign so their children can enter the poster contest. (Selected drawings will be used for the poster produced after Global Volunteer Day. See page 28 for more information.)

_____ Please complete and send the enclosed Postproject Information Sheets (see pages 31-33) to David Vineyard, EDS Community Affairs, 5400 Legacy Drive, H3-6F-47, Plano, Texas 75024 USA— or fax it to him at (+1) (214) 605-8625 [8-835]—by close of business **Friday, June 21,** so we can begin tallying the event's results. The Postproject Information Sheet is also available on-line in OfficeVision. Type "GVDPOST" on the command line. Complete the form and press PF6 to send.

VOLUNTEER RECOGNITION

Recognition is important to maintaining the volunteer spirit both before and after the project.

Techniques to help volunteers feel appreciated:

- Important—be sure to recognize employees, customers, and family members within two weeks after the event. Use the enclosed certificate (see following page), or create something unique.
- Ask your local leadership to send a personal letter to each volunteer endorsing both the program and the time spent volunteering (see sample on page 36). If you partnered with your customer, you may also request his or her signature on the thank-you letter.
- Communicate the results of your project to both your volunteers and your leadership.
- Present recognition in a meaningful way, and be sure each volunteer feels special. For example, you might distribute recognition certificates at an employee reception or picnic. Show pictures from the event and honor the volunteers' hard work. If you give certificates, you may have your leaders present these to the volunteers. Or post the volunteers' names on bulletin boards or in busy areas such as coffee areas or the cafeteria.

Some inexpensive recognition ideas:

- Employee identification at a team function or meeting
- Newsletter highlight
- Photo displays
- Personal thank-you notes
- Leadership thank-you and recognition letters to employees–see page 36
- Award certificates—see following page
- Thank-you reception, to which you invite a representative from the recipient organization
  - An ice cream social
  - After-work snacks or drinks
  - Coffee or tea and sweets
- Duplicated thank-you letter from the recipient organization
- Duplicated Global Volunteer Day summaries from Community Affairs in Plano, Texas, available later in 1996

Recipient Organization Recognition

The recipient organization with which you partnered is just as much a part of our success as we are and is an important audience to recognize. Without them, Global Volunteer Day would have no meaning or purpose. Some inexpensive recognition ideas:

- Send a personal note to the executive director and anyone else you worked with at the organization.
- Send the Recipient Organization Certificate (see following page) with your note.
- When you receive the Executive Summary later in 1996, send a duplicate to the organization. It is very important that we communicate the success of the day with this audience—they, too, need to see the big picture!

EXHIBIT A.4 Federated Department Stores, Inc.*

- Partners in Time Q&A

- Partners in Time Overview

- Why Partners in Time is Good for Our Employees, Our Company, and Our Communities

- Process for Approval of Volunteer Project

- Project Request

- Project Evaluation

- Volunteerism Interest Survey

*Reprinted with permission by Federated Department Stores, Inc., Atlanta, GA.

Federated
DEPARTMENT STORES, INC.

Background of Federated Department Stores, Inc.

Federated Department Stores, with corporate offices in Cincinnati and New York, is the nation's largest operator of department stores with annual sales of more than $15 billion. Federated currently operates more than 400 department stores and 150 specialty stores in 36 states. Federated's department stores operate nationally under the names of Bloomingdale's, The Bon Marche, Burdines, Goldsmith's, Lazarus, Macy's, Rich's and Stern's.

Background of *Partners in Time*

Federated already had a long history of involvement in the community when the *Partners in Time* employee volunteer program was founded at Rich's/Goldsmith's in Atlanta in 1989. With the reality of budgetary pressures of the late '80's, our stores were seeking additional ways to contribute to the community, additional ways to take a leadership role. *Partners* was an immediate success, both in terms of contributions to the community and internal benefits of camaraderie and team building. In 1993, other divisions began to create their own *Partners in Time* organizations based upon the Rich's/Goldsmith's example. In 1996, *Partners in Time* volunteers across America volunteered more than 70,000 hours in 1,257 projects, all on their own time.

How does it work?

Throughout the year, group volunteer projects are suggested and developed in which any employee, family member or friend can participate. The opportunities are endless and include school partnership events, park clean-ups, hospital visits, Special Olympics competitions, and efforts to benefit housing and women's issues. At each event, the *Partners in Time* tee shirt is worn.

What types of projects are undertaken?

Partners in Time has been involved in a variety of community and civic projects. They have created their own annual "Instant Traditions," and they have acted quickly in response to crisis situations. Their projects reflect the vast diversity of its participants. Nearly every issue has been addressed, from the environment to AIDS, from homeless children to senior citizens.

What kinds of organizations are eligible?

All organizations must have a 501(c)(3) non-profit tax-exempt status and must be non-partisan, non-controversial, and non-sectarian.

How do we keep everyone informed?

Communication is a major key to our success: recruitment flyers are produced for our major storewide events; a photographer is assigned to major events; we write articles for employee newsletters and magazines and we create photographic story board displays that chronicle the fun and good work. All Coordinators have bulletin boards that are frequently revised.

We utilize several means to keep the public informed of our efforts: free-standing display units positioned in each store's high traffic area; inclusion in newspaper advertising, where appropriate, press releases and the Federated Contributions Annual Report. All contribute to public awareness.

Federated
DEPARTMENT STORES, INC.

Partners In Time Paragons

- In 1997, Federated was selected as one of just 150 companies to participate in the Presidents' Summit for America's Future in Philadelphia. This was the catalyst for our 'Earning for Learning' grants-for-schools initiative which rewards volunteers who commit 20 hours during the school year to educational programs with a $250 contribution to the school.

- *Partners in Time* received a citation from the President's National Volunteer Council counting them in the top two percent of nearly 3,500 nominees for the President's 1991 Volunteer Action Award. The Community Relations Report awarded *Partners in Time* with the "Bellringer Award." The founding division, Rich's/Goldsmith's, was one of four corporations recognized for the best Employee Volunteer Programs in America.

- For the first time, in 1996, Federated's four New-York based divisions—including Bloomingdale's and the Federated Merchandising Group—shared the *Partners* banner for New York City's annual Share-A-Walk. 120 volunteers walked to promote Breast Cancer awareness and raise research dollars.

- With some Partners in Time projects, customers also can get into the act of service. During "Art With A Heart," a project benefiting Harborview Medical Center in Seattle and Children's Hospital in Pittsburgh, hundreds of Bon Marche and Lazarus volunteers issued an open invitation to customers to join them in painting cheery murals and ceiling tiles.

- At Macy's East, contributions and volunteers combine to support the Pine Street Inn, a Boston homeless shelter. Financial aid helps move families from the streets to self-sufficiency, while on a more personal level, 200 Macy's volunteers prepare, cook and serve dinners to shelter residents throughout the year.

- Burdines' volunteers lent their time to 'Taste of the Nation' events in six Florida cities. Thousands of supporters attended the 'Share Our Strength' fund-raising events hosted by renowned chefs and restaurants. The end result was $70,000 to benefit local hunger relief agencies—which translates to more than 350,000 meals for the hungry.

- Benefit Shopping Days at Macy's West, manned by store and charity volunteers, provided almost $2 million in 1996 for civic and non-profit organizations in dozens of cities.

- For several years, Goldsmith's store volunteers have gotten in on the action at the WKNO Action Auction in Memphis. Partners created "Made in Memphis" gift baskets to be auctioned and took phone pledges to raise funds for public television.

- In 1996, Rich's led a parade of 500 volunteers to be the largest corporate team in AIDS Walk Atlanta, raising nearly $30,000. Other Rich's cities have had similarly spectacular results.

- Stern's launched its Partners program in 1996, gathering more than 100 volunteers from five New Jersey stores to unpack, sort and repackage 118 pallets of food for the Community Food Bank. The food was then distributed to 1,500 non-profit agencies serving communities where Stern's operates.

PARTNERS in TIME
EMPLOYEE VOLUNTEER PROGRAM
Federated
DEPARTMENT STORES, INC.

Overview of Partners in Time Volunteer Program Results
1989–1996

Year	Employees Participating	Number of Volunteer Hours	Number of Events
1989	2,584	1,987	47
1990	3,543	8,293	116
1991	5,399	10,300	139
1992	6,406	12,165	149
1993	8,500	19,000	220
1994	14,732	42,207	385
1995	20,460	51,607	642
1996	24,721	71,817	1,257
Total:	86,345	217,376	2,955

Federated
DEPARTMENT STORES, INC.

WHY PARTNERS IN TIME IS GOOD
FOR OUR EMPLOYEES, OUR COMPANY & OUR COMMUNITIES

- Employees at various levels volunteer together and get to know each other in an informal setting. It's a <u>valuable team builder</u>.

- Employees at various levels get an <u>opportunity to assume a leadership role</u> by heading up a *Partners in Time* project. Studies of Employee Volunteer programs around the country show that employees appreciate an opportunity for this type of growth and that it can be a factor in retaining employees.

- Employees <u>feel pride in their company</u>. In our employee surveys, "Showing the community that Federated is a company that cares" is the Number One reason employees volunteer. Employees get more exposure to our philanthropy.

- *Partners in Time* generates <u>positive publicity in the press</u>. *Partners in Time* projects are annually covered in all types of national and local media.

- Even with our contributions budget, we cannot reach all of the organizations and people we would like to benefit. *Partners in Time* helps to fill the void, with projects such as the Valentine card-making party for thousands of senior citizens and visits to shelters for homeless children.

- Because the projects are employee-driven, the company gets a better awareness of issues that are of particular interest to our employees, such as AIDS research, education, women's issues and children at risk.

Federated
DEPARTMENT STORES, INC.

PROCESS FOR APPROVAL OF PARTNERS IN TIME VOLUNTEER PROJECT

STEP 1: HOW CAN A PROJECT BE REQUESTED?

Project ideas can be generated by:
• Individual employees
• Location Coordinator
• Non-profit agency
• Manager of Volunteer Programs
• Executive Committee

STEP 2: HOW DOES A PROJECT GET APPROVED?

All information describing a proposed project and the beneficiary agency should be sent to your *Partners in Time* Regional Coordinator. This information is then reviewed for approval by:
• Regional Executive Committee
• Manager of Volunteer Programs
• VP of Community Affairs

Projects are approved with the guidance of:
• *Partners in Time* Executive Committee
• *Partners in Time* Think Tank

STEP 3: HOW IS AN APPROVED PROJECT THEN IMPLEMENTED?

• Identify the Project Director(s). See description of Project Director role in administrative structure section.
• Meet with the agency well in advance of targeted date of project.
• Plan the event.
  • Establish project scope—what can be accomplished within the time frame?
  • Determine the number of volunteers necessary to achieve the project scope objective.
  • Delegate and encourage people to get involved in leadership aspects of the project.
• Recruit volunteers and communicate project goals.
• Send photos, sign-in sheets and Project Evaluation information, to your Regional Coordinator within 10 days of project.

Federated
DEPARTMENT STORES, INC.

PROJECT REQUEST

IMPORTANT: All project requests must be submitted for approval by the Executive Committee at least four weeks prior to the event. Please send to your Regional Coordinator. *If funding required—eight weeks prior.

<u>PLEASE FILL OUT THIS FORM COMPLETELY AND LEGIBLY</u>

Proposed by _____ SYSM ID: _____

Location Name: _____ Region _____

Phone (   ) _____ Date Submitted _____

Name of Non-profit Organization _____

Address _____

Purpose of Organization _____

Does this organization have a 501 (c) (3) tax-exempt status? _____

Why was this organization selected? _____

_____

_____

Date of Project _____ Time: From _____ a.m./p.m. To _____ a.m./p.m.

Location of Project _____

DESCRIBE VOLUNTEERS INVOLVEMENT (Please be specific) Attach information as needed. _____

_____

_____

_____

Number of Volunteers needed _____

Will this project involve other Locations? Which ones? (Please indicate the type of project activity, etc.) _____

_____

Project Director and Title _____

Location Name: _____ SYSM ID: _____ Phone _____

*What budget or equipment is requested? _____

_____

Review Date _____ Questions Call: _____ Approved ____ Declined ____

Federated
DEPARTMENT STORES, INC.

PARTNERS IN TIME VOLUNTEER PROJECT EVALUATION
PLEASE FILL OUT THIS FORM COMPLETELY AND LEGIBLY

Name of Project _____ Date of Project _____

Project Director _____ House Number _____

City _____ County _____ State _____ Zip Code _____

Location _____ Phone (W)( ) _____ Fax No. ( ) _____

Name of Organization _____

Contact Person and Title _____

Address _____

City _____ County _____ State _____ Zip Code _____

Phone Number ( ) _____ Fax Number ( ) _____

Briefly Describe Activity _____

_____

_____

List Number of Hours:

_____ # People X _____ # Hours Each = _____ Volunteer Hours

Planning Hours of Project Leader(s) _____

Was there any budget expense charged to *Partners in Time?* If so, please detail:

_____

_____

Who would you recommend to chair this event next year? _____

How could we improve this project? _____

_____

Did you receive your *Partners in Time* mug for chairing this project? _____

Did you take photos at the event? _____

Have you sent in the photos or negatives to the Regional *Partners in Time* Coordinator?

_____

Please attach sign-in sheets of all people involved.

Submitted by _____ Date _____

MAIL TO: Please return to your Regional Coordinator within 10 days following this event.

THANK YOU!

Federated
DEPARTMENT STORES, INC.

Partners In Time Volunteerism Interest Survey

Please take a moment to help us understand your volunteer interests. This does not obligate you to participate. It simply helps us prioritize community issues for selecting projects. Please print clearly; your ideas are important to us!

Associate Number: _____ Loc./Dept. Name/# _____
First Name: _____ Last Name: _____
Address: _____
City: _____ County: _____ State: ____ Zip: _____
Home Phone: # (   )   Work Phone: # (   )   Sysmail Code:
_____   _____   _____

Status (Circle):
Associate   Dependent/Spouse   Dependent/Child   Retiree   Other _____

TIME PREFERENCE (for Volunteering)   **TYPES OF PROJECTS**
(Please Circle)   *(Please Circle)*
Weekdays   AM   PM   Company-wide Big Projects
Weekday Evenings   AM   PM   Smaller Projects
Saturdays   AM   PM   Ongoing Projects (ex. Tutoring)
Sundays   AM   PM   Family Projects
                                                     Other _____

CIRCLE ONE OR MORE OF THE FOLLOWING:

INTERESTS   **SKILLS**
AIDS   Animal Mascots (Richie/Lazzie Bear,
Arts   Goldie, etc.)
Education   Carpentry
Elderly   CPR Trained
Environment   Computer Operations
Families in Crisis   Crafts or Sewing
Health (other than AIDS)   Face Painting
Hunger   Hospitality
Homelessness/Housing (Christmas in   Magician
   April/Habitat, etc.)   Musician (instrument) _____
Museums & Other Attractions   Painting
Special Olympics   Photography
Sports and Recreation   Recreation Sports
Women's Issues (i.e., battered women,   Simple Repairs (household handy
   breast cancer, etc.)   person)
Youth at Risk   Teaching/Training
Other _____   Other _____

What specific non-profit organization(s) would you like Partners to help? _____
_____

Are you a current volunteer? _____ What is your favorite type of volunteer activity? _____
_____

- Questionnaire for Employee/Retiree Volunteers

*Reprinted with permission by the General Mills Foundation, Minneapolis, MN.

Questionnaire for Employee/Retiree Volunteers

General Mills Volunteer Survey

Many General Mills employees have been active as volunteers supporting their communities through service. This survey is designed to explore the experiences of volunteers and to gather information to improve General Mills' ability to assist employees who are looking for volunteer opportunities. We would appreciate a few minutes of your time to provide us with information on your experiences as a volunteer. These may be experiences arranged with the assistance of General Mills and the Volunteer Connection Program as well as those you found on your own. Please circle your answers. If you have not volunteered recently, please answer only the questions indicated by the instructions. The survey should take only about 10 to 15 minutes of your time. Thank you for your assistance.

SECTION ONE

Employment Information

1. **To begin, how many years have you been/were you an employee at General Mills?**
   Less than 1 year 0
   1 to 2 years 1
   3 to 5 years 2
   6 to 10 years 3
   11 to 15 years 4
   16 to 20 years 5
   Over 20 years 6

2. **What were you doing just before you began your current/last job?**
   I was in school or job training 1
   I held another job at General Mills 2
   I was employed at another company 3
   I was not working or in school 4

3. **In what division or department do/did you work at General Mills?**

4. **What is/was your plant/office location?**

5. **What is/was the nature of your job?**
   Non-exempt or hourly employee (including secretarial,
   administrative support, production, etc.). 1
   Salaries exempt:
   Professional/technical (non-manager) 2
   Entry-level manager 3
   Manager 4
   Director or above 5

6. **During the last 3 years, have you participated in any volunteer**
   activities? We are interested both in activities you found on
   your own and those coordinated by the company.
   Yes 1
   No (SKIP TO SECTION 5) 2

If you answered "no," please skip to Section 5. If you answered "yes"
please answer the next two questions and continue with Sections 2, 3 and 4.

7. **During the past year, how often would you say you have done**
   volunteer work?
   More than once a week. 1
   About once a week 2
   Once or twice a month 3
   4 to 6 times during the year 4
   2 or 3 times during the year 5
   Once during the year 6

8. **About how many hours, in total, did you volunteer in the past**
   year?
   _____ hours

(continued)

SECTION TWO

Volunteer Activities

Using the attached chart, please list up to four organizations or projects where you have volunteered recently during the past three years. If there are more than four, please list the four where you spent the most time. For each activity listed, please provide the information requested. (If you have chosen not to volunteer in the past 3 years, please skip to section 5.)

Volunteer Activity One	Volunteer Activity Two
1. Name of Organization	**1. Name of Organization**

2. What did you do there? (Briefly describe)

2. What did you do there? (Briefly describe)

3. What type of organization is this? (Circle all that apply)

School. 1
Other education program . . . 2
Hospital or health 3
Government agency 4
Religious institution 5
Social service agency 6
Political/advocacy group 7
Youth service organization . . 8
Ethnic/cultural group 9
Other (describe) 96

3. What type of organization is this? (Circle all that apply)

School. 1
Other education program . . . 2
Hospital or health 3
Government agency 4
Religious institution. 5
Social service agency. 6
Political/advocacy group. . . . 7
Youth service organization . 8
Ethnic/cultural group. 9
Other (describe) 96

4. What type of services does the organization provide? (Circle all that apply)

Education 1
Food bank/drive 2
Public safety/emergency
   response 3
Health care 4
Substance abuse . . . .
   treatment/prevention 5

4. What type of services does the organization provide? (Circle all that apply)

Education 1
Food bank/drive 2
Public safety/emergency
   response. 3
Health care 4
Substance abuse
   treatment/prevention. 5

Volunteer Activity One

Assist homeless 6
Services for disabled. 7
Youth/child care 8
Parks/recreation 9
Environmental. 10
Conservation. 11
Historic preservation 12
Arts 13
Sports-related 14
Other (describe) 96

5. **What was the nature of your activities?**
   (Circle all that apply)
   Help provide community
      services 1
   Assist with administration of
      organization   2
   Counseling/workshops/talks   3
   Marketing/recruitment 4
   Fundraising 5
   Board member 6
   Staff an event 7
   Other (describe) 96

6. **Who benefited the most from this activity?**
   I did 1
   The organization did 2
   The people served by the
      organization did. 3

7. **Is this activity similar to your job?**
   Similar to my job 1
   Expands on my job skills. . . . 2
   Not similar, but uses some of
      my skills and training. 3
   Not at all similar. 4

Volunteer Activity Two

Assist homeless 6
Services for disabled 7
Youth/child care 8
Parks/recreation 9
Environmental. 10
Conservation 11
Historic preservation. 12
Arts 13
Sports-related. 14
Other (describe) 96

5. **What was the nature of your activities?**
   (Circle all that apply)
   Help provide community
      services 1
   Assist with administration of
      organization 2
   Counseling/workshops/talks   3
   Marketing/recruitment. 4
   Fundraising. 5
   Board member 6
   Staff an event 7
   Other (describe) 96

6. **Who benefited the most from this activity?**
   I did. 1
   The organization did. 2
   The people served by the
      organization did 3

7. **Is this activity similar to your job?**
   Similar to my job. 1
   Expands on my job skills . . . 2
   Not similar, but uses some of
      my skills and training 3
   Not at all similar 4
   (continued)

Volunteer Activity One

8. **How often did you do this activity?**

   More than once a week. . . . 1
   About once a week 2
   Once or twice a month 3
   4 to 6 times a year. 4
   2 to 3 times a year. 5
   One-time event 6

9. **How was this activity organized?**

   I was the only volunteer . . . 1
   Several volunteers did
      different activities 2
   Volunteers worked as a
      team 3
   As a service event
      (e.g., paint-a-thon, food
      drive, fundraising walk) . . 4

10. **How did you learn about this activity?**

   Found it on my own. 1
   Heard about it through prior
      volunteer experience. . . . 2
   Newspaper/TV/radio 3
   Through General Mills. 4
   Through a friend or
      acquaintance. 5
   Other (describe) 6

11. **How would you rate this experience?**

   Very satisfying. 1
   Somewhat satisfying 2
   Neither satisfying nor
      dissatisfying. 3
   Somewhat dissatisfying. . . . 4
   Very dissatisfying 5

Volunteer Activity Two

8. **How often did you do this activity?**

   More than once a week . . . 1
   About once a week. 2
   Once or twice a month 3
   4 to 6 times a year 4
   2 to 3 times a year 5
   One-time event. 6

9. **How was this activity organized?**

   I was the only volunteer . . . 1
   Several volunteers did
      different activities 2
   Volunteers worked as a
      team 3
   As a service event
      (e.g., paint-a-thon, food
      drive, fundraising walk). . 4

10. **How did you learn about this activity?**

   Found it on my own 1
   Heard about it through prior
      volunteer experience . . . 2
   Newspaper/TV/radio. 3
   Through General Mills 4
   Through a friend or
      acquaintance 5
   Other (describe) 6

11. **How would you rate this experience?**

   Very satisfying 1
   Somewhat satisfying. 2
   Neither satisfying nor
      dissatisfying 3
   Somewhat dissatisfying . . . 4
   Very dissatisfying 5

Volunteer Activity One

12. **Was the agency well prepared for you?**
   Well prepared 1
   Somewhat prepared 2
   Not at all prepared. 3

Volunteer Activity Two

12. **Was the agency well prepared for you?**
   Well prepared 1
   Somewhat prepared 2
   Not at all prepared 3

(*continued*)

SECTION TWO (*continued*)

Volunteer Activities

Volunteer Activity Three

1. Name of Organization

2. What did you do there? (Briefly describe)

3. What type of organization is this? (Circle all that apply)
School 1
Other education program . . . 2
Hospital or health 3
Government agency 4
Religious institution 5
Social service agency 6
Political/advocacy group 7
Youth service organization . . 8
Ethnic/cultural group 9
Other (describe) 96

4. What type of services does the organization provide? (Circle all that apply)
Education 1
Food bank/drive 2
Public safety/emergency
    response 3
Health care 4
Substance abuse . . . .
    treatment/prevention 5

Volunteer Activity Four

1. Name of Organization

2. What did you do there? (Briefly describe)

3. What type of organization is this? (Circle all that apply)
School 1
Other education program . . . 2
Hospital or health 3
Government agency 4
Religious institution 5
Social service agency 6
Political/advocacy group 7
Youth service organization . 8
Ethnic/cultural group 9
Other (describe) 96

4. What type of services does the organization provide? (Circle all that apply)
Education 1
Food bank/drive 2
Public safety/emergency
    response 3
Health care 4
Substance abuse
    treatment/prevention 5

Volunteer Activity Three

Assist homeless 6
Services for disabled. 7
Youth/child care 8
Parks/recreation 9
Environmental. 10
Conservation. 11
Historic preservation 12
Arts 13
Sports-related 14
Other (describe) 96

5. **What was the nature of your activities?**
   (Circle all that apply)
   Help provide community
   services 1
   Assist with administration of
   organization   2
   Counseling/workshops/talks   3
   Marketing/recruitment 4
   Fundraising 5
   Board member 6
   Staff an event 7
   Other (describe) 96

6. **Who benefited the most from this activity?**
   I did 1
   The organization did 2
   The people served by the
   organization did. 3

7. **Is this activity similar to your job?**
   Similar to my job 1
   Expands on my job skills. . . . 2
   Not similar, but uses some of
   my skills and training. 3
   Not at all similar. 4

Volunteer Activity Four

Assist homeless 6
Services for disabled 7
Youth/child care 8
Parks/recreation 9
Environmental. 10
Conservation 11
Historic preservation. 12
Arts 13
Sports-related. 14
Other (describe) 96

5. **What was the nature of your activities?**
   (Circle all that apply)
   Help provide community
   services 1
   Assist with administration of
   organization 2
   Counseling/workshops/talks   3
   Marketing/recruitment. 4
   Fundraising. 5
   Board member 6
   Staff an event 7
   Other (describe) 96

6. **Who benefited the most from this activity?**
   I did. 1
   The organization did. 2
   The people served by the
   organization did 3

7. **Is this activity similar to your job?**
   Similar to my job. 1
   Expands on my job skills . . . 2
   Not similar, but uses some of
   my skills and training 3
   Not at all similar 4

(continued)

Volunteer Activity Three

8. How often did you do this activity?

More than once a week. . . . 1
About once a week 2
Once or twice a month 3
4 to 6 times a year. 4
2 to 3 times a year. 5
One-time event 6

9. How was this activity organized?

I was the only volunteer . . . 1
Several volunteers did
different activities 2
Volunteers worked as a
team 3
As a service event
(e.g., paint-a-thon, food
drive, fundraising walk) . . 4

10. How did you learn about this activity?

Found it on my own. 1
Heard about it through prior
volunteer experience. . . . 2
Newspaper/TV/radio 3
Through General Mills. 4
Through a friend or
acquaintance. 5
Other (describe) 6

11. How would you rate this experience?

Very satisfying. 1
Somewhat satisfying 2
Neither satisfying nor
dissatisfying. 3
Somewhat dissatisfying. . . . 4
Very dissatisfying 5

Volunteer Activity Four

8. How often did you do this activity?

More than once a week . . . 1
About once a week 2
Once or twice a month 3
4 to 6 times a year 4
2 to 3 times a year 5
One-time event 6

9. How was this activity organized?

I was the only volunteer . . . 1
Several volunteers did
different activities 2
Volunteers worked as a
team 3
As a service event
(e.g., paint-a-thon, food
drive, fundraising walk). . 4

10. How did you learn about this activity?

Found it on my own 1
Heard about it through prior
volunteer experience . . . 2
Newspaper/TV/radio. 3
Through General Mills 4
Through a friend or
acquaintance 5
Other (describe) 6

11. How would you rate this experience?

Very satisfying 1
Somewhat satisfying. 2
Neither satisfying nor
dissatisfying 3
Somewhat dissatisfying . . . 4
Very dissatisfying 5

Volunteer Activity Three

12. Was the agency well prepared for you?

Well prepared 1
Somewhat prepared 2
Not at all prepared. 3

Volunteer Activity Four

12. Was the agency well prepared for you?

Well prepared 1
Somewhat prepared 2
Not at all prepared 3

(*continued*)

SECTION THREE

About Your Volunteer Experiences

In this section, we are interested in your overall perceptions of the volunteer experiences you have had. Please indicate whether you agree or disagree with each of the following statements based upon your volunteer experiences as a whole.

		Strongly Agree	Agree	Neither Agree nor Disagree	Disagree	Strongly Disagree
1.	While volunteering, I learned new skills that are useful to me outside of work	1	2	3	4	5
2.	Volunteering helped me understand my community better	1	2	3	4	5
3.	I benefit more from my volunteering than the people who receive my services do	1	2	3	4	5
4.	The work I did when volunteering was similar to the work I do on my regular job	1	2	3	4	5
5.	The people who receive my services benefit more than I do	1	2	3	4	5
6.	Volunteering is an opportunity to improve the skills I use at my regular job	1	2	3	4	5
7.	Without the General Mills Volunteer Connection I would volunteer less time	1	2	3	4	5
8.	I plan to volunteer at least as much in the upcoming year as I did this year	1	2	3	4	5
9.	Volunteering provides an opportunity to work with other General Mills employees away from my regular job	1	2	3	4	5

	Strongly Agree	Agree	Neither Agree nor Disagree	Disagree	Strongly Disagree
10. Volunteering is not a good way for me to learn new skills which would help me do my job better	1	2	3	4	5
11. Without the Volunteer Program, the type of activities I volunteer for would be different	1	2	3	4	5
12. I was not properly recognized at General Mills for all of my volunteer activities	1	2	3	4	5
13. Without the Volunteer Program, I would volunteer about the same amount of time as I do now	1	2	3	4	5
14. I was able to learn leadership skills by being a volunteer	1	2	3	4	5
15. I prefer to volunteer with other General Mills employees rather than on my own	1	2	3	4	5
16. When I volunteer, people who need help get services they would not receive otherwise	1	2	3	4	5
17. When I volunteer, people who need help get the same services they would ordinarily receive, but more of them	1	2	3	4	5
18. When I volunteer, it costs less to provide services to people who need help	1	2	3	4	5

SECTION FOUR

About People Who Have Not Volunteered

You have been a volunteer and understand what is involved. You probably know what would make it easier for others to volunteer. Please think about co-workers who have not been able to volunteer, or who do not volunteer often. For these people, do you think the following statements are true or not?

	True	Somewhat True	Not True
1. They do not volunteer because other activities outside of work are more important	1	2	3
2. They would volunteer more if they had help caring for their children or other family members	1	2	3
3. They are too busy at work to volunteer	1	2	3
4. If supervisors at work were more supportive they would volunteer more	1	2	3
5. If more of their co-workers volunteered as a group they would volunteer more	1	2	3
6. They would volunteer more if General Mills provided more help	1	2	3
7. If the agency where they wanted to volunteer was more willing to take their individual skills and interests into account they would volunteer more	1	2	3

8. What other obstacles do you feel make it difficult for your co-workers to participate in volunteer activities?

Please skip Section 5 and continue with Section 6.

SECTION FIVE

For People Who Have Not Volunteered (in the past 3 years)

1. The following are some reasons people may not participate in volunteer activities. How true are these statements for you? I do not volunteer because:

	Somewhat True	Not True	True
a. Other activities outside of work are more important	1	2	3
b. I am too busy at work to volunteer	1	2	3
c. I want to spend more time with my family and friends	1	2	3
d. I am not interested in volunteer activities	1	2	3
e. I did not know how to find volunteer activities I would like	1	2	3
f. I am busy as a primary caregiver in the family	1	2	3
g. The agencies where I would like to volunteer do not take my individual skills and interests into account	1	2	3

2. Are there any other reasons you do not choose to volunteer, or which make it difficult for you to volunteer?

3. If any of the following were provided by General Mills or some other organization, would you be more likely to volunteer?

	No More Likely	Somewhat More Likely	Much More Likely
a. Day care	1	2	3
b. More support from supervisors at work	1	2	3
c. Transportation	1	2	3
d. More information about what opportunities are available	1	2	3
e. Just the right volunteer opportunity	1	2	3
f. Opportunities to volunteer as a group with co-workers at General Mills	1	2	3
g. More help from General Mills	1	2	3

4. Is there any other assistance (or other form of compensation) that you feel would make it easier for you to participate in volunteer activities? If so, please describe briefly.

SECTION SIX

About the General Mills Employee Volunteer Program

In this section, we would like to learn about your experiences, if any, with General Mills and the Volunteer Connection, the General Mills employee volunteer program. Even if you have had no dealings with this service, we are interested in your perception of management's support for employee volunteer efforts within your division or department.

1. Please indicate whether or not you feel each of the following statements regarding the General Mills Employee Volunteer Program is accurate.

	Very Accurate	Somewhat Accurate	Inaccurate
a. I have not heard positive things about it.	1	2	3
b. They do not have the type of volunteer opportunities I want.	1	2	3
c. I value General Mills corporate commitment to volunteerism.	1	2	3
d. I did not know about the volunteer program provided by General Mills.	1	2	3
e. I prefer to use other sources for information.	1	2	3
f. I do not know who to contact.	1	2	3
g. The General Mills Employee Volunteer Program supports employee training and skills building through its projects.	1	2	3
h. The corporate emphasis on volunteer work makes me uncomfortable.	1	2	3

2. Have you ever used the services of the General Mills Employee Volunteer Program to look for volunteer opportunities?

Yes . . . . 1 (Answer question 3)
No . . . . 2 (Answer question 4)

3. Please indicate whether or not each of the following happened:

	Yes	No
a. They had the type of opportunities I sought.	☐	☐
b. I contacted the Volunteer Program manager.	☐	☐
c. I spoke with my area volunteer coordinator.	☐	☐
d. I read their bulletin, posting or other written materials.	☐	☐
e. The people were friendly and helpful.	☐	☐
f. They carefully referred me to the right volunteer situation.	☐	☐

4. What could the General Mills Employee Volunteer Program do to be more helpful to employees who want to do volunteer work in their local community?

5. What could the agencies where you volunteer do to make your volunteer experiences more satisfying and productive?

SECTION SEVEN

More About You

Your responses to the following very important questions are strictly confidential. They will be used only to help classify your answers. General Mills has employed Abt Associates Inc. to ensure your anonymity.

1. Into which of the following age groups do you fall? Are you . . .

Under 21 years of age 0
22 to 29 years old 1
30 to 39 years old 2
40 to 49 years old 3
50 to 59 years old 4
60 to 65 years old 5
Over 65 years old 6

2. What is your employment status at General Mills?

Full-time employee 1
Part-time employee (30 hours or less), or. 2
Retired 3

3. Are you male or female?

Male 1
Female 2

4. What is the highest level of education that you completed?

Grade 11 or less 0
Completed high school (include GED) 1
Completed trade/technical school after high school 2
Attended some college 3
Completed a 2-year college 4
Completed a 4-year college 5
Some graduate school 6
Completed a graduate degree 7

5. How would you characterize the neighborhood or community in which you live? Is it . . .

Rural 1
A small town 2
A suburb 3
Urban 4

Thank you very much for completing this survey. Please return it to the person who has been designated to help distribute and collect these forms.

- Development through Volunteerism

- Introduction

- Employee Development Worksheet

- Competency Checklist

- Development Opportunities Management and Supervisory Skills

- Development Opportunities Professional and Technical Skills

- Development Opportunities Communication Skills

- Development Opportunities Interpersonal Skills

- Employee Development Map

- Evaluation

- Project Commitment

Reprinted with permission by The Pillsbury Company, Minneapolis, MN.

DEVELOPMENT THROUGH VOLUNTEERISM

Introduction

Purpose: To provide opportunities for employees to develop professional skills through volunteerism.

Background: Experiences gained through volunteerism can enhance your professional development.

This kit provides a structure to guide you in using volunteerism to help you meet your developmental goals. Feel free to use the following worksheets as you sort through your interests and goals, and to think about a volunteer activity that will match your needs. The worksheets are optional—use them in a way that is most helpful to you.

How to Use: ■ Review the materials.
■ To explore possible volunteer placements contact:
Human Resource Representative
Volunteer Programs
X-4581

Development Through Volunteerism benefits employees and our community. For further information, please contact your Human Resources representative.

DEVELOPMENT THROUGH VOLUNTEERISM

Employee Development Worksheet

Name: _____

Title: _____   Department: _____

Supervisor: _____   Date: _____

The purpose of this worksheet is to help you identify areas where you could benefit from developmental opportunities through volunteerism. You and your supervisor can use this information to create a developmental plan or refer to your personal Individual Development Plan (IDP). Your plan may include such things as training courses, on-the-job assignments or cross-training opportunities. Other developmental opportunities exist through volunteer service with a variety of community organizations.

What do you see as your talents that help you do your job well?
_____
_____

What types of tasks best utilize these talents? _____
_____
_____

What do you see as your greatest development needs? _____
_____
_____

Is there any area where you think you need additional technical or skill training?_____
_____

If so, what skill or technical area? _____

List any types of volunteer projects that you would be interested in doing to meet your development goals. _____
_____
_____

DEVELOPMENT THROUGH VOLUNTEERISM

Competency Checklist

Following is a list of competencies. Check those that you wish to develop for your current or future job responsibilities.

- ☐ Assertiveness
- ☐ Budget management
- ☐ Change management
- ☐ Computer skills
- ☐ Conflict resolution
- ☐ Cultural awareness
- ☐ Delegating
- ☐ Facilitating
- ☐ Flexibility
- ☐ Interpersonal skills
- ☐ Leadership
- ☐ Listening skills
- ☐ Managing people
- ☐ Motivating others
- ☐ Needs analysis
- ☐ Negotiating skills
- ☐ Networking

- ☐ Organizational skills
- ☐ Planning
- ☐ Presentation skills
- ☐ Problem-solving and decision making
- ☐ Project management
- ☐ Recruitment; personnel evaluation and selection
- ☐ Resiliency
- ☐ Risk-taking
- ☐ Selling
- ☐ Teamwork
- ☐ Time management/prioritizing
- ☐ Verbal communication skills
- ☐ Written communication skills
- ☐ _____
- ☐ _____
- ☐ _____

DEVELOPMENT THROUGH VOLUNTEERISM

Development Opportunities Management and Supervisory Skills

SKILL/DEVELOPMENTAL AREA	WAYS TO PRACTICE
Budget Management	Chair a finance committee Plan events on a budget Chair an event with a budget Volunteer for a board position with finance responsibility Plan promotions on a budget
Change Management/ Strategic Awareness	Help write group bylaws Participate on an organization board Serve on personnel committee Do strategic planning for an organization Help write vision for an organization Participate in a focus group Write/rewrite job descriptions Be an active participant in a changing organization
Leadership	Serve as the chair of a committee or event Supervise volunteers Be the spokesperson for a group or organization Work with young people as a tutor/mentor
Managing People	Manage volunteers Coordinate an event Volunteer to be a facilitator
Developing/Motivating Others	Be a tutor/mentor Work in fundraising activities Chair a committee Be a United Way team captain Promote an event or organization
Problem-Solving and Decision-Making	Answer calls for a hot line Volunteer as a counselor Serve as a mentor/tutor Plan an event Work on a construction project

DEVELOPMENT THROUGH VOLUNTEERISM

Development Opportunities
Professional and Technical Skills

SKILL/DEVELOPMENTAL AREA	WAYS TO PRACTICE
Computer skills	Develop a database Utilize a new word processing program
Information Systems Applications	Apply systems applications on a database
Needs Analysis	Develop a strategic plan Volunteer at a school Develop surveys Organize the acquisition and distribution of resources Serve on a finance committee Volunteer as a counselor
Organizational Skills	Plan an event Edit a newsletter Provide clerical services Coordinate a multi-sponsored event
Planning	Plan an event Help produce a newsletter Serve on a strategic planning committee Coordinate an event or activity
Project Management	Plan an event Be a tutor/mentor Edit a newsletter Coordinate/monitor an ongoing project

DEVELOPMENT THROUGH VOLUNTEERISM

Development Opportunities
Communication Skills

SKILL/DEVELOPMENTAL AREA	WAYS TO PRACTICE
Facilitation	Lead a committee meeting Conduct a class Coordinate a group process
Listening Skills	Volunteer to answer calls for a hot line Serve as a tutor/mentor Provide crisis intervention counseling Work with sick people
Presentation Skills	Become part of a speakers' bureau Serve as a team captain Do public relations work Be a spokesperson Be the master of ceremonies for an event
Verbal Communication	See presentation skills—Ways to Practice Volunteer for an activity that uses the telephone
Written Communication	Write for a newsletter Develop letters for fund-raising Take minutes at meetings Write grants/proposals Serve as the secretary for a group, organization or event

DEVELOPMENT THROUGH VOLUNTEERISM

Development Opportunities
Interpersonal Skills

SKILL/DEVELOPMENTAL AREA	WAYS TO PRACTICE
Assertiveness	Serve as a fundraiser, solicit pledges or support Participate in registration drives Be a recruiter
Conflict Resolution/Negotiation	Serve on a board Negotiate contracts or personnel issues Manage a function or event Participate in the planning/execution of multi-committee events
Cultural Awareness	Volunteer in an activity that works closely with people unlike yourself Be a tutor/mentor Make presentations to diverse audiences Serve on a public relations committee
Flexibility/Resiliency	Volunteer with children, the elderly or persons with disabilities Volunteer in a crisis center Coordinate other volunteers Work on an outdoor event
Interpersonal Skills	Assume a leadership role in an activity that involves a group of people Become part of a speakers' bureau Do the public relations work for an event or organization Recruit volunteers Do fund-raising Volunteer to answer calls for a hot line Be a tutor/mentor

DEVELOPMENT THROUGH VOLUNTEERISM

Development Opportunities
Interpersonal Skills (continued)

SKILL/DEVELOPMENTAL AREA	WAYS TO PRACTICE
Networking	Edit a newsletter Do public relations work Acquire resources Conduct surveys Solicit funds or participation Recruit volunteers or members Serve on a board
Reliability/Followup	Voter registration Coordinate an adopt-a-family project Be a mentor/tutor
Risk-taking	Coordinate volunteers Get involved with a new activity Participate in the start-up of a new organization or event Plan an outdoor activity or event
Selling	Assist with fundraising Recruit volunteers Serve as an organization sponsor/liaison
Taking Initiative	Serve as a fund-raiser Participate in the start-up of a new organization or event Recruit volunteers Solicit resources
Teamwork	Work on a construction or rehab project Be a coach Collaborate with others on a project Plan/coordinate an event Board service
Time Management/ Prioritizing	Volunteer at a school Manage resources Facilitate meetings

DEVELOPMENT THROUGH VOLUNTEERISM

Employee Development Map

Remove this form from your Development Through Volunteerism booklet. As you complete the other materials, transfer the appropriate information to this form. When complete, this form will serve as a single document outlining your development selection.

Name: _____

Title: _____ Department: _____

Supervisor: _____ Date: _____

Top Three Developmental Area(s)
Refer to Competency Checklist:

_____   _____   _____

Way(s) to Practice
Refer to the Development Opportunities Chart:

_____   _____   _____

Area(s) of Interest
Consider the type of organization with which you would like to work.

_____
_____

Experience Objectives
Write a specific goal(s) for your experience as it relates to the developmental area(s) listed above:

_____
_____
_____
_____

Time and Location Preferences
How much time and what location will best fit your situation?

_____

DEVELOPMENT THROUGH VOLUNTEERISM

Evaluation

EMPLOYEE VOLUNTEER   Date: _____

Name: _____

Briefly describe your volunteer project:

_____

_____

Rate the effectiveness of this project in meeting your developmental needs(s):

1	2	3	4	5
did not meet	partially met	met	exceeded	greatly exceeded

Briefly describe how the project met your developmental objective(s):

_____

_____

How will you apply this learning at Pillsbury?

_____

_____

Would you recommend *Development Through Volunteerism* to other Pillsbury employees?

            Yes   No

AGENCY   Date: _____

Contact Person's Name: _____

Rate the volunteer's effectiveness in meeting the project objective.

1	2	3	4	5
did not meet	partially met	met	exceeded	greatly exceeded

Describe how the volunteer met or did not meet the project objectives:

_____

_____

Would you work with another *Development Through Volunteerism*
Pillsbury employee volunteer?

                Yes   No

Please outline any suggestions for improving the program:

_____

_____

_____

_____

EMPLOYEE'S SUPERVISOR   Date: _____

Name: _____

Would you recommend *Development through Volunteerism* to other
employees?

                Yes   No

Please outline any suggestions for improving the program:

_____

_____

DEVELOPMENT THROUGH VOLUNTEERISM

Project Commitment

Use this commitment form to guide your discussion with the agency representative.

EMPLOYEE VOLUNTEER   Date: _____

Name: _____

M.S. _____ Ext. _____

Title: _____

Employee's objective for the project:

_____

_____

Competency(ies) to be developed:

_____

_____

How much time are you able to give to the agency?
(___ hrs/wk X __ wks)

_____

What support will you need from the agency? (i.e., supplies, equipment, training, access to people and information)

_____

_____

_____

AGENCY   Date: _____

Agency: _____

Contact Person: _____

Address: _____

_____

Phone: _____

Agency Project Objective(s):

_____

_____

_____

_____

What are your expectations of this employee volunteer? (i.e., time
commitment, expected outcome of project, etc.)

_____

_____

_____

COMMITMENT

Duration of this commitment: _____

We agree to the above expectations.

_____   _____
      Employee Volunteer   Agency Contact Person

▼9 A Strategic Approach for Maximizing Volunteering's Value for the For-Profit Organization

9.1 INTRODUCTION

Corporate leaders recognize the value of volunteering in creating, recruiting, and retaining a quality workforce. They understand that the characteristics of top-producing workers can be improved and refined through volunteer activity.[1] A number of studies have documented the immense value of business involvement in the community. A set of studies commissioned by IBM and conducted by UCLA's Professor Lewin examined 156 companies and found that employee morale was up to three times higher in corporate businesses that actively engaged in community activities. The studies concluded that this, in turn, had a positive effect on financial performance.[2]

Chapter 9 will illustrate how a business can develop an employee volunteer program that promotes return value and how existing employee volunteer programs can refine the process. A good plan can greatly increase the return benefit ratio for employees while providing significant benefits for employers.

A number of companies that have employee volunteer programs have noted that volunteering is the newest major benefit for employees. These are companies that have successfully secured quality return value for their employees.

Volunteer employee programs have been successful in businesses of all sizes including the largest global concerns and the smallest local firms. The success of these programs can be attributed to many factors, but every successful program has followed at least two important rules:

1. The plan must be in the interest of the employees; and
2. The business must be sincere in wanting to make a positive contribution to the community.

Traditionally, businesses that successfully engage in an employee volunteering program also have a third motive—improving the image of the business within the community. Most businesses that have developed programs using these three goals have been successful.

Some companies are discovering that there is a lot more to gain from employee volunteer programs, however. This is particularly true in the current work environment which requires greater people skills. Volunteering provides opportunities for employees to learn and experiment with actual experiences in working as a team member, performing leadership tasks, and associating with a diverse group of individuals who have come together to reach a common goal. It is an exciting way to educate employees on contributing and excelling in the new work environment.

A number of companies discussed in this chapter are industry giants who have discovered that employee volunteer programs are good for business. It is not necessary to be an industry giant to have an employee volunteer program in place, however. The development of a program can have a positive effect on the bottom line of any business. Equal benefits can be enjoyed by small firms and Fortune 500 firms alike.

A great deal of material has been devoted to employee volunteer programs such as literature from the Points of Lights Foundation. You should avail yourself of these sources. This chapter will reinforce much of the available literature and it will focus primarily on the return value that the individual employee can receive from a volunteering experience. It will also focus on how employee volunteer programs can benefit an employer.

The exhibits will illustrate, by example, the methods of administering an employee volunteer plan. Blank versions of the exhibits and examples of *actual* business materials created by visionary corporate leaders can be found on the computer disk attached to the inside back cover of this book. Several of the exhibits are sample forms or agendas that can be used by the reader. In the book, the forms have been completed to bring the process alive. The computer disk contains blank versions of these forms that can be downloaded for individual use.

The case study for this chapter will illustrate the value of employee volunteer programs that emphasize return value. It is based on the Jarrett-Anderson Company. Jarrett-Anderson is a small manufacturing business that was established nearly 100 years ago. The founders developed a small engine that could be used for a number of tasks. The engine was reliable and the company gained a reputation as a quality enterprise.

The company started out in a mid-Atlantic state in a small town called Norrisville and remained there. The company expanded and built a manufacturing site in the South and a sales office on the West coast. The company currently has 2500 employees: 1600 at the Norrisville site, 700 in the South, and 200 on the West coast.

The company has been successful for nearly 100 years due to a superior product and little competition. Although the small engine is still their primary product, additional products have been produced in the last ten years in an attempt to diversify. Unfortunately, global competition has affected the sales of small engines. As a result, the company has been forced to cut production and lay off employees, something they have never had to do before. These cutbacks have been a wake-up call for the leaders of the company. They are determined to develop a strategic plan that will help the business survive *and thrive* in this new environment. If the company is to remain vital, however, the leaders will have to do a lot of strategic thinking and they will have to take immediate action. In order to reach a solution to this problem, we will need to focus on the human resources of Jarrett-Anderson. The employees of this company have a sterling reputation for producing quality products that are sought globally. The company's leaders, on the other hand, were slow to recognize significant shifts in the marketplace and vast changes in the way business was being conducted.

The company's human resource department consists of four people at the headquarters and one person at each of the company's other locations. This is not a large department. One of the functions of each of the human resource departments is overseeing an employee volunteer program. The company's program is a basic service that assists employees in finding volunteer positions.

The leaders of Jarrett-Anderson realize that they need to closely examine their entire operation just as the original owners of the company did at the beginning. Due to the complexity of the situation, they felt that an outside expert would be appropriate so they sought and secured a management consultant who specialized in strategic planning, who has agreed to help.

The management consultant reviewed the entire operation and discovered that the company was financially stable and that it produces quality products. The consultant then focused on the people assets of the company and found a quality group of employees who seem to be loyal. He also found that the group has changed over the last ten years, particularly with the expansion to the South and to the West coast. The diversity of the employees increased as transfers became commonplace and as the company hired individuals for new positions.

Cultural differences at the three locations are apparent. The southern plant resulted from a buyout of an existing operation and much of the culture of the old employer is still in place. Although a sales force is located at all three locations, the West coast office is the only location where sales is the exclusive operation. The sales force does most of their business by phone. Customer service is also handled mostly by phone.

The consultant began to understand the problem and, while one part of the company spent time on the development of new products, he began to investigate ways to train employees for the new work environment. A number of new programs were created within the company that proved very beneficial.

The management consultant then began the process of creating an external training program for employees which would educate the employees and place them in actual situations that would demonstrate teamwork, group dynamics, working with individuals in a diverse setting, leadership skills, and many other valuable benefits.

The consultant outlined the basic steps that will assist him with implementing and revitalizing the employee volunteer program. Here are the recommended steps:

1. Institute a corporate needs assessment;
2. Develop a community needs assessment for each of the company's locations;
3. Discover which assets of the company can assist in the full development of the plan;
4. Make sure that the volunteer employee plan is linked to the company's strategic plan;
5. Create a volunteer standard that can measure volunteering's return value;
6. Create opportunities for partnerships with the company;
7. Develop an employee volunteer promotional plan;
8. Determine which areas and not-for-profits to target;
9. Create a volunteer agreement for employees;
10. Conduct an employee volunteer orientation program;
11. Make the first approach to the targeted not-for-profits;
12. Develop the volunteer agreement between not-for-profits and the company;

13. Implement an evaluation plan; and

14. Establish a meaningful recognition program.

9.2   INSTITUTING A CORPORATE NEEDS ASSESSMENT

Jarrett-Anderson's corporate needs assessment should focus on the human element of the company. Jarrett-Anderson needs to increase the value of its personnel so that they can remain competitive.

In order to do this, the company needs to discover the individual needs of each employee. This is an important step in ensuring that the employee volunteer program provides the necessary components for providing maximum value to meet corporate priorities, community needs, and employee interests.

A review of the corporate needs or priorities that can be supported by a volunteer program are highlighted. An employee volunteering program can assist Jarrett-Anderson in a number of ways:

1. Employees can experience how important decisions are accomplished through collective interaction;
2. Employees can learn that challenging and exciting changes are occurring;
3. Employees' morale can be increased through the satisfaction of helping others;
4. Employees can experiment with management techniques in real situations;
5. Professional skills, such as group dynamics and leadership traits, can be gained;
6. Teamwork training can be accomplished individually or with other employees on group projects;
7. Individuals' personal needs can be satisfied;
8. The company and the community can work together in reaching mutual goals;
9. The company can offer a lot to the community; and
10. The community can provide a wealth of support for the company.

Employees' interests can be discovered and heightened through surveys and focus groups. This also provides a great opportunity to meet with employees individually to discuss their needs. The information gained through this process can be incredibly valuable.

The consultant understands that the employee volunteer program that was already in place provided some of the traditional benefits that the company made as past priorities, namely service to the employee and to the community. The company feels that these services were good for employee morale and that they projected a positive image to the community.

While this is an accurate assessment, the management consultant wants to build on this tradition by looking at company *and* employee needs to discover the best way to design the employee volunteer program for increased return value. When the data was collected from the needs assessment forms, it became obvious that the most important need was people skills training. Thus, company and employee needs are interwoven with each other.

The consultant developed a list. Exhibit 9.1 provides a review of part of that list. The list was divided into four major employee levels or categories of positions at Jarrett-Anderson—executive and management, sales force, assembly areas, and office staff. Each individual employee is listed under the appropriate category. A comment was made under the remarks column next to the name of each employee. The comments varied, but they reflect the most urgent need for each particular employee to address.

EXHIBIT 9.1 The Corporate Needs Assessment

Company:	Jarrett-Anderson
Chief Executive Officer:	Ann Anderson, President
Outside Council:	The Management Consultant
Date:	November 10, 1997

Level	Individuals	Remarks	Action Step
Executives/ Management	Henry Jarrett, Exec. VP Jane Curtis, HR Dir	Next CEO More creative	External network Other operations
Sales Force (All three locations)	Richard Smith (List additional names)	Face-to-face selling	Human relations skills
Assembly Crews (Both locations)	Joseph Ryan (List additional names)	Increase production	Diversity skills
Office Staff (At headquarters)	Kate Johnson (List additional names)	Overall operations	Project development

Henry Jarrett, Executive Vice President, needs to be prepared to become the next president of the company. This is not a simple task. Where will he receive this training? Richard Smith, a sales representative, needs to acquire face-to-face sales experience because most of the company's sales have been over the telephone. Joseph Ryan, a line supervisor, needs skills in motivating employees to be more productive. Kate Johnson, an office manager, needs to discover ways of refining the office's operations. This list includes all 2,500 employees. The process will prove to be a valuable way of focusing on the internal personnel needs of the company.

9.3 DEVELOPING A COMMUNITY NEEDS ASSESSMENT FOR EACH OF THE COMPANY'S LOCATIONS

The company needs assessment for Jarrett-Anderson is quite revealing. It documents the need for company employees to gain insight and training from external sources. The consultant knows that there are ample volunteer opportunities to expose all 2500 employees to the activities that will provide the training each individual needs.

The consultant set about accomplishing this task. He created a community needs assessment form. Exhibits 9.2, 9.3, and 9.4 show the model that he used for each of the company's three locations. While several models exist, he felt that this model was the easiest to work with and it could be used in all three sites. The assessment consisted of a descriptive overview of each community and their political and social structures. Most importantly, the assessment listed the leading not-for-profits in each area, the key contacts at each institution, and the company employees that are closest to that person. An actual community assessment should be more detailed, but for our purposes the three reviews provide the information and differences needed to illustrate the proper points.

It was fascinating to discover the differences in the locations and how they related to the company. The Norrisville community where Jarrett-Anderson's headquarters and its major plant operations are located has a number of advantages and disadvantages. Its mid-Atlantic location provides a number of "quality of life" advantages; however, the employees in this area do not have a great deal of experience in dealing with diversity issues.

The southern community location, on the other hand, deals well with diversity issues but it does not have a stable employee base. The West coast sales office is completely different from the other two locations. They

EXHIBIT 9.2 The Community Needs Assessment—Norrisville

Company:	Jarrett-Anderson
Community:	Norrisville
Chief Executive Officer:	Ann Anderson, President
Marketing Director:	James Edison, Vice President
HR Director:	Jane Curtis, HR Director
Date:	November 11, 1997

Description of Community

A small rural town in a mid-Atlantic state situated near several key business/
metro areas. Most of the employees live within 12 miles of the headquarters and
reside in a variety of communities: rural areas 35%, small towns 30%, and suburban areas of mid-size city areas 35%.

Political and Social Structure of the Community

The area has a variety of local government structures within the 12-mile radius of
the company's headquarters. There are five service clubs, seven United Ways,
and 43 not-for-profits. Most of the community structure depends on its linkage
with external groups or organizations in the nearby metro areas.

The Organizations and/or Services within the Community That Have a Reputation for Quality

1. The Norrisville United Way
2. The Sports Group
3. The High Adventure Brigade
4. Bread for the Homeless
5. The Greater Region School District

Key Contacts Made within the Community

Contact	Company Representative Closest to Individual
1. Joyce Keyes, Superintendent of Schools	Jane Curtis, HR Dir.
2. Douglas Fairway, CEO of QWE, Inc.	James Jarrett, IV, Chairman 1997 Chair, United Way
3. Kathy Single, Program Chair, The Sports Gp.	Ann Anderson, President
4. Wayne Green, Ex. Dir., High Ad. Brigade	John Anderson, Vice Chair
5. John Gill, Chair, Bread for the Homeless	Jane Curtis, HR Dir.

EXHIBIT 9.3 The Community Needs Assessment—Southern Community

Company:	Jarrett-Anderson
Community:	Southern Community
Plant Manager:	Paul Brown, Manager
HR Coordinator:	Roberto Rodriguez, HR Representative
Date:	November 13, 1997

Description of Community

The plant operations are located near a mid- to large city near the Mexican border. Most of the employees live within five miles of the company facilities. The employee base, like the community, is highly diverse.

Political and Social Structure of the Community

Although the area near or around the plant has one form of government, a mayor/city council model, the city and surrounding areas are governed by a number of local or neighborhood groups who can make or break the election of a city council representative. One United Way and 67 not-for-profits serve the needs of the community.

The Organizations and/or Services within the Community That Have a Reputation for Quality

1. The Southern United Way
2. The Neighborhood Alliance
3. The Hispanic Coalition for Education
4. Youth in Action
5. The Southern Business Council

Key Contacts Made within the Community

Contact	Company Representative Closest to Individual
1. John Harrison, Ex. Dir., S. United Way	Paul Brown, Manager
2. Mary Robinson, Pres., The Neigh. All.	Roberto Rodriguez, HR Representative
3. Diego Rivera, Dir., Hispanic Coalition	Roberto Rodriguez, HR Representative
4. Kim Quan, Coordinator, Youth in Action	William Wallace, Line Supervisor
5. Jason Simon, VP TFR., Inc., Board Member of Southern Bus. Council	Paul Brown, Manager

EXHIBIT 9.4 The Community Needs Assessment—West Coast Community

Company:	Jarrett-Anderson
Community:	West Coast Community
Sales Manager:	Janet Johnson, Sales Manager
HR Coordinator:	James West, HR Representative
Date:	November 15, 1997

Description of Community

The sales office for Jarrett-Anderson on the West coast is located in a suburban area near a major city. Most employees live within a 25-mile radius of the office in a number of bedroom communities throughout the area.

Political and Social Structure of the Community

The political structure of the communities that surround the office varies. While the nearby city does not have official jurisdiction, it does have a great influence on the social aspects of the overall community. The area has 12 United Ways and 141 not-for-profits. Although the area is highly populated, it does not have a sense of community.

The Organizations and/or Services within the Community That Have a Reputation for Quality

1. The West Coast United Way
2. The Greater Arts Council
3. The Business Leaders Alliance
4. The Environmental Coalition
5. Greater Area Food Pantry

Key Contacts Made within the Community

Contact	Company Representative Closest to Individual
1. Thomas Tilus, board member, W.C. United Way	Janet Johnson, Sales Manager
2. Anthony Rizzo, Ex. Dir., G. Arts Council	James West, HR Representative
3. Doris Hanson, President, Bus. Ldrs. Alliance	Janet Johnson, Sales Manager
4. Henry Aaron, board member, Environmental C.	Daniel Lion, Sales Representative
5. Marin Adams, Dir., Greater A.	Linda Short, Sales Representative

do not have plant operations but they do have a group of employees who need training in the art of selling face-to-face.

In each location, the consultant identified not-for-profits that are leaders in the community. In addition, key contacts from each of the not-for-profits were identified as well as a Jarrett-Anderson representative who had the ability to contact and meet with the contact. The not-for-profits varied in mission, but each had the potential to assist Jarrett-Anderson in the revitalization of its employee volunteer program.

9.4   ASSESSING COMPANY ASSETS

In preparing for the development of a dynamic employee volunteer program that emphasizes return value for its employees and has a powerful effect on the company, the management consultant knew that the company would need to come to the table with something of value for the not-for-profit. Therefore, he went on a mission to discover the hidden assets of the company.

Although the research process revealed pages of valuable information, the consultant condensed everything into one page. Exhibit 9.5 provides an example of what the consultant found. The document is divided into two listings for each of the company's locations—overall assets and local assets. It is fascinating to discover what kinds of areas can become major benefits.

(a)   Overall Assets

1. The company is well known by the average consumer. This has always been a plus and it may be of assistance in attracting partnerships with not-for-profits on various projects;
2. Employees have good feelings about the company. They are proud of their association with Jarrett-Anderson. This provides a positive base and it will be of great help in working closely with each employee to increase the return value of their future volunteering experiences; and
3. The primary product the company sells, a small engine, can become a resource in creating new volunteer experiences.

(b)   Headquarters: Norrisville

1. Jarrett-Anderson is the only major company in the area. This places the company in a powerful bargaining position. In fact, not-for- profits have traditionally approached the company for volunteers and funding;

EXHIBIT 9.5 Assessment of Company Assets

Company:	Jarrett-Anderson

Overall Assets

- The company is known by most consumers;
- The main product, the small engine, is a fine product that can be used for a number of applications;
- The employees overall have been loyal and productive;
- The company has a network that spans the globe; and
- The company is known for standing behind its products.

Headquarters - Norrisville

- The company is highly respected in the area;
- It is the largest employer in the area;
- Hundreds of employees are highly skilled mechanics;
- The company leadership, although descendants of the original owners, are involved and knowledgeable about the product they sell; and
- The company has facilities that could be used for a number of activities.

The Southern Plant

- Although the company name is well known, the plant was once run by another company whose culture is still part of the operations. Part of the culture could be beneficial at the company's other two sites.
- The workforce has kept up to the level needed to produce quality engines; and
- The plant is located in an area that would make it accessible for use for volunteer activities.

The West Coast Office

- The employees are all highly skilled salespeople;
- The sales office is in the heart of one of the busiest locales in the country; and
- The sales office has the ability to help refine the image of the company.

2. The employees at this location have a variety of skills that lend themselves well to volunteering. This includes group volunteering efforts and top leadership opportunities; and
3. The company has facilities that can be used to further the volunteer plan.

(i)   The Southern Plant

1. The culture of the operations varies a great deal from the headquarters facility, yet certain of these qualities can be real assets in the Norrisville or West coast locations;
2. The southern employees understand the needs of the community; and
3. The plant is located close to community needs. The company facilities can be used to fulfill these needs.

(ii)   The West Coast Office

1. The West coast office is far different from the other sites. It is located in an office building in a large suburban area outside of a large city. It is not visible or known by the general public but it is known within the profession as a highly skilled group;
2. The office is near one of the largest media hubs in the world; and
3. The most flexible and creative employees are at this location.

The management consultant was pleased with what he found. A number of assets are already in place. All that is needed is a repackaging process that will create attractive bargaining chips to present to targeted not-for-profits who will assist in revitalizing the company's employee volunteer program.

9.5   MAKING SURE THAT THE VOLUNTEER EMPLOYEE PLAN IS LINKED TO THE COMPANY'S STRATEGIC PLAN

The management consultant was getting more and more excited about the prospects of the employee volunteer program being the key to the Jarrett-Anderson turn-around plan. In this case, the company had a strategic plan that only needed a few refinements. He knew that the volunteer employee plan needed to be part of the company's strategic plan. In fact, he could recall a number of companies who had initiated ideas to assist communities and fulfill corporate goals at the same time.

Shell Oil Company's National-Disaster-Relief-Efforts provided a wonderful example of how a company can assist the community through the direct help of employees. In fact, Shell received help from employees at all levels, from local retailers to corporate headquarters. When Hurricane Andrew struck southern Florida, local Shell dealers, jobbers, and employees contacted Shell to see how they could help William Schutzenhofer, Vice

President for Marketing, put together a relief plan within 24 hours.[3] This would never have been possible if the concept had not been in the employee volunteer plan at Shell. The genius of the plan is that it provided instant value in a situation that needed an immediate response. It involved employees who were attracted to the volunteer experience and it involved the use of Shell equipment, products, and skills to make it work.

Linking the employee volunteer plan to the strategic plan of the company ensures that return value for the employee and the business gets the attention that it deserves. In the case of Jarrett-Anderson, the consultant saw three main areas in which the employee volunteer plan could be linked to the strategic plan: personal, corporate giving, and marketing plan goals. Exhibit 9.6 is an outline of possible relationships.

EXHIBIT 9.6 Linking the Employee Volunteer Plan to the Company's Strategic Plan

Area	Reason
Personnel	-The ability to train employees in skills that are needed to remain competitive. -To focus training on each employee's need. -To have the ability to place employees in teams of highly motivated and dedicated people. -To encourage a more diverse multi-cultural experience. -To increase morale and, therefore, individual productivity. -To determine the value that is given to the community and also the return value received by the employee who volunteered.
Corporate Giving	-To link corporate giving with the goals of the company. -To develop package programs that include both volunteers and financial giving. -To determine the value that is given to the community and also the return value given back to the community through a link of the employee volunteer program to the corporate giving program.
Marketing Plan	-Certain aspects of the marketing plan can be enhanced through the employee volunteer program.

(a)   Personnel

Strategic planning goals that pertain to company personnel often have a direct relationship to employee volunteer programs. One of Jarrett-Anderson's prime goals is to teach employees skills that will help them remain competitive. Individual or focused training will be needed to accomplish this goal.

The need for training in multi-cultural experiences due to the increased diversity of the workforce is another major goal. So is improving morale and increasing productivity. These goals seemed daunting until Jarrett-Anderson realized that these needs could be satisfied through an employee volunteer program that places emphasis on return benefits. They will simply need to seek and obtain the proper return value to bring employees up to speed and to keep them there.

(b)   Corporate Giving

Corporations have a long tradition of being generous to not-for-profits through their corporate giving programs. These programs have included everything from direct donations to gifts for local United Way campaigns that direct the money to individual programs.

Jarrett-Anderson has provided $2 million a year to various charities near the corporate headquarters, $1 million to charities near the southern plant, and $200,000 to charities near the West coast sales office. Although the company has received recognition for these gifts, they have not gotten much more. In many cases, the gifts were totally unknown to the general public.

The management consultant saw an opportunity to use the same money to gain greater recognition and an increased return on their investment. He did this by linking most of the corporate giving to the employee volunteer program. The company's new volunteer program will offer a combined package of funding and employee volunteers to targeted not-for-profits. In the process, they will accomplish worthwhile activities but there will be an understanding that the projects must be engineered to fulfill employee and company needs.

(c)   Marketing Plan

The employee volunteer plan has a natural link to a company's marketing plan. For example, Jarrett-Anderson could use its small engine in various ways to assist the community. This is a wonderful way to show the company's dedication to the community and it is a great way to expose potential customers to the product. Training young people on how to build the engine and how to use it provides a source of future employees and customers. Jarrett-Anderson discovered a number of ways that the company can fulfill its marketing goals by supporting the employee volunteer program.

9.6   THE VOLUNTEER STANDARD

The management consultant created a standard so that Jarrett-Anderson could measure its employee volunteer program. The standard is simple and direct. Exhibit 9.7 provides an outline.

The company decided that it will only conduct business with organizations that have been documented as not-for-profit by the government. In the case of most organizations, the governing body with jurisdiction is the Internal Revenue Service who assesses potential not-for-profits under the requirements listed in Section 501(c) of the Internal Revenue Code. Foreign not-for-profits possess similar credentials.

The services of each volunteer employee must benefit individuals or the community. They must not be a self-serving exercise because this would destroy the entire purpose of volunteering.

Each volunteer act needs to be documented to determine its worth for everyone involved. This is not designed to fulfill personnel records. Rather, it is to make certain that each volunteer experience fulfills the required needs.

Recognition is an important factor and it should be part of all volunteer experiences. It should include both the employee volunteer and the

---

EXHIBIT 9.7 The Volunteer Standard

1. The volunteer experience must be conducted with a not-for-profit organization that is actively classified in good standing under the laws and regulations of the country(s) where it is conducting business.
2. The volunteer acts by each employee must provide a service or goods to an individual(s) and/or community.
3. The volunteer experience needs to be documented by the employee who volunteers and by the company representative.
4. Recognition needs to be given to the employee and to the not-for-profit for their service.
5. A full evaluation of the volunteer experience takes place to ensure that the experience was beneficial for all who were involved.

---

not-for-profit that is involved. Jarrett-Anderson developed a plan that provided enough recognition to meet this standard.

Finally, an evaluation program will be put in place that assists in maintaining and enhancing proper standards. This is important because it ensures that the plan is always evolving and improving.

9.7   CREATING OPPORTUNITIES FOR PARTNERSHIPS WITH THE COMPANY

The management consultant now has enough background information on Jarrett-Anderson and the needs in each of its communities. The next step is making a value judgment about the general activities and projects that the company's employee volunteer program could be of assistance to. At this point, the ideas will provide a basis to begin to form plans. Not all these ideas will be appropriate and some additional ideas will surface.

Exhibit 9.8 outlines the opportunities that the consultant thought would provide quality volunteer experiences while also providing a significant service to the community. The projects were created based on the company's needs and they focused on the top five not-for-profits in each of the company's locations. The projects are designed to provide value to the not-for-profit and to the community in general.

Henry Jarrett, Executive Vice President and heir apparent to the presidency, will be able to network and act in a leadership role through his work with the Norrisville United Way. The small sales force at the Norrisville headquarters will be able to improve their sales techniques by becoming coaches for the local athletic league. The technicians will help out with the High Adventure Brigade's annual jamboree which will give them experience in working with a diverse population. The office staff will assist the Bread for the Homeless by helping to feed 600 people over three weekends. This will give them organizational skills. Finally, young supervisors will have an opportunity to improve their training skills by helping the Norrisville Regional School District train students on small engine repair.

The southern plant and the West coast sales office have planned similar programs that provide new and exciting volunteer opportunities. All of these experiences will provide real growth potential for employees. In addition, they are solid methods for fulfilling company strategic goals and they provide great opportunities to make quality contributions to the community.

EXHIBIT 9.8 Partnership Opportunities

Company:	Jarrett-Anderson
Date:	December 2, 1997

Headquarters: Norrisville

-The use of top executives as key leaders in the Norrisville United Way;

-To provide coaches for the spring sports programs with the Sports Group;

-To provide technical support for lighting the Jamboree for the High Adventure Brigade;

-To provide employee volunteers and funding to help feed the homeless through Bread for the Homeless; and

-To develop an ongoing relationship with the Greater Region School District to train students on small engine repair.

The Southern Plant

-To provide teams of employees to assist the Southern United Way campaign;

-To provide funding and employee volunteer time to assist in strengthening the Neighborhood Alliance;

-Work with the Hispanic Coalition for Education to ensure that youth are given the opportunity to be taught various trades and pre-college programs;

-Create a program to promote youth activities through Youth in Action; and

-Get top management involved in the Southern Business Council.

The West Coast Sales Office

-Offer key sales executives as loan executives to the West Coast United Way;

-Find a way for Janet Johnson, sales manager, to secure a volunteer position with the Greater Arts Council;

-Make sure the company becomes an active player with the Business Leaders Alliance;

-Offer funding and volunteer assistance to a meaningful project that could be developed and managed by the company for the Environmental Coalition; and

-Offer assistance to the Greater Area Food Pantry in a sales and marketing area.

9.8 DEVELOPING AN EMPLOYEE VOLUNTEER PROMOTIONAL PLAN

The management consultant is now ready to develop the approaches that the company will need to make to the selected not-for-profits. Exhibit 9.9 provides a guide for this part of the process.

Now that the general needs of the company have been determined and the general volunteer program ideas are listed, it is time to engage employees in the process. The preliminary ideas listed on the employee surveys now need more clarification.

The management consultant has suggested that an employee task force be developed. This can help the company clarify the existing volunteer ideas and assist them with any new ideas that may surface from internal or external sources. The task force would help link potential projects with employees' interests.

A key person will be designated by the company to make the initial approach to the not-for-profit. The approach will vary depending on who is being contacted and who is making the contact. A meeting will be arranged with each not-for-profit to review the idea or concept and to determine the targeted organization's interest. Of course, there will be a detailed sum-

---

EXHIBIT 9.9 The Employee Volunteer Promotional Plan

1. Determine the personal needs of the company and how volunteering may be able to assist;
2. Develop a task force of employees to determine the types of volunteer opportunities that they might be interested in doing in relationship to both community and employee needs;
3. Link the needs expressed to appropriate not-for-profit groups in the area;
4. Develop a cultivation plan for each targeted not-for-profit;
5. Find a key person to make the initial contact;
6. The key person makes the contact with the not-for-profit(s);
7. Meet with the not-for-profit(s);
8. Determine interest and discover if the not-for-profit is able and willing to provide return value. Schedule a second meeting with the not-for-profits who wish to partner;
9. Develop a volunteer agreement/brief proposal based on the agreed plan; and
10. Meet with not-for-profits who have agreed to partner and present the volunteer agreement/proposal brief.

---

mary of the benefits that the company wants its employees to receive and the benefits that the company is willing to provide in return. If everything works out, an agreement will be created that outlines each important provision and it will be presented to the not-for-profit for approval.

9.9 DETERMINING WHICH AREAS AND NOT-FOR-PROFITS TO TARGET

The management consultant is ready to assist the company in selecting the initial areas and not-for-profits that they might create partnerships with to implement meaningful projects and activities. Most of the final decisions are based on the previous data that determined the leading not-for-profits in each company location. Exhibit 9.10 provides an outline of the results.

In each case, a key person has been identified. These individuals have various roles within their not-for-profits and may be everything from volunteers to professionals. Each person was selected, however, for the influence they have within their organization.

In order to access these individuals, a key employee who has the best relationship with the individual from the not-for-profit has been chosen. Each employee will be briefed on the project and will be requested to make an initial contact with the person from the not-for-profit.

The selection of each project or not-for-profit is based on the needs of the company and the type or quality of organizations that are available. It is important that this is based on a comprehensive research plan that involves company officials and various levels of employees. The management consultant is well aware of this preparation and he will base his selection on the ample information and ideas derived from company records and from Jarrett-Anderson employees directly.

9.10 THE INITIAL MEETING WITH THE TARGETED NOT-FOR-PROFITS

The time has come to meet with the targeted not-for-profits to determine if either entity is interested in working together. The management consultant has met with each of the key employees to coach them on the best way to approach each not-for-profit. He has also determined who should attend the face-to-face meeting with them.

Exhibit 9.11 shows the suggested agenda prepared by the management consultant. The agenda emphasizes the necessary preparation for

EXHIBIT 9.10 Determining the Areas and Not-For-Profits to Target

Company: Jarrett-Anderson
Date: December 18, 1997

Company Locales	Not-For-Profits	Key Employee	Key Person
Norrisville	-Norrisville United Way	Jim Jarrett	Doug Fairway
	-The Sports Group	Ann Anderson	Kathy Single
	-The High Adventure Brigade	John Anderson	Wayne Green
	-Bread for the Homeless	Jane Curtis	John Gill
	-The Greater Region School Dist.	Jane Curtis	Joyce Keyes
Southern Plant	-The Southern United Way	Paul Brown	John Harrison
	-The Neighborhood Alliance	Roberto Rodriguez	Mary Robinson
	-The Hispanic Coalition for Ed.	Roberto Rodriguez	Diego Rivera
	-Youth in Action	William Wallace	Kim Quan
	-The Southern Business Council	Paul Brown	Jason Simon
West Coast Sales Office	-The West Coast United Way	Janet Johnson	Thomas Tilus
	-The Greater Arts Council	James West	Anthony Rizzo
	-The Business Leaders Alliance	Janet Johnson	Doris Hanson
	-The Environmental Coalition	Daniel Lion	Henry Aaron
	-Greater Area Food Pantry	Linda Short	Marin Adams

such a meeting. This preparation includes having an agenda in the first place and creating a volunteer proposal based on the requirements of the proposed project.

The meeting should be held away from the company's offices and, if possible, at the not-for-profit's facilities. This is a visible demonstration that the company does not wish to be the center focus of the project.

The heart of the agenda is the development of a relationship between the not-for-profit and the company. This area provides an opportunity for

---

EXHIBIT 9. 11 The Initial Meeting with the Targeted Not-For-Profit

---

I. Pre-meeting
   -Develop an agenda to follow even though the meeting may be on a casual basis; and
   -Bring a brief volunteer proposal to present.

II. The Meeting
   -Thank the volunteer representative for meeting with you;
   -Note that you have an opportunity to work in partnership with the not-for-profit;
   -Present the volunteer proposal;
   -Note the highlights of the volunteer opportunity and how it can benefit the not-for-profit;
   -Also note how it can help your employees as well;
   -Provide time for a reaction and take notes;
   -Negotiate and try to develop a plan that will also fit the needs of the not-for-profit;
   -Inquire about how the not-for-profit provides recognition; and
   -Be sure to get information on the evaluation process to be used.

III. Post-meeting
   -Send a thank you letter and confirm the arrangement.

---

each side to become acquainted with the other and to discuss the proposed project to see if it fulfills the not-for-profit's mission. Not-for-profits cannot afford to engage in unrelated projects that take away from the core work of the institution. It is always best to develop a project around a specific need or, at least, to be flexible enough to adapt your needs to a current need of the not-for-profit.

It is unusual for a company to present such a proposal, so do not be surprised if this takes some explanation during your initial approach. Most not-for-profits approach for-profits with sections of a project or requests for funding that fit their current agendas. For-profits presenting projects that provide volunteer and funding support will be more than welcomed, however, if the company is flexible enough to ensure that it addresses a real need.

The initial meeting is an important first step in a relationship that can last for years. Make sure that the not-for-profit understands your needs and make sure you understand their needs. The best part of a well-designed volunteer partnership is that everyone can benefit from it, including the not-for-profit, the community, the employee volunteer, and the company.

9.11 DEVELOPING THE VOLUNTEER AGREEMENT BETWEEN THE NOT-FOR-PROFIT AND THE COMPANY

The volunteer agreement between a not-for-profit and the company is not designed to be complicated or restrictive. It is simply designed to contain the goals that each side wants to meet. The agreement can be more detailed and it can contain more return value provisions. The best agreements, however, are as short and clearly defined as possible. Exhibit 9.12 is a sample document.

Notice that Jarrett-Anderson and the Bread for the Homeless has decided to develop a joint project called, "Feed the Hungry." The company will provide a number of resources including volunteers, funding, food, and management personnel. Bread for the Homeless has agreed to provide sufficient support and to allow two management support persons to see how the not-for-profit is organized.

9.12 CONDUCTING AN EMPLOYEE VOLUNTEER ORIENTATION PROGRAM

The employee volunteer program is now official. Jarrett-Anderson has made a commitment as a company, the local not-for-profits have an interest, and the employees have helped to formulate the plan.

Now it is time to inform all of the employees about the plan and to articulate the advantages of becoming involved. The program now needs quality support literature. This kind of literature will be different for every company and for every project. The Points of Light Foundation, however, is an excellent source of materials that may give you some ideas. The Points of Light Foundation locations can be found on the computer disk on the inside back cover of this book.

The agenda listed in Exhibit 9.13 is a good outline of an orientation session. This orientation plan calls for a formal meeting of company employees to make them fully acquainted with the employee volunteer program. This may not be practical for a number of employee groups, however. If it is not appropriate to hold a gathering, there are several other ways to inform employees about the program. The important thing is that employees become aware of the program and how it can help both them and the local community.

The most important part of the orientation plan is to ensure that all employees understand the advantages of being involved.

EXHIBIT 9.12 The For-Profit and Not-For-Profit Volunteering Agreement

Company:	Jarrett-Anderson
Key Contact:	Jane Curtis, HR Director
Not-For-Profit:	Bread for the Homeless
Key Contact:	John Gill, Chair
Project:	"Feed the Hungry"
Date:	December 21, 1997

The Company:

Jarrett-Anderson agrees to support the "Feed the Hungry" project with the following resources:

-75 volunteers for three weekends to prepare and serve food;

-$25,000 to assist Bread for the Homeless operating expense;.

-6 tons of assorted food ordered via Bread for the Homeless; and

-2 management support persons.

The Not-For-Profit:

Bread for the Homeless agrees to support the volunteers from Jarrett-Anderson in the following ways:

-Six support staff will be coordinating the three weekends and will provide direct guidance;

-The facility will be prepared to meet the support that will be needed;

-Special recognition at the event will occur for each volunteer and a special recognition certificate will be given to each volunteer at our next major meeting;

-As per our agreement, we will ensure that the two management support persons will be provided opportunities to work with the board during the process to obtain more insight on the management function of the organization; and

-An evaluation component will also be in place.

This is a flexible agreement that is designed to provide all parties, and in particular the volunteers, with a beneficial volunteer experience. It is also designed to ensure that the project provides the end result intended—to feed homeless people with nourishing food.

Jane Curtis	Date	John Gill	Date

EXHIBIT 9.13 The Employee Volunteer Orientation Session

Opening	Conducted by the highest corporate executive possible
History of Employee Volunteering Program at the Company	Community Relations Director (CRD)
Important Role of Volunteering in Community	CRD
The Return Value of Volunteering	CRD
The Company's Investment	CRD
The Recognition Plan	CRD
The Evaluation Component	CRD
The Review of Volunteer Opportunities	CRD
How to Select a Volunteer Position	CRD
Questions/Answers	CRD

9.13   THE EMPLOYEE VOLUNTEER AGREEMENT

The Employee Volunteer Agreement is an important step for the company and for the employees who will volunteer. Exhibit 9.14 is an example of a simple agreement.

Roberto Rodriguez has agreed to chair a major project at the Hispanic Coalition for Education. The agreement cites all of the goals that Roberto will need to achieve and it includes the support that the company will provide to ensure that the project is successful.

This can be a dynamic learning experience for the volunteer. It can provide a meaningful project for the not-for-profit and the company can receive a wealth of information and knowledge. The agreement simply clarifies these points and pinpoints the important roles that everyone will play.

9.14   IMPLEMENTING AN EVALUATION PLAN

The evaluation of each volunteer experience or group project is important. The evaluation is not designed as a tool for dwelling on the negative outcomes. Rather, it is a positive review of the exciting experiences that

EXHIBIT 9.14 The Employee Volunteer Agreement

Company:	Jarrett-Anderson
Employee:	Roberto Rodriguez
Not-For-Profit:	The Hispanic Coalition for Education
Project:	The Pro-Education Project
Volunteer Position:	Project Chair
Date:	December 20, 1997

Jarrett-Anderson is delighted to provide the opportunity for you to develop a partnership project with The Hispanic Coalition for Education. This is a highly visible position that will demand significant time and energy for you to succeed. This is a volunteer position that you have created to assist in the implementation of this important project and that you are committed to for at least two years to ensure its success.

In order for the position and the project to be successful, you will need to meet the following standards:
- Act as an active chair of the project;
- Recruit 35 members of the committee who have leadership potential;
- Preside over the quarterly meetings of the project;
- Attend the monthly board meetings of the coalition to report progress and to coordinate;
- Recruit 32 students for the first year, and 64 students for the second year.

Jarrett-Anderson will support you and the project in the following manner by:
- Allowing you to spend eight hours per week as a loan executive to the project;
- Making available use of company facilities in rooms 7, 9, and 11 upon written request;
- Providing three instructors for 40 hours each; and
- Contributing $50,000 year one and $100,000 year two, or a total of $150,000, to the Coalition to assist in their expenses.

The evaluation component will be conducted as a joint effort between you, Jarrett-Anderson, and the Coalition. This process is designed to ensure that your volunteer experience will be productive for you and the other parties involved. We are delighted that you have developed and accepted this challenging and rewarding volunteer opportunity.

Roberto Rodriguez	Date	Paul Brown	Date

individuals had through volunteering. Specifically, it is a method of refining the program, encouraging personal growth, fostering additional partnerships, and improving the quality of life within the community.

Exhibit 9.15 illustrates one way to evaluate a volunteer project. This particular evaluation comes from a partnership between Jarrett-Anderson and the Greater Arts Council. The project involved the Greater Arts Exhibit. Twelve employees were involved and each employee completed an evaluation form. A composite and totals are placed in the exhibit. The nine questions were easy to understand and complete, yet they were important ways of measuring success for Jarrett-Anderson.

Questions one and two provide insight on the support that the not-for-profit provided. This is good information to obtain because it is one way of determining if the company should entertain another project with the not-for-profit. Questions three through eight are core questions that help determine the return value that the company received. Question nine will help to determine whether or not the experience provided the return value for the community.

The last part of the questionnaire provides room for the volunteer to deliver a personal response. Did the experience fulfill personal needs and how could the volunteer activity have been a better experience? There is also room for additional comments.

This questionnaire can assist in refining future projects, ensuring that volunteers' desires are fulfilled, and seeing that the company benefits as well.

9.15   THE EMPLOYEE VOLUNTEER RECOGNITION PLAN

It is important to have a quality recognition program for volunteers. Most not-for-profits will have a recognition program in place as well, but it should never be a substitute for a separate, company plan. The forms of recognition can range from very basic awards to extravagantly elaborate banquets. It is up to each individual company to decide what they want to do.

Exhibit 9.16 is an example of what Jarrett-Anderson provided for individual employee volunteers and for volunteers who were involved in group employee volunteering experiences. The management consultant advised the company that powerful symbols of value could take the form of thank-you letters, recognition pieces, recognition for tenure, and a review of the return value that each employee received.

EXHIBIT 9.15 The Employee Volunteer Evaluation Questionnaire

Company:	Jarrett-Anderson
Volunteer Activity:	The Greater Arts Exhibit
Not-For-Profit:	The Greater Arts Council
Number of Volunteers Involved:	12
Number of Hours:	135
Contribution:	$15,000
Number of Participants:	625

Please answer the following questions based on individual opinions of the employees who volunteered for this project (with 1 being the lowest and 5 the highest).

Question	Answer
1. Leadership role of the not-for-profit	4
2. Guidance given	3
3. Real value to the community	4
4. Teamwork skills gained	2
5. Strategic planning conducted	1
6. Opportunity to work with different constituencies	2
7. Making new contacts	4
8. Committee and board experience	3
9. Satisfaction of helping others	4
Total	27/45

10. How did the experience fulfill your personal needs?
    (List all comments)

11. What would you change to make this a better experience?
    (List all comments)

12. Other comments?
    (List all comments)

_____   _____

Employee Volunteer Program Coordinator   Date

EXHIBIT 9.16 The Employee Volunteer Recognition Plan

Company:　　　　　　　　　Jarrett-Anderson
Date:　　　　　　　　　　　December 28, 1997

Individual Employee Plan

All employees who participate in the company employee volunteer program through either an individual or group volunteer experience will be eligible for the recognition program:

1. Each employee will receive a letter thanking them for volunteering.
2. Each volunteer will have their name placed in the annual report on the company volunteer program.
3. Individuals' recognition pieces will be presented at the annual recognition gathering.
4. Each employee will be given one day off for each 150 hours of service.
5. Employee volunteers will be recognized for their tenure starting after the first year. This will be in the form of pins and other recognitions in the workplace.
6. Volunteering service will be placed in the employee record.
7. Employees will be individually assisted, if desired, to gain as much return value as possible from their volunteer experiences.

Group Employee Plan

A number of employee volunteer experiences are conducted through employee group volunteering. Therefore, in additional to the individual benefits provided, our company will provide added recognition for volunteering when it occurs through group activity:

1. Groups will be recognized for each volunteer activity that they perform;
2. Group volunteers will be provided a social event as a group;
3. Groups will be honored on the recognition wall and other appropriate locales; and
4. Groups will be honored in the annual report of the employee volunteer program.

Group volunteering should have recognition programs directed to both the individual and to the group. This can have profound results for the individual volunteer, the group, and the company itself.

Recognition programs can be the bridge to thanking the person who volunteers and they can be a way to enhance the company's employee volunteer program. They can also be a way of marketing volunteering to new employees and a way of making previous volunteers want to repeat the process year after year.

9.16 CONCLUSION

The strategic approach for maximizing volunteering's value for the for-profit organization is an important tool for corporate leaders who want to project a positive community image and experience benefits that can increase productivity. Businesses who do not have employee volunteer programs should seriously consider them. Companies who have programs in place need to refine and develop them so that they complement the for-profit's overall strategic plan.

The employee volunteer program can provide real return value to the employees who are involved. These values range from the personal satisfaction of helping others to gaining tangible career skills. The skills that are gained through volunteering can increase employee morale and make individuals more productive at the workplace. Volunteering, therefore, can have real bottom line value to a company while still providing a vital service to the community.

Meaningful volunteering can only occur, however, if the for-profit realizes the potential of volunteering and understands the process of creating and maintaining a quality employee volunteer program. This effort includes awareness of the individual employee needs and the community resources that are available to fulfill those needs.

Well-designed employee volunteer programs should be a key part of the strategic plan of the business. They should link personnel training functions, marketing, sales, and corporate charitable giving to a strategic effort to practice good corporate citizenship and to maximize the return value that volunteering can provide for employees and for the company.

ENDNOTES

[1]*Corporate Volunteer Programs: Benefits to Business,* The Conference Board, New York, NY, p. 18.

[2]*Principles of Excellence in Community Service: A Plan to A.C.T.,* The Points of Light Foundation, Washington, D.C., p. 2.

[3]"Corporate Community Service: Seeking America's Leaders," *Fortune,* New York, NY, November 28, 1994.

APPENDIX

WORKSHEETS*

*These worksheets can also be found on the computer disk located at the back of the book.

The Corporate Needs Assessment

Company:
Chief Executive Officer:
Outside Council:
Date:

Level	Individuals	Remarks	Action Step
Executives/			
Sales Force			
Assembly Crews			
Office Staff			

The Community Needs Assessment—Norrisville

Company:
Community:
Chief Executive Officer:
Marketing Director:
HR Director:
Date:

Description of Community

Political and Social Structure of the Community

The Organizations and/or Services within the Community That Have a Reputation for Quality

Key Contacts Made within the Community

Contact	Company Representative Closest to Individual

Assessment of Company Assets

Company:

Overall Assets

Headquarters - Norrisville

The Southern Plant

The West Coast Office

Linking the Employee Volunteer Plan to the Company's Strategic Plan

Area	Reason
Personnel	
Corporate Giving	
Marketing Plan	

The Volunteer Standard

1. The volunteer experience must be conducted with a not-for-profit organization that is actively classified in good standing under the laws and regulations of the country(s) where it is conducting business.
2. The volunteer acts by each employee must provide a service or goods to an individual(s) and/or community.
3. The volunteer experience needs to be documented by the employee who volunteers and by the company representative.
4. Recognition needs to be given to the employee and to the not-for-profit for their service.
5. A full evaluation of the volunteer experience takes place to ensure that the experience was beneficial for all who were involved.

Partnership Opportunities

Company:

Date:

Headquarters: Norrisville

The Southern Plant

The West Coast Sales Office

The Employee Volunteer Promotional Plan

1. Determine the personal needs of the company and how volunteering may be able to assist;
2. Develop a task force of employees to determine the types of volunteer opportunities that they might be interested in doing in relationship to both community and employee needs;
3. Link the needs expressed to appropriate not-for-profit groups in the area;
4. Develop a cultivation plan for each targeted not-for-profit;
5. Find a key person to make the initial contact;
6. The key person makes the contact with the not-for-profit(s);
7. Meet with the not-for-profit(s);
8. Determine interest and discover if the not-for-profit is able and willing to provide return value. Schedule a second meeting with the not-for-profits who wish to partner;
9. Develop a volunteer agreement/brief proposal based on the agreed plan; and
10. Meet with not-for-profits who have agreed to partner and present the volunteer agreement/proposal brief.

Determining the Areas and Not-For-Profits to Target

Company:
Date:

Company Locales	Not-For-Profits	Key Employee	Key Person

The Initial Meeting with the Targeted Not-For-Profit

 I. Pre-meeting
  -Develop an agenda to follow even though the meeting may be on a casual basis; and
  -Bring a brief volunteer proposal to present.

 II. The Meeting
  -Thank the volunteer representative for meeting with you;
  -Note that you have an opportunity to work in partnership with the not-for-profit;
  -Present the volunteer proposal;
  -Note the highlights of the volunteer opportunity and how it can benefit the not-for-profit;
  -Also note how it can help your employees as well;
  -Provide time for a reaction and take notes;
  -Negotiate and try to develop a plan that will also fit the needs of the not-for-profit;
  -Inquire about how the not-for-profit provides recognition; and
  -Be sure to get information on the evaluation process to be used.

 III. Post-meeting
  -Send a thank you letter and confirm the arrangement.

The For-Profit and Not-For-Profit Volunteering Agreement

Company:
Key Contact:
Not-For-Profit:
Key Contact:
Project:
Date:

The Company:

The Not-For-Profit:

_____   _____
                    Date   Date

The Employee Volunteer Orientation Session

Opening

Conducted by the highest corporate executive possible

History of Employee Volunteering Program at the Company

Important Role of Volunteering in Community

The Return Value of Volunteering

The Company's Investment

The Recognition Plan

The Evaluation Component

The Review of Volunteer Opportunities

How to Select a Volunteer Position

Questions/Answers

The Employee Volunteer Agreement

Company:
Employee:
Not-For-Profit:
Project:
Volunteer Position:
Date:

Date	Date

The Employee Volunteer Evaluation Questionnaire

Company:
Volunteer Activity:
Not-For-Profit:
Number of Volunteers Involved:
Number of Hours:
Contribution:
Number of Participants:

Please answer the following questions based on individual opinions of the employees who volunteered for this project (with 1 being the lowest and 5 the highest).

Question	Answer
1. Leadership role of the not-for-profit	
2. Guidance given	
3. Real value to the community	
4. Teamwork skills gained	
5. Strategic planning conducted	
6. Opportunity to work with different constituencies	
7. Making new contacts	
8. Committee and board experience	
9. Satisfaction of helping others	

Total

10. How did the experience fulfill your personal needs?
    (List all comments)

11. What would you change to make this a better experience?
    (List all comments)

12. Other comments?
    (List all comments)

_____   _____

Employee Volunteer Program Coordinator   Date

The Community: An Opportunity to Form Volunteer Partnerships for the Common Good

If you have read this book from the beginning, the thought may have crossed your mind that there should be a coordinated effort to seek volunteers and place them in needed positions. Well you are not alone. There are a number of dedicated groups that do just that.

Federated groups like the United Way coordinate such activity. The Points of Light Foundation's volunteer centers provide leadership for linking individuals to quality volunteer positions. They also work with local employers through corporate volunteer councils which act as independent coalitions of corporations who have active employee volunteer programs. Many local affiliates of regional, national, and international organizations such as the National Society of Fund Raising Executives and the American Society of Association Executives all play a role in attracting individuals to volunteer for the purpose of making a difference in the community.

Yet, even with all of this effort, there does not seem to be a coordinated program to promote, encourage, and motivate volunteering's return value.

Volunteering is not a growing industry. In fact, it has leveled off. While millions of individuals still volunteer and great worth is being produced from these experiences, the percentage of volunteers is not increasing in any significant increments.

The methods of attracting and maintaining volunteers need to be re-examined in order to discover new approaches that will excite current volunteers to continue and, perhaps, to increase their efforts. Even more importantly, new ways need to be discovered to attract people who do *not* volunteer. These new approaches need to be directed to our youth but we must not forget people of all ages, including the growing senior citizen population.

If you have volunteered, think about how you were first introduced to this wonderful experience. Did your parents instruct you on the fine art of volunteering? Did your school have special classes that encouraged volunteering? Did your local community conduct sessions on the advantages of volunteering?

If you answered no to the questions above, you are not alone. Most people who began to volunteer early in life did so to help others in some way or to pay back the community for all it had given. Some of these people also volunteered to receive self-satisfaction. The process is amazing. While volunteering has had an immense impact on humankind, it has done so in a very decentralized way.

This book was written to provide a new awareness of two products of volunteering—the benefits that volunteering provides for the community and the return value that volunteering provides for the individual who performs the act.

This book provides several approaches for maximizing the value of volunteering. Part I provided methods on how individuals who volunteer can increase the worth of the experience by properly selecting and molding a volunteer opportunity so that it enhances both the benefits for the community and the return value for themselves. Part II illustrated ways that not-for-profits can enhance their volunteer recruitment programs by emphasizing the return value that volunteers receive from the experience. Part III demonstrated the ways in which the increased value of the volunteer experience can increase return value to the employee who volunteers and can enhance bottom line value for the employer who promotes volunteer programs.

Each of these approaches can work well independently, yet it makes a lot more sense to create a plan that brings all of these elements together. A community effort that promotes volunteering is a natural extension of this concept. This could be a process that provides real worth to the community and ample return value to the individuals who volunteer.

Part IV provides an example of how a community should work together to increase volunteering based on the overall value of the process. It is a simple process that can save time and resources. Such a cooperative arrangement would involve a partnership of not-for-profits, for-profits, and the public sector working together to attract individuals to volunteer.

10 ▼ A Community Approach That Can Increase the Rate and the Worth of Volunteering

10.1 INTRODUCTION

Volunteering's contribution to the community has been enormous. The process proves time and time again that an individual can make a difference. It is fitting, therefore, that the leaders of the community should get together to provide increased emphasis on the kind of volunteering that will bring new life to the process and help everyone involved achieve significant goals.

Volunteering needs to be taught when we are young children and reinforced for the rest of our lives. Parents need to be educated on the value volunteering has for their children. Schools need to teach volunteering and they need to promote student volunteering in the community. Adults need to be reminded of the overall value of volunteering and how it opens new opportunities and fulfills individual needs.

Parents play a significant role in how a child views volunteering. If a child witnesses others who are volunteering early in life, they think of volunteering as a positive thing to do. Parents need to emphasize the important role that volunteering provides for the community. This can be accomplished each time a volunteer act occurs around the child. This shows the child how volunteering benefited everyone involved.

Parents should also encourage children to volunteer themselves. It may be a simple act at first but it will reinforce the worth of volunteering.

Parents can provide a "jump start" to a lifetime of volunteering that will bring countless acts of good work to the community and a wealth of return value for the child.

Schools need to teach volunteering as a role that good citizens play in the community. Students should also be taught the abundant return value that can be derived from volunteer experiences and how it can enhance their lives.

A number of school districts currently require community service credits as a requirement for graduation from high school. While this is a fine idea, it can backfire if it is not reinforced with a sound educational program that promotes volunteering as a positive part of our lives. Programs must be more than just a way of forcing students to give up their free time in order to fulfill some arbitrary requirement. Instead, they must educate students on the joy and personal worth of volunteering. They must also educate them on the direct, career-enhancing benefits that can be derived from the process.

Colleges could require a three-hour course that teaches students about the role of a volunteer. The students should be taught how volunteering benefits the community and how it can benefit the students' personal and professional lives. In addition, students should be taught about how they can obtain volunteer positions and what they should look for in a particular position to get the most out of the experience.

Adults should receive reinforcement and training on the worth of volunteering throughout their lives. Such instruction can take the form of public service announcements, materials provided by the government or other organizations, religious instruction, or employee volunteer programs at the workplace.

Not-for-profits play a very important role in ensuring that volunteering is kept alive and well. This role includes the promotion of volunteering but it also includes maintaining and ensuring quality volunteer experiences that produce the desired result that each individual is seeking. Not-for-profits also need to create new volunteer roles and add excitement and benefits to existing ones. This can be difficult at times. Not all volunteer positions can change the world, but every volunteer experience has a way of providing worth for the community and return value for the individual who volunteers.

For-profit businesses have a unique role to play in the promotion of volunteering. Employers typically spend more time with their employees than the employees spend with their families. The worksite is often an ideal place to encourage volunteering. Employers can provide unique incentives to promote volunteering. Companies realize that employees who volunteer create a positive relationship between the business and the community. In fact, community relations is traditionally one of the major reasons why companies promote volunteering. Astute companies, however, realize that volunteering provides more than a positive image. They realize that it can provide return value to the employee who volunteers and, therefore, a measurable asset for the business itself. As a result, sharp business leaders understand that volunteering can be a powerful way of enhancing their bottom line.

The community has the most to gain through the volunteer process. If volunteering is thriving, the community will be too. Of course, the reverse is true as well. The community is a collective body. Therefore, everyone has a great stake in the success of volunteering. Every community should commit itself to ensuring that volunteering continues and thrives. While this can occur through the individual methods outlined in the first three parts of this book, it makes far more sense to combine this energy into a coordinated effort.

This chapter will illustrate this point by developing a plan based on the approaches found in this book. The plan is based on:

1. The development of individual volunteers;
2. The coordinated efforts of not-for-profits;
3. For-profit business leadership; and
4. The involvement of the public sector.

What would have happened if a community effort was in place when James Jones in Chapter 1 began his search for the ideal volunteer position on his own? Would he have achieved better results than the volunteer opportunity he found as the Public Relations Chair of the Northwest Area Health Center? Would the Jacksonville Environmental Coalition in Chapter 6 have been able to secure more or better quality volunteers than they did through their comprehensive approach? Would Jarrett-Anderson's corporate leaders in Chapter 9 have been able to increase the value of their employees any more if a community plan was in place?

It might not have made a great deal of difference in these cases but at least some of the outcomes would have been more favorable. Certainly, the process would have been a lot easier.

The important question, however, is what the overall results of a community plan would be. Remember, the examples in the previous chapters involved individuals and entities that made an active and strategic effort to improve their situations. James Jones aggressively sought a good volunteer position. The Jacksonville Environmental Coalition sought quality partnerships and skilled volunteers. Finally, Jarrett-Anderson strategically mapped out ways that volunteering could improve its business.

A coordinated effort on behalf of the community would enrich the area to a much higher degree because it can assist individuals and entities who do not take such an active role in finding volunteer positions or volunteers. A community volunteer effort can increase volunteer involvement overall by making appropriate matches and providing attractive benefits packages to individuals and entities.

A community volunteer plan needs to address the desires and requirements of every element of the volunteer process. This includes the needs of individuals, not-for-profits, for-profits, and the public sector. The public sector includes federal, state, and local governments, and it can play a significant role within the community model.

Here are the recommended steps for forming a community volunteer plan:

1. A core group or organization needs to assume the leadership role to develop and maintain a community-wide volunteer program. The program should emphasize both traditional community benefits and return value for the individuals who volunteer;

2. The leadership group needs to set up a meeting with all of the organizations that will be involved to determine if a coordinated plan is possible. These organizations should represent all four elements of the volunteer process. If a plan is possible, the group should investigate ways of integrating everyone's needs into one coordinated community effort;

3. Individuals' needs should be addressed first to determine how they can be met;

4. Not-for-profits should play a leadership role since they are the source of volunteer positions. This will ensure that they have the capacity and resources to fulfill volunteers' needs;

5. For-profit businesses should be invited to play a major role;

6. The public sector should map out the role that they will play in the process;

7. The promotional plan should be standardized for the volunteer program in the community;

8. A community-wide recognition program for volunteers should be put into place;

9. A comprehensive evaluation plan should be developed; and

10. The volunteer program should have the ability to be recycled.

The case study in this chapter will focus and expand on the cases contained in previous chapters. It will illustrate that a community-wide volunteer plan can be coordinated if all the sectors of the community work together. In this example, the Jacksonville Environmental Coalition, the Jarrett-Anderson Corporation, and James Jones are involved with the Harford Community Volunteer Program.

10.2 A CORE GROUP OR ORGANIZATION MUST ASSUME THE LEADERSHIP ROLE IN DEVELOPING THE COMMUNITY VOLUNTEER PLAN

The first and most important step of establishing a community volunteer plan is identifying the organization who will take the lead in this effort. This organization must have a number of attributes in order to successfully administer such a program. Exhibit 10.1 provides five guidelines to use in identifying and selecting the appropriate group.

The group needs to be an established and highly respected institution that is noted for getting things done. This will create a highly charged program that will command performance by the lead group. The group must also have the reputation of being able to bring individuals and groups together. The group's leaders will need to be able to engineer the process and come to a common goal quickly. The group will also need to have the capacity to administer the program. This includes both physical needs and psychological needs.

EXHIBIT 10.1 Necessary Attributes of a Core Group Who Will Lead the Community Volunteer Program

---

1. The group or organization needs to be an established, well-known, and respected institution in the community;
2. The group or organization needs to have a reputation for bringing together the various sectors of the community;
3. The group or organization must have the capacity to perform the leadership role that it will need to make the volunteer program a success;
4. The group or organization needs to understand and appreciate the important role that volunteering plays in furthering the needs of the individual and the community; and
5. The group or organization needs to be committed to the promotion of the full benefits derived from volunteering including both the worth that the community receives from the process and the individual return value that can be created as well.

The selected group must understand the important role that volunteering plays in the community. It needs to know exactly what it means if the community increases to levels of volunteering. A group that understands the value of volunteering will have a better understanding of how the process works.

The most important attribute to look for in the core group is a commitment to the promotion of volunteering's benefits. This includes the value that volunteering provides for the not-for-profit and for the community. It also includes the return value that it provides for each individual who volunteers.

The community volunteer plan cannot entice volunteers if only part of the value of volunteering is promoted. The core group needs to be sold on the "full benefit package" that volunteering can provide. It must be willing to develop and implement a plan that includes all the elements needed to provide full value to everyone involved.

The Harford United Way will be the group that leads the volunteer plan in the Harford community. They were selected because they possess many of the qualities that are needed to successfully create and deliver a successful community volunteer plan.

10.3 BRINGING IN ORGANIZATIONS THAT REPRESENT THE OVERALL COMMUNITY

The next step is bringing the leaders of the community together to present the community volunteer plan and to win their support. The group needs to include all of the various factions in the community. It should also include individuals, not-for-profits, and for-profits. Basically, it should include a representative sample of citizens and organizations since the success of the plan is dependent upon the entire community buying into the concept.

The key leaders of the community also need to be a part of the planning process. The entire community will not have a say in the plan but they will be more apt to approve of the plan and to participate if proper representation is ensured. Exhibit 10.2 provides guidelines on selecting which organizations will best contribute to the development of a quality community volunteer program.

The Harford United Way decided that an advisory group would be the best way to attract leading citizens to the community volunteer plan. The advisory group is an impressive array of individuals and it includes a representative from the mayor's office and a state delegate. Several entities are

---

EXHIBIT 10.2 Getting Key Organizations to Participate in the Community Volunteer Program

---

The key elements or sectors of a community need to be part of the community volunteer effort. These elements will vary from community to community but the core institutions tend to be similar. Here are the core groups or elements required:

1. The individual needs to be represented. This is the most difficult one to identify. It may be a representative(s) from a citizen's group or an individual(s) who represents the overall community;
2. The not-for-profit sector needs to be represented. This should include a representation of organizations that are in the community. The factors to consider are both the type and size of the institutions;
3. For-profit businesses need to be represented. They can play a key role in the success of the program. Participants need to represent various industries and sizes of companies in the area; and
4. The public sector—federal, state, and local government leaders who have a logical link to volunteering through educational, community, and public welfare interests.

---

also on the advisory group, including the local volunteer center, the area corporate volunteer council, the local chapter of the National Society of Fund Raising Executives, and the local allied group of the American Society of Association Executives. Other entities that are on the board include the local association of nonprofit organizations, the Jacksonville Chamber of Commerce, and the Clean Air Association. Finally, the Citizens Action League has two local individuals on the advisory group who represent the average citizen's point of view.

10.4 FULFILLING INDIVIDUALS' NEEDS THROUGH A COMMUNITY VOLUNTEER PROGRAM

The community volunteer program must be designed to fulfill the needs of the individuals who will be volunteering. This, of course, is the major selling point to a prospective volunteer. Even if the volunteer simply wishes to help someone within the community, they will have personal goals or desires that will need to be addressed.

When James Jones searched for a volunteer position in Chapter 1, he wanted to provide a quality volunteer experience to the community. More importantly, however, he had a number of personal goals that he wanted to fulfill. He conducted his search on his own. It was his push and his drive that made the process work.

Most volunteers are not as aggressive as Mr. Jones. For the most part, individuals want to be encouraged and cultivated to volunteer. The process has to be open and readily available to people. Individuals should be encouraged to investigate potential opportunities and to make educated decisions on the type of positions that they would like to devote their time to. Exhibit 10.3 provides a listing of needs that should be addressed in alerting individuals in the community to the volunteer positions that are available.

A system needs to be developed that identifies the volunteer opportunities within the community. The Harford United Way has developed a central location to post volunteer positions. The local volunteer center took on this task. Not-for-profits were alerted to this process and they were told how their messages could be listed. New positions can be mailed or e-mailed and they are posted under various categories to assist the prospective volunteer in finding the proper position.

The general public was alerted to this service and they were told how they could access the information. The information can be obtained by requests over the telephone or through the mail. It can be sent out by mail or by fax. Individuals with Internet capability can access the information as well. A hard copy of the Web page list is available at several locations throughout the area, including local libraries, city hall, and not-for-profits. The lists are updated on a weekly basis.

EXHIBIT 10.3 Addressing an Individual's Needs through a Community Volunteer Program

1. Develop a system that identifies volunteer opportunities within the community;
2. Create a method that alerts the community about the volunteer opportunities;
3. Educate the public on the methods in which to seek and obtain a volunteer position;
4. Ensure that local not-for-profits are part of the process ; and
5. Provide a way for individuals to contact a community representative for assistance.

The information on these lists makes it easy for the public to follow up on each opportunity. Each position has a contact person and telephone number to call. The list provides information on the position and its qualifications. This is of great assistance because it improves the pool of volunteers who apply for a position. Groups who participate in this listing service must contact prospective volunteers within 24 hours of receiving a call from them. This helps to keep up individual interest and it helps to fill the volunteer positions quickly.

A central location was created to assist prospective volunteers who have any questions or difficulties. This assists in identifying areas that need refinement and it helps to keep the interest of prospective volunteers high. The key to success for the Harford Community Volunteer Program is the openness of the process. It is clear that everyone wants to be involved and wants to see the plan succeed.

10.5 NOT-FOR-PROFITS NEED TO PLAY A LEADERSHIP ROLE SINCE THEY ARE THE SOURCE OF VOLUNTEER POSITIONS

Since not-for-profits are the source of volunteer positions in the community, they need to play a key role in the development of a community plan which encourages individuals to volunteer. This will ensure that there are enough resources and capacity to fulfill volunteers' needs and the requirements of the community plan.

Participating not-for-profits need to look within themselves to determine which volunteer positions fit the profile of a full benefit program that provides both community worth and return value to individuals who volunteer. Exhibit 10.4 lists a number of areas that not-for-profit organizations need to examine if they want their participation in the program to be successful.

In our example, not-for-profit organizations provide a listing of all the positions that are currently available. Each list is updated weekly and sent to the Harford United Way so the positions can be posted and made available to the entire community. The process of forwarding the names is kept simple—data can be mailed or e-mailed. Prospective volunteers are happy with this system because they can be confident that the central list is current and they can also rely on the position being available.

Each volunteer position a not-for-profit creates needs to provide full benefits to both the community and to the individual. To accomplish this,

---

EXHIBIT 10. 4 The Not-For-Profit's Role in the Community Volunteer Program

1. Not-for-profit organizations provide the listing of volunteer opportunities to the community;
2. They develop volunteer positions that encourage the full range of benefits including the value to the community and the not-for-profit as well as the return value that the individual who volunteers can receive from the experience;
3. Individual organizations develop a position standard for each volunteer position;
4. They agree to use the volunteer standard developed by the community;
5. They establish or refine their volunteer orientation program;
6. They agree to use the standard volunteer agreement form, based on the community model, for all employer/employee volunteer experiences;
7. They provide a recognition program that complements the community recognition program;
8. They work with the community to ensure that their evaluation program is uniform and complements the community evaluation program; and
9. They commit to the community volunteer program for an extended period of time.

---

the entire culture of the organization needs to adapt itself to designing, promoting, executing, recognizing, and evaluating their volunteer positions with regard to the benefits they can provide.

The organization needs to develop a job profile for each position. The job profile should be written in a standard format, provide information on a particular volunteer need, and be recognized by everyone in the community. This simplifies the process and makes it easier for volunteers to compare positions.

Not-for-profits must agree to use the standard format that the community adopts. The standard format should specify which terminology to use and should require certain basic information to be posted. This will allow the process to work more effectively. In addition, all of these basic components will help the community to focus on the real challenge of attracting and retaining volunteers.

The community should develop an orientation model that local organizations can adapt to fit their needs. Each not-for-profit organization should then develop an individual volunteer orientation plan based on the community model. The plan should outline the core principles of volunteering and the needs that are unique to the not-for-profit itself. This is the first major meeting with the new volunteer and it is important to inform and to inspire the newcomer.

The not-for-profits in the community should use a standard volunteer agreement to promote uniformity. Developing such an agreement provides an opportunity to network with other participants in the community program, including for-profit businesses. A standard agreement also supports the community goal of working with individuals to create exciting and worthwhile volunteer experiences.

The volunteer recognition program should be standardized as well. Of course, individual not-for-profits should create their own recognition programs, but these programs should complement the community plan. If the overall plan is well designed, each volunteer should be individually recognized by the not-for-profit organization, the community, and their employer.

This is as it should be because each of these entities owes thanks to the volunteer. The not-for-profit should recognize the volunteer for their direct work at the organization, the community should recognize the volunteer for service to the community, and the volunteer's employer should recognize the volunteer for improving their skills and helping to boost the bottom line of the business.

The evaluation process should be standardized, too. Of course, the not-for-profit should evaluate the plan from the standpoint of how it assisted or fulfilled the mission of the organization. It is vitally important, however, to ensure that the evaluation is conducted in such a way that the findings can be collected and compared with other parts of the community effort.

Perhaps the most important requirement that the community should place on the not-for-profits is a stipulation that each organization be committed to the effort for an extended period of time. If you want to expand the volunteer base in an area, the community volunteer program cannot be a short-term exercise. It must be long-term.

When a community commits to this concept, they need to do it for an amount of time that can yield measurable and scientifically sure results. If a community wishes to create a pilot program, they need to make sure that enough resources are available for a minimum of three to five years. This will be enough time to accurately measure the success of the plan

10.6 FOR-PROFIT BUSINESSES MUST BE INVITED TO PLAY A MAJOR ROLE

For-profit businesses will take a different approach to the proposed community volunteer program. They will see the benefits that can be derived from the process and they will want to play a role in the leadership phase, especially in the areas that affect their business. They will want to visualize how the plan affects their employees and the company. Exhibit 10.5 provides a check list for businesses who want to participate in the community volunteer program.

It is important that businesses review the needs of their employees and the needs of the company to determine the appropriate relationship to have with the proposed community volunteer program. The needs of the business and its employees will come first, but for-profits will soon discover that many of their needs can be met through a community volunteer program.

Businesses need to prepare in ways similar to not-for-profits. This includes reviewing their internal requirements. From a business standpoint, this includes both employee and company needs. This process may be quite revealing for companies who have never measured these needs and who have never thought about the community resources that are available to fulfill these needs.

The next step is to look at the picture in reverse and visualize how the business may be able to solve some of the community's needs. It is often surprising how similar the community's needs and the company's needs are. This process will make the future partnership much easier.

EXHIBIT 10.5 The For-Profit Approach to the Community Volunteer Program

1. Review the internal needs or goals of the employees and the company that may relate to a community volunteer program;
2. Evaluate the community needs and how the business could assist;
3. Make a review of the company's assets that could be used;
4. Make an evaluation of the company employee volunteer plan to see how it relates to a benefits driven community volunteer plan. Make adjustments where necessary;
5. Agree to use the volunteer standard developed by the community;
6. Find ways for the company to act as a partner in area volunteer projects;
7. Develop a promotional plan for introducing the community volunteer plan to employees, including an ongoing orientation and recognition program for all employees;
8. Agree to use the standard volunteer agreement form, based on the community model, for all employees;
9. Work with the community to ensure that the evaluation program is uniform and complete; and
10. Commit to the community volunteer program for an extended period of time.

If the company already has a volunteer plan, the plan should be evaluated by an outside source. The outside source should determine if the plan meets the needs of the employees and the company. Most importantly, the plan should be evaluated to determine if it is compatible with the community volunteer program. This is the time to make sure that return value is a vital part of the plan. Employers must also agree to use the uniform community volunteer standard to ensure consistency throughout the system.

Business participants can provide a number of important components for a community volunteer plan. Businesses need to discover ways of forming partnerships with the community for the common good. This is a great way for all parties to benefit from the process. Community projects can affect a company both positively and negatively, however. It is the positive aspects that need to be explored and exploited for mutual benefit.

The businesses within a community can have a major effect on the success of the community volunteer program. They can inform employees about the plan, encourage participation, and provide incentives to ensure volunteer enthusiasm and success.

Businesses need to be encouraged to use the volunteer agreement form that the community develops. The form will simplify the process and it will increase volunteering. Businesses also need to work with the community to ensure that the company's evaluation process is compatible with the overall community evaluation model. This effort will ensure that data can be used to measure employee involvement and how it has affected the company's objectives. Good data can also measure how the community volunteer plan affected the business' volunteer program.

Just like not-for-profits, companies need to commit to the process for an extended period of time. For-profits can be a highly effective part of a community plan but they need to be involved for a sufficient period of time. This commitment allows the evaluation process to obtain accurate data on the effectiveness of the community program.

10.7 THE PUBLIC SECTOR NEEDS TO PLAY AN IMPORTANT ROLE IN THE PROCESS

By definition, the public sector represents the government and the roles that they play within the community. These roles can come from local, state, or federal sources and they can affect volunteering through laws and regulations that are applicable to the local community.

The public sector can play a productive role in the development of a community volunteer program. They have the power to promote volunteering through existing networks. This can be a powerful force in increasing public awareness of the scope of volunteer programs in the area. The public sector can also provide a number of resources that can greatly enhance a community volunteer program.

Exhibit 10.6 lists some of the ways that the public sector can support a community volunteer program. These include the use of facilities, various communications channels, and people.

More likely than not, the facilities that the public sector have under its control are more extensive than any other sector. These facilities can be used for meetings and for other activities. The public sector's communications network can be another major asset. These networks include everything from public television to the Internet. Finally, the public sector has a staggering pool of individuals at its disposal, including a vast array of experts that can be called on to assist in supporting and promoting the community volunteer plan. These experts can include teachers, social workers, health professionals, or transportation experts.

Public sector employees should not be overlooked as potential volunteers. In many cases, they represent the largest employer in the area. The same process that applies to for-profit businesses and their employees can apply to the public sector as well. This will help to fill the pool of potential volunteers that is needed to keep the community volunteer program alive.

The public sector can provide significant help in assessing community needs. After all, that is what they do. They can provide the data and, often, they can pinpoint the key areas of the community to focus on. Including

---

EXHIBIT 10.6 The Public Sector's Role in the Development of a Community Volunteer Program

---

1. To keep the public aware of the benefits of volunteering and the current opportunities that are available;
2. To offer facilities and experts who can assist;
3. To encourage their own employees to participate;
4. To assist in the assessment of community need;
5. To provide financial support where appropriate;
6. To help in the evaluation of the community volunteer plan;
7. To support and to help recognize individuals who volunteer in the community; and
8. To support the continued development of the community volunteer program.

---

the public sector in the leadership of the program will ensure that the group is not overlooking important areas or concerns in the community. This is even more important as the government continues to cut social programs.

Even with serious cutbacks in social programs, however, the government might still be a source of financial support for the community volunteer program. The reduction of funding for social programs makes it even more important for the government to work closely with the not-for-profit and for-profit sectors to ensure that sufficient support remains in place to help those who are in need. A volunteer effort on behalf of the community will make the government's money go further in helping needy individuals. This might be one of the most important and timely parts of the community volunteer plan. This relationship should address the challenge of serving increased needs with reduced government resources.

The public sector can be of great assistance in reviewing the community evaluation plan. The government has the resources and motivation to make sure that the community has programs to assist its citizens. This operates as a powerful incentive to ensure that a community volunteer program is in place and that it is well-supported.

The recognition program is a great way to bring the public sector on board. It provides an opportunity to recognize local citizens who have made a difference in the community and, more importantly, it provides a way of making the public sector feel that they have played a significant part in the process.

The public sector can have a profound effect on a community volunteer program. It can assist in developing the plan and in assuring the continued use of the plan for an extended period of time. The public sector should not be overlooked as a major resource in developing and maintaining a quality volunteer plan in the community.

10.8 STANDARDIZING THE COMMUNITY VOLUNTEER PROGRAM'S PROMOTION PLAN

The promotion of the community volunteer program needs to be a coordinated effort. After all, it is the sum of the individual parts that strengthens the process and motivates the community to increase their involvement in volunteering. Exhibit 10.7 lists the steps needed to successfully promote a community volunteer program.

EXHIBIT 10.7 The Promotion of a Community-Wide Volunteer Program

1. Create a united effort within the community through obtaining consensus from the major players in the area;
2. Develop a yearly calendar of events;
3. Create standard materials for use by all parties;
4. Develop a communications-marketing effort to create enthusiasm for the plan;
5. Use public forums, i.e., public meetings, church services, and schools to keep the plan in front of the community;
6. Provide an ongoing worksite emphasis on the community volunteer program;
7. Feature not-for-profit programs and their various positive outcomes;
8. Ensure that the promotional effort features the overall benefits of volunteering, including return value;
9. Encourage new ideas and methods for volunteering; and
10. Provide ample levels of recognition to all who are involved with the community volunteer program.

The Harford United Way knows that they need an approach that will generate new excitement in the community's volunteer process. They decided to promote the benefits that volunteering can offer to both the community and the individual who volunteers.

The first step in the plan called for building consensus among the people who have agreed to participate in the community volunteer program. This was a challenge, but emphasis was placed on how the plan could benefit the overall community and how it could fulfill the goals of all who were involved.

Jason Smith, President of the Harford United Way, decided that the best way to bring greater attention to this effort was to bring in an outside expert. The expert selected was a management consultant who had successfully implemented similar programs in other communities.

The management consultant started the process by setting up individual meetings with key players from every sector. The purpose of the meetings was to discuss the collective and individual benefits of volunteering and to figure out how a community volunteer plan could enhance these benefits.

When the timing was right, Jason Smith; Mary Jackson, Chair of the Board of the Harford United Way; and the Chairman of R. F. Financial Services held a prestigious gathering of key players from the community at an exclusive club in town. The management consultant was there but she was not the center of attention. She had staged the meeting and added a few comments, but the meeting was officially called by the group that would lead the community volunteer program, the Harford United Way.

The meeting was a great success due to the individual meetings prior to the gathering and the careful staging of the gathering itself. Everyone knew that they needed to develop an aggressive plan that included exciting support materials. Local funding sources promised to find financial support for the program. These funding sources included a community foundation, a handful of corporations, and the local government.

The Harford United Way was charged with creating a multi-year budget and developing a plan to secure the funds. Jason Smith immediately suggested that two task forces be appointed:

1. A task force dedicated to developing the budget; and
2. A task force dedicated to creating a fund development plan.

The task forces were made up of key leaders from every sector of the community. Leaders from major funding sources were invited to act as advisors or participants on the development task force. Community leaders were now involved and every effort was made to make sure all the resources were in place to launch the task force. With everyone in place, the public awareness campaign could begin.

The management consultant was retained to provide advisory support to ensure that the process continued on schedule. More importantly, she was kept around to make sure that the successful concepts used in other communities could be emulated in the Harford community.

A calendar of events was published that contained the activities for the community volunteer program's first year. The year will begin with a formal kick-off rally to gain community-wide attention and it will end with a major recognition event to honor the thousands of volunteers who participated. During the year, there will be events of all types and descriptions that reinforce the volunteer plan. Standard materials will be created to promote the program, but they will be flexible enough to provide ways to insert individual logos or personalize them for various audiences.

The community volunteer leadership realized that the plan would be unsuccessful unless the general public understood the concept and saw a value in participating. In order to accomplish this, a community volunteer communications plan was instituted. The community really backed this effort. Local media sources donated time to help develop the plan and they also provided space and time in their individual media outlets to provide maximum exposure to the general public.

This provided the proper support to reinforce the more direct approaches that were being made throughout the community. It brought universal enthusiasm to the process and it generated a feeling that everyone wanted to be involved in this worthwhile effort.

A grass-roots approach was used to inform people about the community volunteer program. Citizens began to understand that the community was serious about creating and maintaining a volunteer program. More importantly, they began to understand that the program could be beneficial for the local area and for the individuals and entities that participated. The public was continually reminded of the program and its benefits. Individuals took the opportunity to remind the public of the volunteer program at several community functions and gatherings, including public meetings, church services, and local school classrooms.

A major effort to inform individuals of the volunteer program took place at worksites in the community. Thousands of employees were told about the new program and the benefits that they could receive from the program personally. A number of companies took this opportunity to announce new or refined employee volunteer programs that would bring an even higher level of return value to their employees.

Not-for-profits individually announced their support for the community volunteer program and provided information on how individuals could participate. Thus, the community was assured that the plan had the backing of the not-for-profit sector and that there were many new and exciting ways to volunteer.

All of the promotions emphasized the important role that the volunteer process can play in the community. It also helped the community focus on the return value that volunteering can provide for an individual if the volunteer process is properly created and maintained.

The community volunteer program encouraged the creation of many new kinds of volunteer activities. The family volunteering program quickly became one of the biggest successes in the community plan. In family volunteering, the entire family volunteers as a unit.

This method of volunteering started at two area companies and it caught on quickly at other companies, not-for-profits, and, even in the public sector. With most adult members of the family working outside the home, it was a great way to bring the family together while helping the community at the same time. These new volunteering ideas were being generated at a rapid pace and a number of the new ideas were transferable to other parts of the community.

Finally, the program's promotion plan provided ample levels of recognition for everyone involved, including volunteers, employers, and anyone else that made the community volunteer program a success.

10.9 A COMMUNITY-WIDE RECOGNITION PROGRAM MUST BE PUT INTO PLACE

Recognition is one of the most important elements of the Harford Community Volunteer Program. While volunteers never expressed a need for it, it was always welcomed.

Recognition, however, needs to be individualized for each person or entity that you wish to thank. Some individuals and entities will not want public recognition but there may be another way of recognizing their work. This can make all the difference in their continued participation. In many cases, these acts of recognition can be as simple as a thank you letter. The important thing is to know each volunteer's needs and desires and to make an effort to fulfill them.

The Harford Community Volunteer Program's leadership knew that their recognition program should be multi-leveled. Exhibit 10.8 is a good check list to follow. The program's leaders knew that general recognitions needed to be uniform from the top down. They also knew that each volunteer would be recognized by several different entities including the not-for-profit that they volunteered for, their individual employers, and the community.

All of these levels of recognition needed to complement and reinforce each other. They also needed to complement the personal needs of each volunteer. For example, space in local newspapers that acknowledges citizens for good deeds and philanthropy is very limited, so this form of recognition is given only to volunteers who want public exposure. Other forms of appropriate recognition are created for individuals who do not desire public exposure.

The community needed to develop standard materials and awards that would complement the expected awards programs of individual not-

---

EXHIBIT 10.8 The Recognition Plan for the Community Volunteer Program

1. Develop a plan that is uniform from the top down;
2. Use a standard package of materials at all levels;
3. Create a recognition program that focuses on the individuals who have volunteered while also encouraging others to volunteer;
4. Recognize everyone who has assisted in the development of the community volunteer program; and
5. Continue providing recognition, through verbal, print, and other methods, throughout the next cycle of the community volunteer plan.

---

for-profits and businesses in the area. This effort took a lot of time to accomplish but the final product made the coordination effort worth it.

The recognition plan is designed to honor those who have given their time and efforts to the community volunteer plan. The people who created this plan, however, also designed it so that it could be used to increase awareness of the community program and to encourage further volunteering.

The recognition plan emphasizes the enormous benefits that volunteering has provided for the community. More importantly, it also emphasizes the return value that volunteers received from the process and it stresses the benefits that the volunteers' families and employers received as well. This is accomplished by providing a number of individual examples. The plan recognizes individuals who gained significant personal benefits. Written reviews of each of these experiences are sent to the appropriate media channels.

10.10 DEVELOPING A COMPREHENSIVE EVALUATION PLAN

Most of the leaders in the Harford area had thoughts about the evaluation of the community volunteer program from the very beginning. How could the plan be effectively measured? Who should do the evaluation? What are the desired outcomes?

Often, it is difficult to measure the effectiveness of a program that spans an entire community. That is why it is important to set the plan into motion at the very beginning. Exhibit 10.9 provides some insight into this process.

EXHIBIT 10.9 The Community Volunteer Program Evaluation Plan

1. The evaluation plan should be flexible enough to be used at all levels;
2. The evaluation plan needs to gauge the method or process for an individual to volunteer;
3. The working relationships between the main divisions of the process, i.e., the individual, the not-for-profit, and the for-profit business should be measured;
4. The public sector's role and how it affected the outcome should also be measured; and
5. The level of volunteering should be compared to past data to see the influence of a community volunteer program.

First, everyone who participates in the community volunteer program needs to approve the evaluation process before it is put into place. This means that the evaluation process needs to be simple and flexible and that it must strive to provide data that everyone can use.

The plan should focus on a system that encourages growth rather than striving to set a standard for everyone to meet. For example, each entity involved should set their own realistic goals instead of trying to meet some predetermined, impossible standard. This will make the evaluation process much more successful.

If measurements are used, make sure that the goal or objective is calculated by percentages instead of raw numbers. For example, if a not-for-profit has increased its number of volunteers from 200 to 220, it is much better to indicate this as a 10 percent increase than an increase of 20 volunteers. This encourages growth by putting the numbers into a context and helps to eliminate contests of who can outdo each other.

The evaluation plan should be an ongoing process. This process can really assist in refining the planning process as you go along. The evaluation component can be accomplished by individuals within the organization but it is often best to bring in outside help.

The Harford community felt that they would like to have an outside person assist them in the evaluation process. Wisely, they chose the same person who had helped them develop the community volunteer program—the management consultant.

The management consultant welcomed the opportunity to evaluate the plan. She met with the key leaders in the Harford community and they agreed to a plan that would evaluate the entire process from the beginning. The management consultant also welcomed involvement from all of the area's leaders.

When the plan was completed, the consultant presented it to the community's leaders. Everyone was impressed by how simple it was. The paperwork was simple, the process of submitting it was simple, and the reports were simple to read. The evaluation was applicable to all of the sectors in the community but it could be used to focus on individuals, organizations, or coordinated projects. The evaluation plan was a great success. It was simple, yet it provided the information that everyone needed.

The desired results were as simple as the evaluation process itself. The Harford community wanted to increase volunteering rates and they also wanted to increase the levels of return value to the individuals who volunteered.

The first objective was simple to measure. It was a quantitative measurement of what was and what will be. The evaluation of this objective was accomplished by documenting past performance and measuring the progress from that base figure.

The second outcome, increasing individual return value, was not as easy to measure because it was a qualitative measurement. It requires detailed information that cannot be expressed in numbers. In addition, it also requires information that some volunteers may not wish to provide.

In response to this problem, the management consultant wisely developed a simple and short questionnaire for each volunteer to complete at regular intervals during their volunteer experience. The forms did not contain the name of the volunteer but, instead, used a number that would match the proper forms at the end of the process. The form asked five questions and provided a method of quantitative measurement for each question:

Question	Answer	Level (1 to 5)
1. Do you like the volunteer position that you have chosen?	Yes	2
2. Do you feel that your volunteering is helping the community?	Yes	3
3. Are you receiving the return value that you expected?	Yes	3
4. How do you rate your overall volunteer experience?		3
5. Would you consider another volunteer experience after this one?	Yes	

The management consultant knew that these five answers could provide the information needed to make an evaluation of the individual volunteer experience. The evaluation also provided additional value because volunteers had the ability to express their thoughts during the process. If there are ever any problems, the volunteer and the organization can make adjustments before the whole experience becomes a waste. Finally, this question gets the volunteer thinking about future volunteer opportunities.

10.11 CREATING A VOLUNTEER PROGRAM WHICH IS ABLE TO BE RECYCLED

A successful community volunteer program is one that lasts. It needs to be an ongoing effort; not a one- or two-year promotional project. If a program is going to last, however, it must be recycled after each time period and, in most cases, the time period is one year.

The most critical recycling period is the first one. Even the most successful community volunteer program can lose steam in the second year. Everyone may be excited and pleased to participate the first time around but there is a natural tendency for people to move on after the initial year.

How can a plan be recycled and be even more successful in the second year? Exhibit 10.10 provides a few ways to keep the plan going after the first year.

The planning for the second period needs to start about halfway through the first period. This will ensure that momentum is not lost and that key players are secured for the next time period. Holding on to the momentum and to the people can be accomplished by bringing the leaders of the community together to discuss the recycling plan.

This meeting is the time to obtain commitments from those who wish to continue to hold leadership positions and to find out who is leaving. The purpose of the meeting is to give sufficient time to recruit new people. Do not disregard the outgoing volunteers, however. Often, they can be of great assistance in the recruiting process. They normally want to see the process continue and they will often be instrumental in identifying and recruiting the right people for the effort.

The evaluation process will have produced valuable information that is relevant to next year's program. Be sure to use this information to expand on successes and to fill in any gaps in the program for the following year.

The Harford community developed a general plan and brought the plan to the recycling strategy meeting. The management consultant was brought into the meeting to help sell the plan and to facilitate the planning process. The general plan helped to reveal a number of new and exciting ideas to consider for the next time period.

The plan that is developed at this meeting should be general in nature but key elements that need to be handled immediately have to be decided

---

EXHIBIT 10.10 Recycling the Community Volunteer Program

1. Bring together the principal players in the community volunteer program at the midpoint of the current cycle;
2. Have the preliminary evaluations of the volunteer plan available;
3. Develop a general plan for year two;
4. Begin to work on the second year's plan, immediately overlapping the completion of year one;
5. Continue to base the build-up on the findings discovered with the first year plan; and
6. Gear the ending of the first year plan to be a kick-off for year two.

---

on to ensure that the recycling process will be successful. Successful community volunteer programs spend at least half of their time working on plans two to three cycles ahead of the current cycle. This is the only way to ensure continued success.

The recognition event for the current cycle is a great place for the public kick-off of the next cycle. It helps to provide a smooth transition into the next cycle and it eliminates any lags that cause a loss of momentum. The process should look seamless. Everyone involved needs to know that the community volunteer program is ongoing. They need to know that it is a stable and established organization that serves the common good and advances the goals of its volunteers.

10.12 STANDARDIZING THE COMMUNITY VOLUNTEER PROGRAM PROCESS

The success of the community volunteer program depends on building close relationships with the leaders of the entities that make the process work. Once that has been accomplished, certain standards need to be adopted to ensure that the plan produces the desired values.

Exhibit 10.11 provides some basic standards to measure volunteer experiences within a community volunteer plan. This exhibit is a combination of the not-for-profit and for-profit volunteer standard. See Exhibits 4.4 and 9.7. The Harford community adopted this standard since it combines the needs of not-for-profits and for-profits.

The standard provides for minimum requirements rather than maximum requirements. Under the standard, the volunteer experience must be conducted at an active not-for-profit, it must be designed to improve the community, and it must be documented in order to ensure quality control. The standard also provides that recognition must be a part of the process and that a comprehensive evaluation plan must be in place. Finally, each volunteer position must have a standard job profile that the community can recognize and understand.

Exhibit 10.12 was adopted by the Harford community and used for all its volunteer positions. The standard made it possible for every position to be listed identically. Participating not-for-profits used the same form to alert the community to new or vacant volunteer positions. In addition, the standard made it easier to process information and made it easier for individuals to find quality positions.

EXHIBIT 10.11 The Volunteer Standard for the Community Volunteer Program

1. The volunteer experience must be conducted with a not-for-profit organization that is actively classified in "good standing" under the laws and regulations of the country in which it is conducting business;
2. The volunteer acts of each individual must provide an unselfish service or good to a person(s) and/or to the community;
3. The volunteer experience needs to be documented by the volunteer, the not-for-profit coordinator, and the company representative if appropriate;
4. Recognition needs to be given to all who have been involved in the process;
5. A full evaluation of the volunteer experience needs to take place to ensure that the experience was beneficial for all who were involved; and
6. Each volunteer position standard brief needs to contain the following information:
   -The not-for-profit;
   -Who the volunteer reports to;
   -Who the volunteer will supervise;
   -Duties of the position;
   -Meeting requirements;
   -Time requirements;
   -Skills required; and
   -Evaluation component.

Most of the formal agreements that the Harford Community Volunteer Program adopted came from the not-for-profits and the for-profits in the community. They provide a simple way of ensuring that every party receives the full benefits from each act of volunteering. Exhibit 10.13 is the agreement that the Harford community adopted.

Every agreement lists the names of all the parties. The volunteer's duties are spelled out on the form next to the duties of the not-for-profit for which they are volunteering. The duties of the not-for-profit include providing adequate support for the volunteer position and providing specific return value for the volunteer. If a for-profit business is involved, their role is clearly stated as well. Spelling out these roles ensures that everyone gets what they expected from the experience.

The evaluation requirement of the agreement should be discussed and each party should know their role in the evaluation process. When everything is completed, the agreement will contain the signatures of all the parties. The document should be treated as a contract once it is signed.

EXHIBIT 10.12 The Volunteer Position Standard

The Jacksonville Environmental Coalition
Volunteer Position Standard
Water Environment Chair
December 5, 1997

Report to:	Volunteer Chair, John Paul
Supervises:	A committee of 12

Duties:

To develop and implement a regional public awareness program concerning the quality of water in the area's rivers and lakes.

Meeting requirements:

1. Hold a quarterly meeting of the Water Environment Committee;
2. Attend the monthly board meeting; and
3. Represent the Coalition at the Clean Air Association quarterly meeting.

Time requirements:

It is estimated that 20 hours a month will be needed to successfully perform this volunteer opportunity. The initial commitment for this position will be for one year.

Skills required:

To have five years experience in water quality issues and to have a professional position that relates to the field.

Evaluation:

The position and committee progress will be evaluated quarterly through a team approach. The team will include the volunteer chair and the Water Environment Chair.

EXHIBIT 10.13 The Volunteer Agreement for a Community Volunteer Program

1. List all parties involved including individuals, not-for-profits, and companies, if appropriate;
2. List the duties, in detail, that the volunteer will perform;
3. List the support and return value that the not-for-profit will provide to the volunteer;
4. List the support that the for-profit will provide if the volunteer is employee-based;
5. Fill out an evaluation component; and
6. All interested parties should sign and date the document.

Exhibit 10.14 was adopted by the Harford community as the standard form for the not-for-profit and individual agreement. They felt that this agreement was a simple way to outline the role that the volunteer and the not-for-profit should play in ensuring that each entity will receive the proper benefits from the volunteer experience.

Exhibit 10.15 was adopted by the Harford community as the standard guide that a for-profit and not-for-profit should use to arrange volunteer experiences for area employees.

10.13 CONCLUSION

The Harford Community Volunteer Plan was a huge success. The community experienced a major growth in volunteering and the people who participated experienced a significant increase in their quality of life.

Individuals were delighted with the process. They could select exciting volunteer opportunities from a central location or they could contact not-for-profits directly. They could even discover volunteer opportunities at work through their employee volunteer program.

All of the volunteer activities were coordinated through the community. This simplified and improved the system and it did so with fewer resources.

The plan also focused on the full benefits of volunteering. This assisted in increasing the worth for the community and for the organizations involved. It also provided greater return value to the individuals who volunteered.

EXHIBIT 10.14 The Volunteer Agreement

Not-For-Profit Organization:	The Jacksonville Environmental Coalition
Volunteer Position:	Water Environment Chair
Name:	Jane Weber
Date:	2/9/98

It is our pleasure to offer you the opportunity to chair the Water Environment Committee. This decision was based on your past volunteer record and your professional interest in water quality. This is a highly visible position that will demand significant time and energy for you to succeed. It is my understanding that this is a position that you seek and that you will be able to commit at least one year to this important volunteer position.

In order to be successful, the following standards will need to be met:
- Act as the active chair of the Water Environment Committee;
- Recruit 12 members of the committee who have background and interest in water quality;
- Preside over the quarterly meeting of the Water Environment Committee;
- Attend the monthly board meeting;
- Represent the Coalition at the Clean Air Association quarterly meeting; and
- Become a sustaining member of the Coalition.

The Coalition will assist you to be successful by:
- Providing an orientation meeting to review the duties of the position;
- Providing past meeting and board minutes for the Water Environment Committee and the Clean Air Association;
- Providing a list of the key leaders of the Coalition;
- Providing an opportunity for you to represent the Coalition at the national meeting of CAA;
- Assisting your company, the Environment Research Corporation, to become an active partner in the Quality Water Project; and
- Assisting you to better understand the board of directors role.

The evaluation component will be conducted as a team effort between the Volunteer Chair and you. This process is designed to ensure that your volunteer experience has been productive for you and the Coalition. Upon your official appointment, you are encouraged to make your sustaining membership commitment. Welcome to the volunteer leadership ranks of the Jacksonville Environmental Coalition. We are delighted to have you involved with our program and look forward to working together to improve our environment.

_____	_____	_____	_____
Jane Weber	Date	Helen Brown	Date

EXHIBIT 10.15 The For-Profit and Not-For-Profit Volunteer Agreement

Company:	Jarrett- Anderson
Key Contact:	Jane Curtis, HR Director
Not-For-Profit:	Bread for the Homeless
Key Contact:	John Gill, Chair
Project:	"Feed the Hungry"
Date:	December 21, 1997

The Company:

Jarrett-Anderson agrees to support the "Feed the Hungry" project with the following resources:
- 75 volunteers for three weekends to prepare and serve food;
- $25,000 to assist Bread for the Homeless operating expense;.
- 6 tons of assorted food ordered via Bread for the Homeless; and
- 2 management support persons.

The Not-For-Profit:

Bread for the Homeless agrees to support the volunteers from Jarrett-Anderson in the following ways:
- Six support staff will coordinate the three weekends and will provide direct guidance;
- The facility will be prepared to meet the support that will be needed;
- Special recognition at the event will occur for each volunteer and a special recognition certificate will be given to each volunteer at our next major meeting; and
- As per our agreement, we will ensure that the two management support persons will be provided opportunities to work with the board during the process in order to obtain more insight into the management function of the organization.
- An evaluation component will also be in place.

This is a flexible agreement that is designed to provide all parties, and in particular the volunteers, with a beneficial volunteer experience. It is also designed to ensure that the project provides the intended end result—to feed homeless people with nourishing food.

Jane Curtis	Date	John Gill	Date

The entire community benefited from the plan. Individuals wanted to volunteer and businesses encouraged employees to volunteer to increase their bottom line. The public sector viewed the program as a way of downsizing the government and reducing funding without sacrificing services.

The community volunteer plan was so successful that other communities sought out the program's leaders for advice. The leaders, in turn, gave these communities everything they could to encourage them to develop a volunteer program in their communities that provides a full range of benefits to individuals, not-for-profits, for-profits, and the community. The leaders also encouraged other communities to seek the wisdom and expertise of a management consultant.

APPENDIX

WORKSHEETS*

*These worksheets can also be found on the computer disk located at the back of the book.

The Volunteer Position Standard

The Jacksonville Environmental Coalition
Volunteer Position Standard
Water Environment Chair
December 5, 1997

Report to:
Supervises:

Duties:

Meeting requirements:

Time requirements:

Skills required:

Evaluation:

The Volunteer Agreement

Not-For-Profit Organization:
Volunteer Position:
Name:
Date:

In order to be successful, the following standards will need to be met:

The Organization will assist you to be successful by:

Date	Date

The For-Profit and Not-For-Profit Volunteer Agreement

Company:
Key Contact:
Not-For-Profit:
Key Contact:
Project:
Date:

The Company:

The Not-For-Profit:

| Jane Curtis | Date | John Gill | Date |

Appendix A
About the Disk

DISK CONTENTS

Directory	Contents
BLANKWS	All worksheets from Chapters 1, 4, 9, and 10 Appendixes
FORMSCH8	Select forms from Chapter 8 Appendix
COMPEDGE	*Volunteering: The Leader's Competitive Edge*
ASAEDIR	American Society of Association Executives
NSFREDIR	National Society of Fund-Raising Executives
POLDIR	Points of Light Foundation Corporate Volunteer Council Communities and Volunteer Centers

The enclosed disk contains files saved in both Microsoft Word for Windows version 2.0 format and ASCII text format. The Microsoft Word files are formatted and can be used with most word processing programs capable of reading Word 2.0 files. If your word processor cannot read Microsoft Word 2.0 files, unformatted ASCII text files are provided for your use.

After installing the files to your hard drive (see instructions below), you can open the files in your word processor and print the forms or begin customizing them to suit your needs. You can add or delete text, adjust the formatting, reset margins and tabs, change fonts, etc. Refer to the user manual that came with your word processing software for instructions on how to make these changes.

SYSTEM REQUIREMENTS

- IBM PC or compatible computer.
- 3.5" floppy disk drive.
- Windows 3.1 or higher.
- To use the formatted files, you will need a word processing program capable of reading Microsoft Word for Windows 2.0 files.
- To use the unformatted files, you can use any word processing program capable of reading ASCII text files.

HOW TO INSTALL THE FILES
ONTO YOUR COMPUTER

If you would like to copy all the files from the disk to your hard drive, run the installation program provided on the disk. Running the installation program will copy the files to your hard drive in the default directory C:\PIDGEON. To run the installation program, do the following:

1. Insert the enclosed disk into the floppy disk drive of your computer.
2. Windows 3.1 or NT 3.51: From the Program Manager, choose File, Run. Windows 95 or NT 4.0: From the Start Menu, choose Run.
3. Type **A:\INSTALL** and press Enter.
4. The opening screen of the installation program will appear. Press Enter to continue.
5. The default destination directory is C:\PIDGEON. If you wish to change the default destination, you may do so now. Follow the instructions on the screen.
6. The installation program will copy all files to your hard drive in the C:\PIDGEON or user-designated directory.

USING THE FILES

Loading Files

To use the files do the following:

1. Load your word processing program.
2. Select File, Open from the pull-down menu.

3. A dialog box will appear. Make the appropriate selections for the drive and directory. If you installed to the default directory, the files will be located in the C:\PIDGEON directory.
4. Select the appropriate subdirectory (e.g., BLANKWS). In the file name list, double click on the file you want to open. If you do not see a listing of all files, under Type of Files, select ALL FILES (*.*).
5. The file should load into your word processor. You can make any changes or revisions to the document.
6. To print the file, select PRINT from the FILE menu.

Note: Many popular word processing programs (including WordPerfect for Windows) are capable of reading Microsoft Word files. However, users should be aware that a slight amount of formatting might be lost when using a program other than Microsoft Word. Also, some users may need to readjust tabs and page margins because of the default font type and default margins set in their program.

Saving Files

When you have finished editing a document, you should save it under a new file name before exiting your word processing program.

USER ASSISTANCE

If you need basic assistance with installation or if you have a damaged disk, please call our product support number at (212) 850-6753 weekdays between 9 A.M. and 4 P.M. Eastern Standard Time.

To place additional orders or to request information about other Wiley products, please call (800) 225-5945.

Index

For information about the disk, refer to Appendix A on pages 307-309.